THE STORY OF LANGUAGE

Probing back to the crudest origins of human communication by sound and tracing the amazing development of speech in many tongues over thousands of years, *The Story of Language* covers a huge subject clearly and concisely.

From the language groups emerging through the centuries the author selects one, 'Indo-European', as being of particular interest, and goes on to describe the growth of the English language as we know it today. From each epoch – Old English, Middle English, the times of Chaucer, of Shakespeare, and later – he introduces charming examples of prose and verse to illustrate his arguments.

In the later chapters, Dr Barber discusses fully the factors that make for constant change in a living language and argues strongly for accepting new words and phrases as they arise.

The Story of Language is an important and brilliantly written exposition of a subject of the greatest interest.

THE STORY OF LANGUAGE

CHARLES BARBER

A PAN ORIGINAL

PAN BOOKS LTD : LONDON

First published 1964 by
PAN BOOKS LTD
8 Headfort Place, London S.W.1

© Charles Barber, 1964

Printed in Great Britain by Richard Clay and Company, Ltd.,
Bungay, Suffolk

CONTENTS

PREFACE

THIS is a book about the history of language: about the process of change which goes on continually in any language which is actually in use. It is intended for the reader without any previous knowledge of the subject, and does not require any technical equipment. Nor does it require any knowledge of foreign languages, though of course these are always a help. Since every reader has an intimate, if unsystematic, knowledge of his own language, I have centred the book on English, and the second half of it is in effect a history of the English language. The first half deals with more general topics, such as the nature of language, its origins, the causes of linguistic change, and language families.

Although the book is intended for the general reader, I have not hesitated to introduce a certain number of technical terms, but I have tried to explain these in non-technical language, and have also brought them together in a Glossary at the end of the book. A number of these technical terms occur in the first chapter; you may find this less interesting than some of the later parts of the book, but it is worth trying to master it, because it will make many later things a good deal clearer. I have however denied myself such technical aids as phonetic and phonemic transcriptions, since I thought these required a bigger effort than the average reader would wish to make. And I have sometimes made simplifications in transcribing words from other languages (e.g. Sanskrit). Indeed, some simplification is inevitable in a book of this kind.

I have included in different places a fair number of short passages of English from various periods, in their original spelling, to show concretely what linguistic change means. Where I give modern translations of such passages, I aim at giving a 'crib', not at producing idiomatic modern English.

In a book covering such a wide field as this, it is impossible to acknowledge all the many sources and authorities that have been drawn on in one way or another. Indeed, for many familiar ideas I should be hard put to it to say what the original source was. Acknowledgments are however made to the following for permission to reproduce copyright material:

W. Heffer and Sons Ltd, for permission to adapt my Figures 2 and 3 from diagrams in *An Outline of English Phonetics*, by Daniel Jones; the Smithsonian Institution, Washington, for permission to reproduce my Figure 5 from Garrick Mallery's *Picture-Writing of the American Indians*, in the Tenth Annual Report of the Bureau of Ethnology to the Secretary of the Smithsonian Institution; Routledge and Kegan Paul Ltd, for permission to adapt my Figure 7 from a diagram in *A Study of Writing*, by I. J. Gelb; the Syndics of the Cambridge University Press and the Delegates of the Oxford University Press, for permission to quote a passage from *The New English Bible*; the Council of the Early English Text Society, for permission to quote a passage from Parson Haben's Sermon, printed in their volume *The Fraternitye of Vacabondes*, by John Awdeley, edited by Edward Viles and F. J. Furnivall; Longmans, Green and Co. Ltd, and Harcourt, Brace and World, Inc., for permission to quote a passage from the novel *By Love Possessed*, by James Gould Cozzens.

I am also grateful to Mr Stanley Ellis, M.A., of the University of Leeds, for providing the material for Figure 9, and to the Survey of English Dialects, from whose archives the material came.

CHAPTER I

WHAT IS LANGUAGE?

IT IS language, more obviously than anything else, that distinguishes man from the rest of the animal world. At one time it was common to define man as a thinking animal, but we can hardly imagine thought without words – not thought that is at all precise, anyway. More recently, man has often been described as a tool-making animal; but language itself is the most remarkable tool that man has invented, and is the one that makes all the others possible. The most primitive tools, admittedly, may have come earlier than language: the higher apes sometimes use sticks for digging, and have even been observed to break sticks for this purpose. But tools of any greater sophistication demand the kind of human co-operation and division of labour which is hardly possible without language. Language, in fact, is the great machine tool which makes human culture possible.

Other animals, it is true, communicate with one another, or at any rate stimulate one another to action, by means of cries. Many birds utter warning calls at the approach of danger; some animals have mating calls; apes utter different cries expressive of anger, fear, pleasure. But these various means of communication differ in important ways from human language. Animals' cries are not *articulate*. This means, basically, that they lack structure. They lack, for example, the kind of structure given by the contrast between vowels and consonants. They also lack the kind of structure that enables us to divide a human utterance into *words*. We can change an utterance by replacing one word in it by another: a sentry can say 'Tanks approaching from the north', or he can change one word and say 'Aircraft approaching from the north' or 'Tanks approaching from the west'; but a bird has a single indivisible alarm cry, which means 'Danger!' This is why the number of signals that an animal can make is very limited: the Great Tit has about twenty different calls, whereas in human language the number of possible utterances is infinite. It also explains why animal cries are very *general* in meaning. These differences will become clearer if we consider some of the characteristics of human language.

What Is Language?

A human language is a signalling system. As its materials, it uses vocal sounds. It is important to remember that basically a language is something which is *spoken*: the written language is secondary and derivative. In the history of each individual, speech is learned before writing, and there is good reason for believing that the same was true in the history of the race. There are primitive communities that have speech without writing, but we know of no human society which has a written language without a spoken one. Such things as the sign language of deaf and dumb people are not exceptions to this rule: even if used by people who cannot speak, and have never been able to speak, these languages are derived from the spoken language of the community around them.

Vocal Sounds

The vocal sounds which provide the materials for a language are produced by the various *speech organs* (see Figure I). The production of sounds requires energy, and this is usually supplied by the diaphragm and the chest muscles, which enable us to send a flow of breath up from the lungs. Some languages use additional sources of energy: it is possible to make clicking noises by muscular movements of the tongue, and popping noises by movements of the cheeks and lips, and such sounds are found for example in some of the languages of Africa. But in English we rely on the outflow of air from the lungs, which is modified in various ways by the 'set' of the organs that it passes through before finally emerging at the mouth or nose.

First the air from the lungs passes through the vocal cords. These are rather like a small pair of lips attached to the walls of the windpipe, and we are able to adjust these lips to various

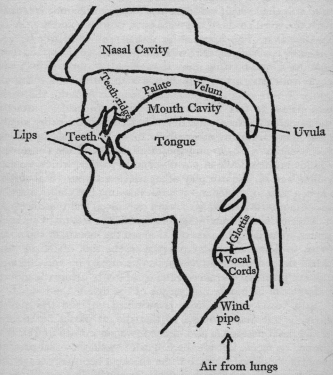

FIG. 1. Main speech-organs. Tongue is usually divided (l. to r.) into tip, blade, front, back, and root. The glottis is the opening between the vocal chords. Alternative names – *soft palate* (for *velum*) and *alveolar ridge* (for *teeth-ridge*).

positions, from fully closed (when the flow of air is completely blocked) to wide open (when the flow of air is quite unobstructed). In one of the intermediate positions, the vocal cords vibrate as the air passes through, and produce a musical

tone called *voice*. We can vary the pitch of the voice (how high
or low the tone is on the musical scale), and the pitch of our
voice varies constantly as we speak, producing the characteristic melodies of English sentences. Sounds in which voice is
used are called *voiced* sounds, but some speech sounds are made
with the vocal cords in the wide open position, and are therefore *voiceless*. The presence or absence of voice can be de-
tected by covering the ears with the hands: voiced sounds then
produce a loud buzzing noise in the head. If, for example, you
cover your ears firmly and utter a long continuous *v* sound,
you will hear voice; if you change it to an *f* sound, the voice
disappears. In fact the English *v* and *f* are made in exactly
the same way, except that one is voiced and the other voiceless. There are many other similar pairs in English, including
z and *s*, the *th* of *this* and the *th* of *thing*, and the consonant
sounds in the middle of *pleasure* and of *washer*, which we can
call *zh* and *sh*. We can play other tricks with our vocal cords:
we can sing, or whisper, or speak falsetto: but the two really
important positions for speech are the voiced and the voiceless.

After passing through the vocal cords, the stream of air continues upwards and passes out through the mouth, or the nose,
or both. The most backward part of the roof of the mouth,
called the soft palate or velum, can be moved up and down to
close or open the entrance to the nasal cavity, while the mouth
passage can be blocked by means of the lips or the tongue.

In a vowel sound, voice is switched on, and the mouth
cavity is left unobstructed, so that the air passes out freely.
If the nasal passage is also opened, we get a nasal vowel, like
French *on* or *un*, but for the English vowels the nasal passage
is normally closed (though some speakers habitually leave the
door ajar and speak with a nasal 'twang'). The quality of a
vowel is determined by the position of the tongue, lower jaw,
and lips, because these can change the shape of the cavity that
the air passes through, and different shapes give different
resonances. The tongue is the most important. If we raise
some part of our tongue, we divide the mouth passage into two
cavities of different sizes, one at the back and one at the front;

the quality of the vowel is largely determined by the relative sizes of these two cavities. To describe any vowel sound, therefore, we specify the position of the highest part of the tongue; we can do this in terms of its height (open, mid, or close) and its retraction (front, central, or back). A little experimentation with your finger in your mouth, or with a torch and a mirror, will demonstrate the way the tongue changes

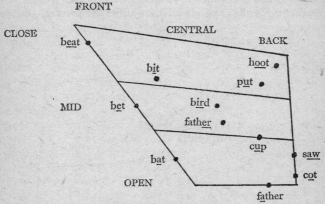

FIG. 2. Tongue position for 12 vowels of present-day English (educated speakers, South-East England).

position for different vowels. It is convenient to represent the tongue position for different vowels by means of a vowel diagram. This is a conventionalized cross section of the mouth cavity seen from the left-hand side, on which a vowel is marked as a dot, representing the position of the highest point of the tongue. Figure 2 shows a vowel diagram for the English vowels as spoken by educated people in the southeast of England.

The quality of a vowel is also affected by the position of the lips, which can be spread wide, or held neutral, or rounded more or less tightly. In most forms of English, lip rounding plays no independent part, for it is an automatic accompaniment of the backmost vowels, and the tightness of the rounding varies directly with the closeness of the vowel; you can easily check this with the help of a mirror and of the vowel diagram (but it may not be true if you are Scots or Irish). But this is not so in all languages: in French, the *u* of *lune* is made with almost the same tongue position as the *ea* of English *lean*, but is made with rounded lips, which gives it quite a different sound.

Vowels can also differ in length. In fact, other things being equal, the English vowels all have different lengths, but it is

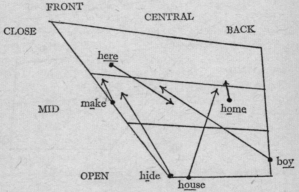

FIG. 3. Vowel Diagram for six diphthongs in present-day English (educated speakers, South-East England).

convenient to make a broad division into two groups, the long and the short. The short vowels are those heard in *pick*, *peck*, *pack*, *put*, *cut*, and *cot*, together with what we can call 'the short *er* sound', which is heard in the *er* of *father* and the *a* of *about*.

The vowel diagram of Figure 2 assumes that the vocal organs remain stationary while the vowel is uttered. But this is not always the case, for there are vowels in which the speech organs change their positions in the course of the sound. These are called glides or diphthongs. An example is the vowel heard in the word *boy*; here the speech organs begin quite near the position they have for the vowel of *saw*, but almost immediately move towards the position they have for the vowel of *bit*, though they may not go all the way there. During most of the sound, the speech organs are moving, though they may remain for a short time in the initial position before the gliding movement begins. Other English diphthongs are heard in the words *hide*, *house*, *make*, *home*, *hare*, *here*, and *poor*. On the vowel diagram, diphthongs can be represented by arrows, and some examples are given in Figure 3. Notice that my definition of a diphthong is concerned with *sound*, not with *spelling*. In popular usage, the *au* of 'cause' and the *æ* of 'mediæval' are often referred to as diphthongs, but these are not diphthongs in my sense of the word: they are pure vowels which happen to be represented in spelling by two letters (the digraph *au* and the ligature *æ*). Conversely, a diphthong may be represented in spelling by a single letter, like the *y* of 'fly'.

I have spoken of diphthongs as single vowel sounds, not as combinations of two vowel sounds. One good reason for doing so is that a diphthong forms only one syllable, not two. A syllable is a peak of loudness in the chain of utterance. If you could measure the acoustic power output of a speaker as it varies with time, you would find that it goes continually up and down, forming little peaks and valleys; the peaks are syllables. The words *hare* and *poor* form only one peak each, and so only one syllable, whereas the words *layer* and *newer* are usually pronounced with two peaks and so contain two syllables. It is thus desirable to distinguish between a diphthong (which is one syllable) and a sequence of two vowels (which is two syllables). Alternatively, a diphthong can be analysed as the combination of a vowel with a semivowel (a non-syllabic glide, like the *y* in *yes*), and this analysis is in fact adopted by many linguists, especially Americans.

In all vowels, the mouth passage is unobstructed. If the mouth passage is obstructed at any time during the production of a sound, it is a consonant. In English, there are three major types of consonant: fricatives, stops, and resonants.

Fricatives are made by narrowing the air passage so much that the stream of air produces audible friction. In *f* and *v*, the constriction is made by pressing the lower lip against the top teeth, while in *th* the tip of the tongue is pressed against the upper teeth. In *s* and *z*, the front of the tongue is pressed against the roof of the mouth (the palate), and the air allowed to flow down a narrow channel in the middle of the tongue, while for *sh* and *zh* the passage is made wider and flatter. In southeastern English, *r* is often a fricative, but in some dialects of English it is a trill, in which the tip of the tongue vibrates rapidly. In some languages, the consonant written as *r* is quite a different sort of sound: in the best known varieties of French and German, it is not made with the front of the tongue, but with the uvula (the small fleshy appendage to the soft palate, which can be seen hanging at the back of the mouth); and in some Indian languages there is an *r* made by curling the tongue right back and articulating against the roof of the mouth.

In stop consonants, the flow of air from the lungs is completely blocked at some point, and pressure built up behind the blockage; then the blockage is suddenly removed, and there is an outrush of air. The exact sound produced will depend on where and how the blockage is made, and on the speed of the release. In *p* and *b*, the blockage is made by pressing the two lips together; in *t* and *d*, the tip of the tongue is pressed against the teeth ridge, i.e. the convex part of the roof of the mouth immediately behind the upper teeth (not against the teeth themselves, as in many other languages); and in *k* and *g* the back part of the tongue is lifted and pressed against the soft palate. In these six sounds, the release is very sudden. In *ch* and *j*, which are made in much the same position as *t* and *d*, the release of the blockage is slower, and this gives a different effect, so that *ch* sounds something like a *t* followed very rapidly by a *sh*. Stops with rapid release are called plosives, and those with slow release affricates.

In the resonant consonants, use is made of resonant cavities, as in the vowels, but there is some kind of obstruction in the mouth passage. The English resonants are the nasals, *m*, *n*, and *ng* (as in *sing*), and the lateral consonant *l*. In the nasals, the nasal passage is open but the mouth passage blocked; in the lateral, the centre of the mouth is blocked by the tongue, while the air is allowed to escape down one side, or down both. These are all normally voiced in English, though they may become voiceless or partially voiceless under certain conditions, for example when they follow an *s*. In Welsh, you will hear an *l* sound (spelt *ll*) which is regularly voiceless, but this is a fricative consonant rather than a resonant. In English, resonant consonants can form syllables; it is sometimes asserted that every syllable must contain a vowel, but this is not so, as can be seen from words like *table* and *button*: in normal pronunciation, each of these has two syllables, the second of which contains no vowel.

This brief account has perhaps given some idea of the kind of vocal material used in the human signalling system. Let us now turn to the word *system*, which is very important.

SYSTEM IN LANGUAGE

A language consists of a number of linked systems, and structure can be seen in it at all levels. For a start, any language selects a small number of vocal sounds out of all those which human beings are able to make, and uses them as its building bricks; and the selection is different for every language. The number of vocal sounds that a human being can learn to make (and to distinguish between) is quite large – certainly running into hundreds – and if you know a foreign language you will be familiar with speech sounds which do not occur in English, like the vowel of the French word *peu* or the consonant of the German *ich*. But out of all these possible sounds, most languages are content with a mere twenty or thirty as their basic material. In English, if you treat the diphthongs as independent sounds, the number is about forty-five; if you treat the diphthongs and the long vowels as combinations of a vowel and a semivowel, the number comes down to about thirty-five. Some languages are more modest in their demands: Italian, which is fairly average, uses only seven different vowels, and manages with twenty-seven basic sounds altogether; Hawaiian is said to manage with only thirteen. Some languages, on the other hand, use sixty or more.

You may have thought of an objection to my suggestion that English makes use of no more than forty-five basic sounds: pronunciation varies from speaker to speaker. Speakers from Manchester, from Edinburgh, from New York use different sounds. Doesn't this mean that there are hundreds of different sounds in English? This is obviously true. These variations, moreover, occur between different social groups as well as between different regions, for there are class dialects as well as regional dialects. The important thing is, however, that all these speakers use what is essentially the same *system* of sounds. When they pronounce the word *man*, they may all use a rather different vowel sound, but all these sounds occupy the same position in the system: they all contrast, for example, with a different vowel sound in *men*, but fail to contrast with the vowel sound heard in a whole number of other words, like *fan* and *can*. Consequently, these different speakers can understand one another without too much difficulty. This assumes, of course, that many sounds will not vary greatly from one speaker to another, and this is in fact true: the *m* and the *n* of the word *man* are pronounced in pretty well the same way by speakers of English all over the world, and it is only the vowel in the word that varies.

Not only do the forty-five basic sounds of English vary from region to region, from class to class, and even from speaker to speaker within a class and region: they also vary in a systematic way within the speech of each individual. These variations depend on the position of the sound – the other sounds that are adjacent to it, the part of the word that it occurs in. Take the English *p* sound. This is a voiceless stop, made by blocking the flow of air through the mouth by pressing the two lips together, and then suddenly releasing the blockage by opening the lips. In the speech of most English people, the release of the *p* is normally followed by a little rush of air, which makes a kind of *h* sound between the stop and the sound that comes next in the word; but when the *p* follows an *s* which belongs to the same syllable, this rush of air is missing, so that we use slightly different variants of the *p* sound in the words *park* and *spark*. You can test this by holding the palm of your hand about an inch in front of your mouth and speaking the two words aloud: in *park* you will feel a strong puff of breath on your hand, but in *spark* the puff is much reduced. If you listen carefully you can also *hear* the difference between the two *p* sounds, but you don't usually notice it in speech because it has no significance for the meaning of what is said: the difference between the two sounds is determined automatically by the neighbouring sounds, and is not used to distinguish between different words.

Another variant of the *p* sound is heard before *m*, as in *top-most*: in this case the stop is released, not by opening the lips, but by letting the air flow out of the nose in an *m* sound, and the lips are not opened until the end of the *m*. Yet another variant is often heard when *p* comes at the end of a sentence, as when you say 'Can I take your cup?'; here it is common not to release the blockage at all, but just to leave the lips together at the end of the sentence. We see, then, that what I have called the English *p* sound in fact consists of a whole group of sounds, slightly different variants being used according to the phonetic context. And this is true of the English sounds generally. For example, you will probably find that you use different kinds of *m* in the words *come*, *triumph*, and *smooth*: different kinds of *l* in the words *old*, *leak*, and *sleek*; and different kinds of long *u* sound in the words *do*, *cool*, and *music*.

You may now feel inclined to ask what has happened to my forty-five basic sounds of English, the building bricks that the language is made up from. It has become clear, at any rate, that the word 'sounds' is hardly suitable: let us say instead that the sound-system of English has forty-five basic terms or positions, each of which is represented by a whole group of related sounds. The sounds of any one group have a good deal in common, but there are small variations which depend on the context; these variations are normally unnoticed by the native speaker, because they are produced automatically, but they may be very obvious to a foreigner, whose language has a different sound-system. Such groups of related and non-contrasting sounds are called *phonemes*; and we can now amend my earlier statement and say that the English language has about forty-five phonemes (the exact number depending on how you decide to treat diphthongs, and a few similar points).

System can also be seen in the ways in which the phonemes can be combined into words. As far as I know, there is no English word *grust* or *blomby*, but there is no reason why there shouldn't be; whereas the groups *ngust* and *glbombr* (although perfectly pronounceable if you care to try) will immediately be rejected by a native speaker as not conforming to the pattern of English words. There are restrictions on the combinations in which English phonemes can occur. The *ng* sound (as in *sing*) cannot occur at the beginning of a word, nor can the *zh* sound (though it can in French, as in the word *je*). Some of the short vowels (for example, that heard in *man*) never occur as the last sound in a word, nor does *h*. (Don't be misled by the *spelling*, and say that there's an *h* sound in *oh* or an *a* sound in *China*.) Again, at the beginning of a word we can have the cluster of consonants *spl-*, but not the cluster *sgl-*; and at the end of a word we can have the cluster *-thmz* (as in *rhythms*) but not the cluster *-gbz*. And so on. These rules, of course, apply only to the English language; other languages have their own systems, and combinations that are impossible in English, and which may even seem quite jaw-breaking to us, may be perfectly normal in another language, and will not seem at all difficult or surprising to the speakers of that language, who are used to them.

When we consider, not isolated words, but whole utterances, we notice such things as stress, pitch, and rhythm, which are also systematic. We have already spoken of the small peaks of loudness which form syllables, but syllables themselves vary in loudness, and in any English utterance of any length there are syllables of many different degrees of loudness; broadly speaking, however, they fall into two groups, those that are relatively loud and those that are not; we can call these stressed and unstressed syllables respectively. In English, stress is closely linked with rhythm. Some languages, such as French and most of the languages of India, have a rhythm in which the syllables are evenly spaced: if a Frenchman speaks a sentence containing twenty syllables, and takes ten seconds to speak it, then the syllables will follow one another pretty regularly at half second intervals. But this is not true of English. Try speaking the following two sentences as naturally as you can, stressing in each the four syllables marked:

There's a new manager at the works today.
There's a new boss there today.

Although the first has eleven syllables, and the second only seven, you will probably find that the two sentences take about the same time to speak. The reason for this is not hard to see: a speaker of English tries to space the *stressed* syllables evenly, so that both sentences contain four time units. In the first sentence, the interval between *new* and *man-* is about the same as that between *man-* and *works*, so that the sequence *manager at the works* has to be taken very quickly.

I have already mentioned the way in which the musical pitch of the voice changes during an utterance, giving the characteristic melodies of English. The use of melody for conveying meaning can be shown very simply by speaking the two sentences:

He's going to be there?
He's going to be there.

In the first we have a rising melody at the end, and in the second a falling melody, and this makes the difference between a question and a statement. We can also use pitch for singling out the part of a sentence that we want to emphasize. Take the sentence 'Is John going to wear those trousers?'. We can select for special emphasis any word in this sentence except *to* ('*Is* John going to wear those trousers?', 'Is *John* going to wear those trousers?', etc.). If you examine what is going on when you speak the sentence with these various emphases, you will see that it is not just a matter of stressing the chosen word more strongly: you also begin it on a higher pitch than the other words, and make the pitch of your voice fall in the course of it.

In English, we only make use of musical pitch as a feature of a whole phrase or group of words: we use intonation (melody) to distinguish between different sentences, but not between different words. But in some languages, musical pitch is a distinguishing feature of the single word, and if you change the intonation it becomes a different word. For example, in the Thai language there are five different word tones: (1) mid tone, in which the voice remains on a level tone of medium pitch; (2) low tone, in which the voice remains on a level tone of low pitch; (3) high falling tone, where the voice begins just above medium pitch, rises, and then falls to below medium; (4) rising-falling tone, in which the voice rises from medium to high pitch and then falls a little; and (5) high rising tone, where the voice begins just below medium pitch, falls a little, then rises high. If the word *kaa* is spoken with mid tone, it is the name of a kind of weed; with low tone, it means 'ginger plant'; with high falling tone it means 'I'; with rising-falling tone it means 'to trade'; and with high rising tone it means 'leg'. Similarly, according to the tone used, *naa* can mean 'rice field' or 'face' or 'aunt'; *maa* can mean 'to come' or 'dog' or 'horse'; and *mii* can mean 'a bear' or 'to have' or 'a kind of noodle'.

System is found in many other aspects of a language. It is found in the ways words are constructed from smaller parts: for example, the way words like *beautiful, mirthful, mindful* are constructed with the suffix *-ful*, or *quickly, slowly, happily* formed from *quick*, *slow*, *happy*. It is found in the ways in which words change their form for different grammatical purposes, as in *boy* / *boys* or *talk* / *talks* / *talking* / *talked*. It is found in the rules for combining words into utterances – the *syntax* of the language. We say 'the good old times', not 'the old good times', and there is a complicated set of rules regulating the way a group of words of this kind is put together in English. Again, we say 'The dog bit John', and it seems almost like part of the order of nature that this shall mean that it was the dog that did the biting and John that suffered it: but it is not at all part of the order of nature, but just one of the conventions of our language; if the conventions were different, it could quite well mean the opposite. Or the conventions might demand a totally different order; for example, 'Bit John dog the'; and if you know any foreign languages, you will indeed be aware that the permissible arrangements of words, and the meanings of particular arrangements, vary from language to language.

System is also found in the realm of meaning. Words tend to form sets, and the meaning of a word depends on the other words in the set, with which it can be contrasted. This is very clear in sets of words denoting such things as military ranks (*captain*, *major*, *colonel*, etc.), where the meaning of each term depends on its position in the hierarchy. Similarly with the words for family relationships, where the categories are different in different languages: Swedish, for example, has no word exactly corresponding to our *uncle*, but has *farbror* (paternal uncle) and *morbror* (maternal uncle). Another obvious set is formed by words for colours, where different languages divide up the spectrum differently: for example, Latin *caeruleus* includes both dark blue and dark green, and there is no Latin word exactly corresponding to our *grey*, for *caesius* means 'bluish grey' and *rauus* covers the range from grey to tawny. Other clear sets are series of words corresponding to degrees of intensity of some kind, like *hot*, *warm*, *tepid*, *cool*, *cold*: if any one of these terms were missing from the language, the meanings of the others would be different, since they would have to cover the same range of intensity in a smaller number of divisions.

LANGUAGE IS SYMBOLIC

In all these ways a language shows system, and it is now perhaps clear, at any rate in a general way, what we mean when we say that a language is a system of vocal sounds. These sounds are *symbolic*. That is, they stand for something other

FIG. 4. British traffic signs. (*a*) representational, (*b*) symbolic.

than themselves, and their relationship to the thing that they stand for is not a necessary one, but arbitrary. A symbol is a kind of sign, but not all signs are symbols. This is illustrated in Figure 4, which shows two British traffic signs. The first shows two children running into the road: this is not symbolic, but representational, for it gives an actual picture of the hazard ahead of the motorist, who does not need to be initiated into the meaning of the sign. The second shows a blazing torch; this stands for learning, and indicates that there is a school ahead, but the relationship between a blazing torch and learning is an arbitrary one, and the motorist needs to have its meaning explained to him; the blazing torch is a symbol.

The same kind of distinction applies to gestures: when a chimpanzee shows a companion that he is hungry by pretending to eat, he is using a representational gesture; but when a man nods his head to indicate assent (or, in some cultures, refusal), the gesture is arbitrary and therefore symbolic. Weeping is a sign of sorrow, blushing a sign of shame, and paleness a sign of fear, but these signs are *caused* by the emotional states in question, and so are not arbitrary or symbolic. When a man shakes his fist in anger, he is delivering a blow in pantomime, and the gesture is essentially representational; but when a man raises a clenched or flattened hand in a communist or fascist salute, he has moved into the realm of the purely symbolic.

Animal gestures and cries are largely non-symbolic: they are either of the weeping and blushing kind, that is expressive cries or gestures; or they are representational, as when a chimpanzee pulls a companion in the direction he wants him to go, or pretends to eat. When a parrot or a crane or a gull cries out on the approach of a predator, and so warns its companions, it is reacting automatically to the stimulus of seeing the enemy; its cry triggers off reactions in its companions, which take to flight, but the bird in fact utters the warning cry even if there are no companions present to be warned. The evolutionary process will obviously favour animals where such expressive cries trigger off suitable reactions, but the element of symbolism is very small, perhaps totally absent.

Its symbolical quality is one of the things that makes human language so powerful a tool. The expressive cry or trigger stimulus can refer only to the immediate situation, to what is present to the senses; but the symbolical utterance can refer to things out of sight, to the past and the future, to the hypothetical and the possible. The change from expressive cry to vocal symbol marks the great leap forward of the intellect, from animal to human.

THE FUNCTIONS OF LANGUAGE

It is clear, if we look and listen, that language is used for more than one purpose. The man who hits his thumb-nail with a hammer and utters a string of curses is using language for an expressive purpose: he is relieving his feelings, and needs no audience but himself. People can often be heard *playing* with language: children especially like using language as if it were a toy, repeating, distorting, inventing, punning, jingling; and there is a play element in the use of language in some literature. But when the philosopher uses language to clarify his ideas on a subject, he is using it as an instrument of thought. When two women gossip over the fence, or two men exchange conventional greetings as they pass in the street, language is being used to strengthen the bonds of cohesion between the members of a society. Language, it seems, is a multi-purpose instrument. One function, however, seems to be basic: language enables us to influence people's behaviour, and to influence it in detail, and thereby makes human co-operation possible. Some animals co-operate, especially the social animals like bees and ants: but human co-operation is more thorough, more detailed, more effective than that found anywhere in the animal kingdom, and no animal society has a division of labour or a system of production at all comparable to those of human societies. This human co-operation would be unthinkable without language, and it is obviously this function of language that has made it so successful and so important; other functions can be looked upon as by-products. A language, of course, always belongs to a *group* of people, not to an individual; the group that uses any given language is called the *speech community*.

A language, then, is a signalling system which operates with symbolic vocal sounds, and which is used by some group of people for the purposes of communication and social co-operation. With this definition in mind, let us turn to the problem of the origins and early history of human language.

CHAPTER II

THE ORIGIN OF LANGUAGE AND THE INVENTION OF WRITING

WE ARE profoundly ignorant about the origins of language, and have to content ourselves with more or less plausible speculations. We do not even know for certain when language arose, but it seems likely that it goes back to the earliest history of man, perhaps half a million years. We have no direct evidence, but it seems probable that speech arose at the same time as tool-making and the earliest forms of specifically human co-operation. In the great Ice Ages of the Pleistocene period, our earliest human ancestors established the Old Stone Age culture: they made flint tools, and later tools of bone, ivory, and antler; they made fire and cooked their food; they hunted big game, often by methods that called for considerable co-operation and co-ordination. As their material culture gradually improved, they became artists, and made carvings and engravings on bones and pebbles, and wonderful paintings of animals on the walls of caves. It is difficult to believe that the makers of these Palaeolithic cultures lacked the power of speech. It is a long step, admittedly, from the earliest flint weapons to the splendid art of the late Old Stone Age: the first crude flints date back perhaps to 500,000 BC, while the finest achievements of Old Stone Age man are later than 100,000 BC; and in this period we can envisage a corresponding development of language, from the most primitive and limited language of the earliest human groups to a fully developed language in the flowering time of Old Stone Age culture.

EVIDENCE ABOUT THE ORIGINS OF LANGUAGE

How did language arise in the first place? There are many theories about this, based on various types of indirect evidence, such as the language of children, the language of primitive societies, the kinds of changes that have taken place in languages in the course of recorded history, the behaviour of higher animals like chimpanzees, and the behaviour of people suffering from speech defects. These types of evidence may provide us with useful pointers, but they all suffer from limitations, and must be treated with caution.

When we consider the language of children we have to remember that their situation is quite different from that of our earliest human ancestors, because the child is growing up in an environment where there is already a fully developed language, and is surrounded by adults who use that language and are teaching it to him. For example, it has been shown that the earliest words used by children are mainly the names of things and people ('Doll', 'Spoon', 'Mummy'): but this does not prove that the earliest words of primitive man were also the names of things and people. When the child learns the name of an object, he may then use it to express his wishes or demands: 'Doll!' often means 'Give me my doll!', or 'I've dropped my doll: pick it up for me!'; the child is using language to get things done, and it is almost an accident of adult teaching that the words used to formulate the child's demands are mainly nouns, instead of words like 'Bring!', 'Pick up!', and so on.

One thing that we can perhaps learn from the small child is the kind of articulated utterance that comes easiest to a human being before he has learnt the sound-system of one particular language. The first articulate word pronounced by a child is often something like *da*, *ma*, *na*, *ba*, *ga*, or *wa*. The vowel is most commonly a short *ah* sound, and the consonant a nasal or a plosive. Nearly always, these early 'words' consist of a consonant followed by a vowel, or of a sequence of syllables of this type (*dadada*, etc.). When the child attempts to copy words used by adults, he at first tends to produce words of this form, so that 'grandfather' may be rendered as *gaga*, 'thank you' as *tata*, and 'water' as *wawa*. This explains why, in so many languages, the nursery words for mother and father are *mama* or *dada* or *baba* or something similar: there is no magic inner connexion between the idea of parenthood and words of this form: these just happen to be the first articulated sounds that the child makes, and the proud parent attributes a suitable meaning to them. Such words may also have been the first utterances of primitive man, though hardly with this meaning.

The languages of primitive peoples, and the history of languages in literate times, may throw some light on the origin of language by suggesting what elements in it are the most archaic. But again we have to be careful, because the language of the most primitive people living today is still a very ancient and sophisticated one, with half a million years of history behind it; and the earliest written records can take us back only a few thousand years. It is probable, of course, that in early times language changed more slowly than in historical times. The whole history of human culture has been one of an accelerating rate of change: it took man about half a million years to develop through the Old Stone Age to the higher material culture of the Middle and New Stone Ages, but a mere 5,000 years or so for these to give way to the Bronze Age, and perhaps 1,000 for the Bronze Age to develop into the Iron Age; and since the Industrial Revolution, the pace has become dizzying. It is perhaps arguable that the rate of change in language has been parallel to that in material culture, and in that case the gap of half a million years between the origin of language and the first written records becomes a little less daunting. It remains daunting enough, however, and we must obviously be careful in theorizing about the remote past.

Still, we may be able to pick up some hints. For example, it is noticeable among primitive peoples how closely their languages are adapted to their material needs: in Eskimo, there is no single word for 'snow', but a whole series of words for 'new fallen snow', 'hard snow', and so on; and in general a primitive people tends to have words for the specific things that are materially important to it (like the particular birds or plants that it eats), and to lump together other things (like birds or plants that it does not eat) under some generic expression. We may also find some evidence about the types of word and the types of expression which are oldest: there is a good deal to suggest that words of command (like 'Give!', 'Strike!') are very archaic, since in the earliest known forms of many languages these imperative forms are identical with the simple stem of the verb, without any special ending added. Compare, for example, Latin *dic* ('say!') with *dicit* ('he says'), *dicunt* ('they say'), or *dicere* ('to say'): the form used for giving a command is the shortest, the most elementary. Some of the personal pronouns, like *me*, also seem to be very archaic, and so do vocatives (the forms of words used in addressing people).

A study of the higher animals can help us by suggesting what man was like in the pre-linguistic stage, immediately before he became man. The expressive noises, signals, and gestures of the higher apes show us what man started from in his creation of language; but they cannot show us how he created language, for it is man alone who has broken through to the use of symbols: the apes, however expressive their signals may be, remain on the other side of language. Apes, of course, have smaller brains than men; and man's development, as part of his adaptive evolution, of a larger and more complex brain than any other creature was undoubtedly a prerequisite for the emergence of language.

The last source of evidence, the behaviour of people suffering from speech defects, is probably the least helpful. The condition which has especially been referred to is *aphasia*, in which the power of speech is wholly or partially lost, often as a result of a brain injury. In recovering from aphasia, the patient to some extent repeats the process gone through by a child in learning to speak for the first time, and some psychologists have suggested that he also repeats the history of the human race in inventing language. It is difficult, however, to see the grounds for this belief, since language, though it uses inherited biological skills and aptitudes, is not itself a biological inheritance but a cultural one; and the kind of prehistory of language which has been constructed on evidence of this kind is not a very convincing one.

Emphasis on one type of evidence or another has led to

rather different theories of the origin of language. Different authors, too, seem to mean different things when they talk about the origin of language: some are thinking especially of the pre-language situation, and of the basic human skills and equipment that were a prerequisite for the invention of language; others are thinking more of the actual situations in which the first truly linguistic utterances took place; others again are thinking of the very early stages of language after its invention, and the ways in which it expanded its resources.

THE BOW-WOW THEORY

One theory is that primitive language was an imitation of natural sounds, such as the cries of animals. This has been called the bow-wow theory. Supporters of the theory point to the large number of words in any language which are, it seems, directly imitative of natural sounds – words like *quack*, *cuckoo*, *peewit*. They add that many other words show a kind of 'sound symbolism', enacting in sound whatever it is that they denote; examples of such words in English would be *splash*, *sludge*, *slush*, *grumble*, *grunt*, *bump*, and *sneeze*. It is certainly plausible to believe that a primitive hunter, wishing to tell his companions what kind of game he had found, may have imitated in gesture and sound whatever kind of animal it was – horse, or elephant, or quail; and this may well have played a part in the development of vocal symbols.

This theory, however, does not explain how language obtained its articulated structure. When we invent an imitative word like *whizzbang* or *crump*, we use an already existing language system, with its vowels and consonants, its laws of word structure, and so on, and we make our imitative word conform to this pattern. But man in the pre-linguistic stage had no such language system, and his imitation of a horse or an elephant would simply be a whinnying or trumpeting sound, without the articulation characteristic of speech. Imitation of this kind may explain part of the primitive vocabulary, and it may have played a part in the transition from expressive cry to vocal symbol, but it cannot by itself account satisfactorily for the rise of language.

Moreover, we probably deceive ourselves about the extent and importance of sound symbolism in language. Because of our intimate knowledge of our language since our early years, and the way it is bound up with our whole emotional and intellectual life, the words that we use inevitably *seem* appropriate to what they mean, simply by constant association. It may be retorted that some groups of sounds really are appropriate to certain meanings, and this is shown by their occurrence in a number of words of similar meaning: for example, in English we find initial *fl-* in a number of words connected with fire and light (e.g. *flame*, *flare*, *flash*) and in an even larger number of words connected with a flying or waving kind of motion (e.g. *flail*, *flap*, *flaunt*, *flay*, *flicker*, *flog*, *fluctuate*, *flurry*, *flutter*). But it is difficult to see any *inherent* appropriateness in the *fl-* sound for expressing ideas of flame or flickering motion: the sense of appropriateness surely arises from the fact that it occurs in all these words, not vice versa. And once a group of words like this exists in the language, new words may be coined on the same model (as perhaps happened with *flash* and *flap*), and words of similar form may develop new meanings on analogy with the members of the group (as has perhaps happened with *flourish*). But there are many other words in English which begin with *fl-*, which have nothing to do with flames or flickering, and yet which by long familiarity sound equally appropriate to their meanings, like *flange*, *flank*, *flannel*, *flask*, *flat*, *flesh*, *flimsy*, *flinch*, *flock*, and so on. It is noticeable that, when you learn a foreign language, the words that strike you as particularly appropriate in sound (or, sometimes, as grotesquely inappropriate) are very often ones that do not strike a native speaker in this way.

The Pooh-pooh Theory

A second theory of the origins of language has been called the pooh-pooh theory. This argues that language arose from instinctive emotional cries, expressive for example of pain or joy. On this view, the earliest linguistic utterances were inter-jections, simple exclamations expressive of some emotional state. This theory, it seems to me, suggests some of the ma-terial which language may have used, rather than the process by which it arose. The theory does nothing to explain the articulated nature of language, and it does little to bridge the gap between expressive cry and symbol. We can, indeed, imagine how, by association, an emotional cry may have be-come a signal: a cry of fear or of pain, for example, could easily become a signal which warned the group of danger; but this level has already been reached by the higher animals, which react to signals of this kind; the further step from trigger stimulus to symbol must also be explained. And the theory does not suggest any motivation for this development; a tremendous task like the creation of language would surely have been undertaken only under the pressure of man's needs.

THE DING-DONG THEORY

A third theory is the so-called nativistic theory, nicknamed the ding-dong theory. This begins from a fact we have already noticed, namely that there is an apparently mysterious har-mony between sound and sense in a language. On this basis, the theory argues that primitive man had a peculiar instinctive faculty, by which every external impression that he received was given vocal expression. Every sensory impression was like the striking of a bell, producing a corresponding utterance. The trouble with this theory is that it explains nothing: it merely describes the facts in a different terminology, and so is only a pseudo-theory.

THE YO-HE-HO THEORY

A fourth theory, put forward by the nineteenth-century scholar Noiré, has been called the yo-he-ho theory. This en-visages language arising from the noises made by a group of men engaged in joint labour or effort – moving a tree trunk, lifting a rock. We all know from experience that, while performing work of this kind, we make involuntary vocal noises. While exerting powerful muscular effort we trap the breath in our lungs by tightly closing the glottis (the vocal cords); in the intervals of relaxation between the bursts of effort, we open the glottis and release the air, making various grunting and groaning noises in the process; since a stop is released, these noises often contain a consonantal sound as well as a vowel. Vocal noises of this kind might then develop into words, meaning such things as 'heave!', 'rest!', 'lift!'. This theory has two great virtues: it gives a plausible explanation for the origin of the consonant-vowel structure of language, and it envisages the origin of language in a situation involving human co-operation, with adequate motivation. It also envisages the earliest speech utterances as commands, and we have already seen that there is some linguistic evidence for the antiquity of such imperative forms. Against the theory, it has been argued that it postulates too advanced a form of social co-operation: language, it is argued, would be necessary *before* men could embark on the kind of complex communal labour that the theory demands. I am not sure that this objection is very compelling: we must surely envisage language and co-operative human labour arising *simultaneously*, each making the other possible; they would continually react on one another, so that there would be a progressive development from the simplest utterances and acts of co-operation to the most complex speech and division of labour.

A variant of the theory has recently been elaborated by A. S. Diamond. He agrees that the first articulated words were commands, uttered simultaneously with the execution of violent arm movements, but argues that all the evidence shows that the most primitive words did not mean such things as 'Haul!', but rather such things as 'Strike!', 'Cut!', 'Break!'. He therefore envisages the rise of language in requests for assistance from one man to another in situations where maximum bodily effort was required. He does not speculate on the exact nature of these situations, but presumably they might be such things as tool-making, the breaking off of tree branches, and the killing of animals during hunting. Such things might occur at a more primitive stage of human society than the communal heaving suggested by Noiré.

THE GESTURE THEORY

A fifth theory of the origins of language takes the view that gesture language preceded speech. Supporters of this theory point to the extensive use of gestures by animals of many different kinds, and the highly developed systems of gesture used by some primitive peoples. One of the popular examples is the sign language formerly used by the Red Indians of North America; this was an elaborate system of gestures which was used for negotiations between tribes that spoke different languages. It is certainly true that speech and gesture are closely intertwined; the centres in the brain which control hand movements are closely linked with those that control the vocal organs, and it seems highly probable that speech and gesture grew up together. This does not prove, however, that gesture came *first*. And, while it is true that animals use gestures, it is also true that they use cries: the chimpanzee makes signals and expresses its feelings both by bodily movements and by vocal noises, and the same was probably true of early man.

An extreme form of the gesture theory argues that speech arose very late (round about 3500 BC) and was derived from early pictorial writing; this writing itself, it is argued, was derived from gesture language. I must say that I find this incredible. We are asked to believe that man lacked speech right through the Old and New Stone Ages, and did not develop it until the time of the city civilizations of the early Bronze Age. But it is difficult to believe that man could have built up the elaborate cultural apparatus of the New Stone Age (agriculture, pottery, weaving, house building, religious burial) without the aid of speech; for a gesture language, however highly developed, has grave disadvantages compared with a spoken language. To use a gesture language you have to have your hands free; but as soon as man becomes a tool-maker and a craftsman his hands cease to be free; and the times when primitive man needed to communicate most urgently must have been precisely the times when he had a tool or a weapon in his hand. It is in fact arguable that it was just this pre-occupation of man's hands with tools and weapons that led to the increased importance of vocal language compared with gestures; and this would support the view that spoken language goes right back to the beginning of man's career as tool-maker. Gesture, too, has the disadvantage that it cannot be used in the dark, or when the users are separated by obstructions like trees – a serious disadvantage for a hunting band, which would surely develop hunting calls and similar cries. Nor can a gesture be used to attract the attention of somebody who is looking in another direction, and so it has very limited value as a warning of the approach of danger. None of these disadvantages of gesture can *prove* that early man had a spoken language, but they do suggest that he had very powerful motives for creating one.

A more attractive version of the gesture theory is the *mouth gesture* theory, which was strongly argued by Sir Richard Paget and has recently been supported by an Icelandic professor, Alexander Jóhannesson. Paget argues that primitive man at first communicated by gestures; as his intelligence and technique developed he needed more exact gestures, but at the same time found that his eyes and hands were more occupied by his arts and crafts. But the gestures of the hands were unconsciously copied by movements of the tongue, lips, and mouth; and when the man was unable to go on gesturing with his hands because of their other uses, the mouth gestures continued without them, and he discovered that if air was blown through the mouth or nose the gesture became audible as whispered speech; if he simultaneously sang or roared or grunted, he produced voiced speech. To support his theory of the sympathetic movements of the speech organs, Paget quotes a passage from Darwin's book *The Expression of the Emotions*:

There are other actions which are commonly performed under certain circumstances independently of habit, and which seem to be due to imitation or some kind of sympathy. Thus, persons cutting anything with a pair of scissors may be seen to move their jaws simultaneously with the blades of the scissors. Children learning to write often twist about their tongue as their fingers move, in a ridiculous fashion!

Language was thus produced by a sort of pantomime, the tongue and lips mimicking the movements of the hands in a gesture. As an elementary example, Paget takes the movement of the mouth, tongue, and jaws as in eating, as a gesture sign meaning 'eat'. If, while making this sign, we blow air through the vocal cavities and switch on voice, we produce the sounds *mnyum mnyum* or *mnya mnya*, which, Paget says, would be universally understood. Similarly, the action of sucking a liquid in small quantities into the mouth produces words like *sip* or *sup*. Paget goes on to analyse large numbers of words in terms of mouth gestures of this kind, and this work has been continued by Jóhannesson, who has examined large numbers of the basic words of the earliest known languages. Some of these analyses strike me as fanciful, and there are times when one feels that, with sufficient ingenuity, any movement of the tongue could be construed as a gesture representing anything one liked. Nevertheless, the theory has considerable plausibility, and must be taken seriously. It has the merit of accounting for the articulated nature of speech, and of giving an explanation for the way the linkage was effected between sound and meaning.

THE MUSICAL THEORY

A sixth theory sees the origin of language in song, or at any rate sees speech and music as emerging from something earlier that included both. This theory was put forward by the great Danish linguist Otto Jespersen. He thought that the bow-wow, pooh-pooh, and yo-he-ho theories could all explain the origins of parts of language, but that none of them could explain the whole of it. His own method was to trace the history of language backwards, to see what the long-term trends were, and then to assume that these same trends had existed since the beginning of language. By this means he arrived at the view that primitive language consisted of very long words, full of difficult jaw-breaking sounds; that it used tone and pitch more than later languages, and a wider range of musical intervals; and that it was more passionate and more musical than later languages. Earlier still, language was a kind of song without words; it was not communicative, but merely expressive; the earliest language was not matter-of-fact or practical, but poetic and emotional, and love in particular was the most powerful emotion for eliciting outbursts of music and song. 'Language,' he writes, 'was born in the courting days of mankind; the first utterances of speech I fancy to myself like something between the nightly love-lyrics of puss upon the tiles and the melodious love-songs of the nightingale.' A romantic picture.

It may be doubted, however, whether the trends in language are as constant and universal as Jespersen thinks. His theory assumes that the same kinds of general change have taken place in all languages throughout their history. But we know nothing of languages before the Bronze Age; even if there has been a universal trend in language since the beginnings of Bronze Age civilization (which is by no means certain), it does not follow that the same trend occurred in the Old Stone Age, when man's circumstances were entirely different. Moreover, we have a historical knowledge of relatively few of the world's languages: of the two thousand languages spoken today, only a handful have records going back to the pre-Christian era.

THE CONTACT THEORY

Finally, mention may be made of the contact theory, which has recently been advanced by G. Révész, a former professor of psychology at Amsterdam. He sees language as arising through man's instinctive need for contact with his fellows, and he works out a series of stages by which language may have developed. First comes the contact sound, which is not communicative, but merely expresses the individual's need for contact with his fellows; such are the noises made by gregarious animals. Next comes the cry, which is communicative, but which is directed to the environment generally, not to an individual; examples are mating calls and the cries of young nestlings in danger. Then there is the call, which differs from the cry in being directed to an individual; it is the demand for the satisfaction of some desire, and is found in domestic animals (begging) and speechless infants (crying for their mother); the call is seen as the starting point for both music and language. Finally comes the word, which has symbolic function and is found only in man. Révész thinks that the earliest speech was an 'imperative language', consisting only of commands; this later developed into mature human language, which contains also statements and questions. Révész's sequence of stages is carefully worked out, and is made very plausible. He does not, however, explain how human language came to be articulated; and he places undue emphasis on the instinctive need for contact as a motive for the invention of language, while rather neglecting the urgent practical motives in co-operative labour which must surely have impelled early man.

THE PROBABILITIES

What are we to make of this welter of theories? It is plain that no finality is possible at present, and that it is merely a matter of weighing the probabilities. It seems to me that we should attach great weight to the question of motivation in the origin of language, since such a great intellectual achievement would hardly have been possible except under the pressure of definite needs. Since the basic function of language is to influence the behaviour of our fellow men, this would favour theories that emphasize the origins of language in situations of social co-operation: such for example are the yo-he-ho theory and Diamond's variant of it. However, other theories, such as the bow-wow theory and the mouth gesture theory, can also be adapted to views of this kind. In the second place, I think we should attach great importance to the articulatedness of language, as seen for example in its vowel and consonant structure; and it seems to me the weakness of many theories that they do nothing to explain this structure; the theories that come off best on this count are the yo-he-ho theory and the mouth gesture theory. But at present we cannot reach absolute certainty.

We must also remain in doubt about the nature of the earliest language, and we do not even know if there was one original language or whether language was invented independently at several different times and places. Jespersen, we have seen, postulates a primitive language that was musical and passionate; he believes that it was very irregular; that it dealt with the concrete and particular rather than the abstract and general; that it contained very long words full of difficult combinations of sounds; and indeed that the earliest utterances consisted of whole sentences rather than single words. Somewhat similar views have been advanced by investigators who have attached great significance to the babbling stages of child speech. But Révész thinks that the earliest language consisted solely of commands; so does Diamond, who argues that these were single words and had the structure consonant-vowel-consonant-vowel (like *bada* or *taka*). The bow-wow theory, on the other hand, demands a primitive language full of imitative sounds like the howling of wolves or the trumpeting of elephants. In the absence of certainty about the origins of language, we must obviously lack certainty about the form which that language took (though the kind of language envisaged by Révész or Diamond seems more plausible than that envisaged by Jespersen).

Inevitably we remain in the realm of more or less plausible speculation as long as we are dealing with a period which has left us no record of its language. Once we reach periods in which writing was practised, we are on much firmer ground, and this chapter can well conclude with a few remarks on the early history of writing.

THE ORIGINS OF WRITING

Writing, in the strict sense of the word, is derived from speech, and is in fact an imperfect visual representation of it, for such purposes as communication at a distance and the keeping of records. Not all visual communications and records are writing in this sense: primitive peoples often use systems of knots tied in ropes, or of notches cut in sticks, as aids to the memory; these are not writing, because the symbols do not correspond to particular words or other linguistic items: they speak their meaning to anybody initiated into the code, whatever his language. The same is true of the most primitive communications by means of pictures, which tell a story independently of language. Such pictures, indeed, are important for the development of writing, for it is very largely out of them that writing has grown.

PICTURE WRITING

We have already noticed the artistic leanings of palaeolithic man, which expressed themselves in paintings on rocks, pictures scratched on bone or ivory, and even female figurines made from clay or soft stone. The purpose of such works was probably magical – to enable the hunter to master the beast depicted or acquire its strength, to promote fertility, and so on. Later, pictures were used for keeping records and for sending messages, and both these uses are known among primitive peoples in historical times. Picture writing was used, for example, among the North American Indians until quite recent times; the pictures were scratched or painted on birch bark or animal skins, and could be used for communication between people who spoke different languages. An example of American Indian picture writing, taken from Colonel Garrick Mallery's enormous work on the subject, is given in Figure 5. This was a notice left on a tree by scouts of the Micmac tribe, which was at war with the Passamaquoddy tribe, and is a warning that ten Passamaquoddy Indians have been seen in canoes on the lake, going towards its outlet. The ten marks to the left of the canoe indicate the number of enemy seen. The fact that they *are* enemy is shown by the fish which the canoe is following; this is meant to be a pollock, which is the tribal emblem of the Passamaquoddy. The rest of the picture is a map, with an arrow on the lake showing the direction in which the ten Passamaquoddy have been seen moving.

This message depicts a whole situation. It uses conventional

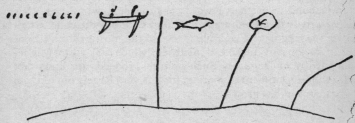

FIG. 5. Red Indian Picture Writing, see text.

signs, such as the tribal emblem and the arrow, but it is not bound to any particular set of words, or even to any one language. We still use pictures in this way, for example the traffic sign showing a boy and a girl stepping into the road (Figure 4), or the silhouette figures of a man and a woman used in many airports to mark men's and ladies' lavatories (the use of pictographs rather than writing being desirable in this case because of the mixed nationalities of the passengers). In some cases, the picture has been simplified and conventionalized; for example, like the Micmac Indians, we often use an arrow to show the way to something or the direction in which people must go, but this arrow has taken on a conventional form, and does not much resemble the feathered flights or metal bolts of longbowmen or crossbowmen. In other cases the sign, whatever its origin, is now completely conventional: such are the signs of mathematics, the signs used by astronomers to symbolize the planets, and the signs used by biologists to denote sex, ♂ for male and ♀ for female. These signs are conventional, but they are not tied to any one language; they can be called *ideograms*, because they stand directly for an idea, without the intervention of any specific linguistic form. They are not therefore *writing* in the narrow sense.

In the development of writing out of pictures, two main processes took place: (1) the pictures were simplified and conventionalized, until they were not recognizable as pictures at all; and (2) they were made to stand directly for linguistic items (first words, then syllables, and finally sounds or phonemes) and arranged in the same order as the linguistic items.

THE CONVENTIONALIZATION OF PICTURES

The process of simplification and conventionalization depended to some extent on the materials used for writing. If symbols are scratched on clay, or incised on wood or stone, there is a tendency to avoid curves, and the writing becomes angular. This can be seen in a very famous and very early form of writing (perhaps the earliest true writing) which was developed by the Sumerians in southern Mesopotamia some time between 4000 and 3000 BC. The Sumerian scribes wrote on clay with a stylus made from a reed. At first they drew little pictures by pulling the tip of the stylus through the clay, but this is not very efficient, for the clay heaps up in front of the stylus and blurs the picture. So later they simply pressed the head of the stylus into the clay as if it were a stamp, thus producing a little wedge shaped mark about a third of an inch long; each picture was made from a group of wedges of this kind. For this reason the writing is called *cuneiform*, which simply means 'wedge shaped'. The scribes tended to avoid wedges pointing in some directions, since they were more difficult to make: for example, wedges pointing from right to left were avoided, because they involved turning the stylus right round. So gradually the marks used became more limited in

number, and the signs became increasingly conventionalized
and remote from the original pictures. Figure 6 shows how
some of the original pictorial signs developed into conventional
cuneiform symbols. You will notice that the ultimate signs are
at right angles to the original pictures. This is due to the way in
which the clay tablet was held: at one period, the tablets were
small and were held in the palm of the left hand, with the

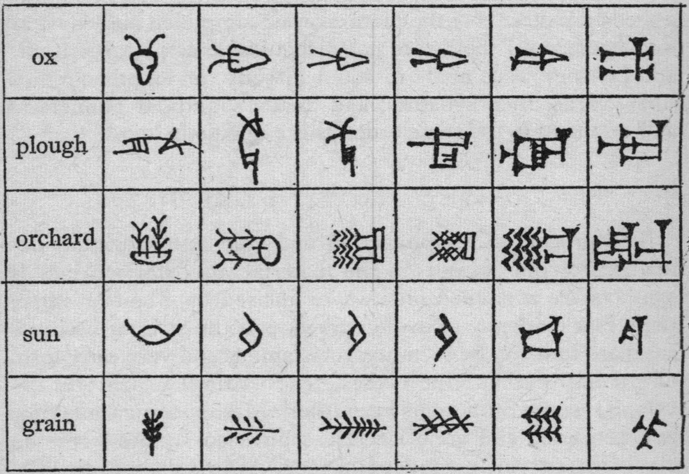

ox						
plough						
orchard						
sun						
grain						

FIG. 6. Development of five Sumerian picture-signs into cuneiform symbols.
The last two columns are classical Babylonian and Assyrian respectively.

fingertips gripping the top of the tablet; while the scribe was
writing on them with his right hand, the top of the tablet would
tend to point to his right rather than upwards, so that the pictures were drawn with their 'tops' pointing towards the left-
hand edge of the tablet instead of towards its top edge. Later,
when tablets became larger and were rested on a table, the
scribes continued to draw the symbols facing this way.

The Sumerians were quite early replaced as the great power
of the Mesopotamian region by various Semitic peoples, such
as the Babylonians and the Assyrians, but the Semites took

over the Sumerian writing and improved it, and for many centuries cuneiform was the almost universal script of the Near East. Besides being used by the East Semitic peoples, it was adopted at one time or another by various peoples speaking non-Semitic languages, like the Hittites and the Persians.

But when scribes write with a pen or a brush on leather or papyrus, a different development takes place: curves, far from being difficult, offer the easiest and most rapid forms, and a

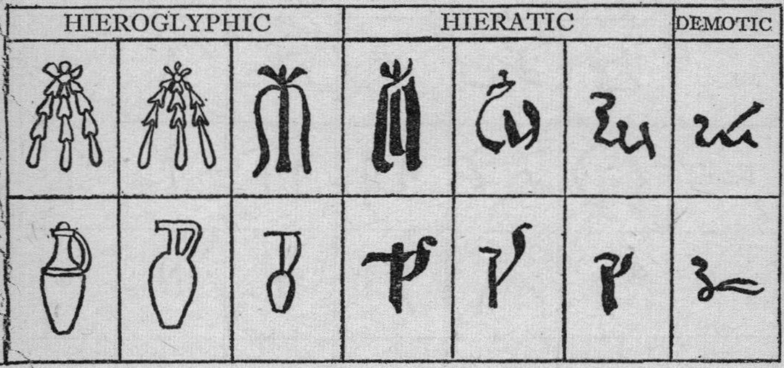

HIEROGLYPHIC			HIERATIC			DEMOTIC

FIG. 7. Development of two Egyptian hieroglyphs into purely conventional hieratic and demotic symbols.

cursive style of writing may arise. This is seen in ancient Egyptian writing. The original Egyptian script, going back to about 3000 BC, was pictorial, and is called *hieroglyphic* writing, from a Greek word meaning 'holy carved (letters)', because the Greeks believed that the Egyptians used this script mainly for religious inscriptions. In fact it could be painted as well as carved, and it was also used for documents written on papyrus, a paper-like writing material made from a sedge plant. For writing on papyrus, the scribes used a kind of brush pen. The hieroglyphic script was used throughout ancient Egyptian times for religious purposes, but for everyday use a more conventionalized form of writing very soon developed from it, less complicated and much quicker to write, which is known as *hieratic*, or priestly writing; from this, in turn, developed in about 700 BC a script called *demotic*, or 'popular' writing.

Examples of hieroglyphic symbols and their development in hieratic and demotic are given in Figure 7.

The conventionalization of a pictorial script seen in Sumerian and Egyptian writing can be paralleled elsewhere, for example in traditional Chinese writing. What about our own alphabet? Where have our letters come from? Our alphabet,

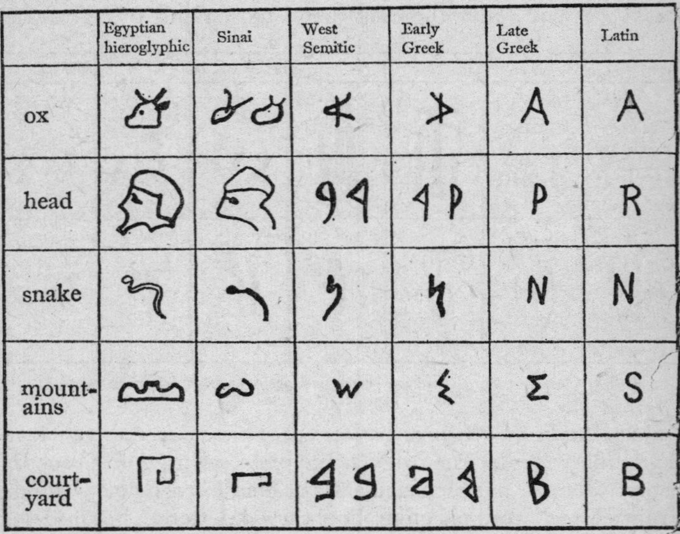

	Egyptian hieroglyphic	Sinai	West Semitic	Early Greek	Late Greek	Latin
ox					A	A
head					P	R
snake					N	N
mountains					Σ	S
courtyard					B	B

FIG. 8. Development of five letters of our alphabet from Egyptian hieroglyphs.

like all those of western Europe, is derived from the Latin alphabet. This in turn is derived from the Greek alphabet, which is also the ancestor of the Cyrillic alphabets (used for Russian and some other eastern European languages). The Greeks in turn got their alphabet from a West Semitic people, almost certainly the Phoenicians (who were great sailors and traders), round about 900 BC. The origin of the West Semitic symbols is not entirely clear, but the most plausible theory is that they are derived from Egyptian hieroglyphic. A link between the Egyptian hieroglyphs and the West Semitic scripts is perhaps provided by some mysterious inscriptions from Sinai, variously dated between 1500 and 1850 BC, which are not fully understood, but which seem to be in a Semitic language. Figure 8 shows some of the symbols of our alphabet and the way they have probably developed from the Egyptian hieroglyphs of 3000 BC.

FROM WORD SYMBOL TO PHONEME SYMBOL

The second process, by which pictures cease to be ideograms and come to stand for specific linguistic forms, is even more important. First, pictorial symbols come to represent single words. The earliest Sumerian writings are just lists of objects with symbols for numbers against them: for example, four semicircles and the picture of an ox's head would read 'four oxen'. It seems that writing arose to meet the needs of the highly centralized city state, and the first writings are records of payments to the temple or city treasury, and similar transactions.

In this way, pictorial symbols come to stand for various words, which are the names of concrete objects like sheep, oxen, the sun, houses, and so on. Next, by a process of extension, the same symbols are made to stand for more abstract words related to the original word. Thus a picture of the sun may come to stand for the words for 'bright' or 'white', and later for the words 'day' and 'time', and a picture of a whip for words like 'power' or 'authority'.

Perhaps the really crucial development, however, is 'phonetization', the association of a symbol with a particular *sound* (or group of sounds). First, a symbol for a concrete object is transferred to some more abstract object which is denoted by the same or a similar word. For example, the Sumerian word *ti* meant 'arrow', and so was represented by an arrow in the script; but there was also a Sumerian word *ti* which meant 'life', so the arrow symbol came to be used for this too. The arrow symbol was then felt to stand for the *sound* of the word *ti*, and was used for the syllable *ti* in longer words. In this way, the original word symbols developed into syllable symbols, which could be grouped together to spell out a word.

An analogous process in English can be imagined on these lines. A picture of a tavern is used to represent the word *inn*. Because of the identity of sound, the same symbol then becomes used for the word *in*. At the same time, a picture of an eye is used for the word *eye*, and then by extension is used for the word *sight*. Finally, the tavern symbol and the eye symbol are combined to write the words *incite* and *insight*, and have now become syllabic symbols. If we wanted to distinguish between *insight* and *incite* in our syllabic script, we could add a third symbol to show which of the two was intended: we could draw a picture of an orator to show that we meant *incite*, or add a symbol for some word like 'wisdom' to show that we meant *insight*. When we used the eye symbol by itself, we might wish to indicate whether it stood for the word *eye* or the word *sight*; one way of doing this would be to add a symbol after it suggesting one of the sounds used in the word intended: for example, if we had a symbol for the words *sow, sew, so*, we could add this after our eye symbol to indicate that the required word began with *s*. These and similar methods are used in ancient Egyptian and Sumerian writing.

Sumerian writing is very mixed, using ideograms, word symbols, syllable symbols, and various kinds of indicators of the types mentioned. Out of it, however, developed the almost purely syllabic system of cuneiform writing which was used for Akkadian (the language of the ancient Babylonians and Assyrians), and which for centuries dominated the writing of the Near East. In this system each cuneiform sign stood for a syllable, such as *ba,* or *lu*, or *ir*. This is a great improvement on systems using signs for whole words, since the number of symbols used can be reduced to about a hundred.

Ancient Egyptian writing also developed into a syllabic system, and was particularly important for the development of true alphabetic writing (i.e. a script that has symbols representing *phonemes*). The important thing about the Egyptian system was that the vowels were not indicated. Most of the signs (about eighty) stood for a group of two consonants, plus any vowels whatever. For example, the symbol for a house (*par*) stood for the group *pr*, and this could mean *par*, *per*, *apr*, *epr*, *epra*, and so on. But there were twenty-four signs which stood for only one consonant plus any vowel; for example, the symbol representing a mouth (*ra*) stood for the consonant *r*, and could mean *ra*, *ar*, *re*, *er*, and so on. When the West Semitic peoples living round the eastern shores of the Mediterranean developed a script, they did so by taking over from the Egyptians just these twenty-four signs. Originally, this must have been a syllable system, in which each of the signs stood for a number of possible syllables, like the Egyptian *ra*, *ar*, *re*, *er*, etc.; but in fact it is formally identical with a purely alphabetic system in which only the consonants are written and the vowels are left out.

The final step, of having fixed and regular symbols for the vowels, was made by the Greeks when they took over this Semitic alphabet. Some of the consonant sounds of Phoenician did not exist in Greek, and the Greeks used the corresponding symbols for vowels. For example, the first letter of the West Semitic alphabet, derived from the picture of an ox, was *'aleph*, and stood for a kind of *h* sound (represented in the spelling by '); the Greeks of that period did not use this sound, and took the letter over as *alpha*, representing an *a* sound. Thus was reached at last a system of writing where symbols stand for phonemes, and all later alphabetic systems are ultimately derived from this Greek achievement. The great advantage of the system is the relatively small number of symbols needed, which makes universal literacy possible. The more unwieldy and difficult the system of writing, the more likely it is to remain the jealously guarded prerogative of an élite, like the priestly caste of the ancient city states or the bureaucracy of classical China: the alphabet is one of the forces making for democracy. It is noticeable, too, that many of the important developments in writing happened when a system was taken over by one people from another: scribes tend to be conservative, and radical changes mostly take place when a system of writing has to be adapted to new conditions.

The importance of the invention of writing hardly needs underlining. Before writing, all cultural traditions had to be memorized. More can be carried in the memory than we tend to think, since we seldom have to exercise ours very hard: pre-literate peoples memorize long genealogical tables, and even whole epic poems. But there is a limit to what the memory can carry, and no very serious expansion of knowledge can take place until permanent records are made in writing.

CHAPTER III

THE FLUX OF LANGUAGE

IN TALKING about the origins of writing, I have referred to several languages that are no longer spoken: nobody today speaks Sumerian, or Akkadian, or Hittite. A language which is no longer spoken by some group of people for the purposes of communication and social co-operation is a *dead* language. A language can continue to be living even though it has no *native* speakers: for several centuries medieval Latin was a living language of international communication even though nobody spoke it as their mother tongue.

One way in which a language becomes dead is that people simply stop speaking it: some other language spreads over the area where it is spoken, and it dies without issue. This is what happened, it seems, to Sumerian: round about 1500 BC, the Sumerian language disappeared from everyday use (though it continued to be used as a liturgical language for another thousand years). The people who spoke it must have changed over to some other language, presumably Akkadian, and the reason for the change was simply that they were conquered by peoples who spoke Akkadian, which became the general currency of the area. Sumerian may have been spoken for a long time as a minority language, but Sumerian speakers would need to speak Akkadian as well, and literature and official transactions would be in Akkadian. Anybody who wanted to get on in the world would have to speak Akkadian, but no native Akkadian speaker would have any incentive to learn Sumerian. If there were intermarriages, the children would tend to speak Akkadian. In such circumstances, the number of speakers of Sumerian would gradually shrink, until finally the language disappeared.

The Retreat of Celtic

My account of the disappearance of Sumerian is hypothetical, but the kind of process involved is well known from more recent times. For example, it is only during the past few centuries that English has become the universal language in Cornwall. Formerly there was a Cornish language, a Celtic language related to Welsh, but this was gradually displaced by English, and finally died out. The last known native speaker of Cornish was an old lady who died in 1777.

The disappearance of Cornish, as a matter of fact, is just one example of a long-term historical trend, in which the whole group of languages called Celtic have retreated before Germanic and Romance languages (like English and French). In the time of Julius Caesar, Celtic languages were spoken over large areas of western Europe, including the whole of the British Isles and France, and parts of Spain, Italy, and southern Germany. Today, the surviving Celtic languages are spoken only by small minorities on the Atlantic seaboard, and are having great difficulties in holding their own, despite intensive efforts by some of their speakers to maintain their traditional language and culture. Irish, indeed, is the first official language of the Republic of Ireland, but the vast majority of Irishmen in fact speak English as their mother tongue, the genuine native speakers of Irish being confined mainly to small communities on the west coast; and it is doubtful whether the attempt to revive Irish as the national language will be successful in the long run. Scottish Gaelic is spoken by less than 100,000 people in the Highlands, out of a total Scottish population of five million, and is retreating. Manx, the old language of the Isle of Man, is almost extinct. In Brittany, over a million people still speak Breton, but most of them speak French as well. Perhaps the most tenacious and vigorous of the Celtic languages is Welsh: there are still country districts in Wales where many children do not understand English, and where many adults pretend not to; and out of a population of two and a half million, nearly three quarters of a million can still speak Welsh.

But even Welsh is in retreat: between 1900 and 1950, the proportion of the inhabitants of Wales who could speak Welsh fell from about 50 per cent to under 30 per cent; the proportion who could speak *only* Welsh fell from about 15 per cent to under 2 per cent. It is difficult to see how even strong national feeling and a genuine love of Welsh traditions can hope to reverse this trend, as long as England and Wales form a single economic and political unit and the Welsh language is in direct competition with English. Indeed, it is doubtful whether even the economic and political separation of Wales would reverse the trend, to judge from the experience of other countries which have more than one language. Switzerland has four official languages (German, French, Italian, and Romansch), and it is the majority language, German, that is spreading at the expense of the others. Belgium has two official languages, French and Flemish; there are rather more native Flemish than native French speakers, but French is spreading at the expense of Flemish simply because French is one of the world languages; and this is happening despite the great care that the Belgians take to maintain parity between their two languages in all fields.

LINGUISTIC CHANGE

This then is one way in which a language becomes dead: it dwindles away until finally nobody speaks it at all. But a language can become dead in another way. Nobody today speaks classical Latin as spoken by Julius Caesar, or classical Greek as spoke by Pericles, or the old Icelandic spoken by the heroes of the Norse sagas. So classical Latin and classical Greek and Old Icelandic are dead languages. But, although dead, they have not *died*: they have changed into something else. People still speak Greek as a living language, and this language is simply a changed form of the language spoken in the Athens of Pericles. The people who live in Rome today speak a language that has developed by a process of continuous change out of the language spoken in Rome in the time of Julius Caesar, though modern Italian developed out of the everyday language of the ancient Roman market place and of the common soldiery, rather than out of the upper class literary Latin that Caesar wrote. And the people who live in Iceland today speak a language that has developed directly out of the language of the great Icelandic sagas of the Middle Ages.

In fact all living languages change, though the rate of change varies from time to time, and from language to language. The modern Icelander, for example, does not find it very difficult to read the medieval Icelandic sagas, because the rate of change in Icelandic has always been slow ever since the country was colonized by Norwegians a thousand years ago and Icelandic history began. But an Englishman without special training will find an English document of the year 1300 very difficult to understand; and an English document of the year 900 will seem to him to be written in a foreign language, which he may conclude (mistakenly) to have no connexion with modern English.

LINGUISTIC CHANGE IN ENGLISH

The extent to which the English language has changed in the past thousand years can be seen by looking at a few passages of English from different periods. Since it is convenient to see the same material handled by different writers, I have chosen a short passage from the Bible, which has been translated into English at many different times. The passage is from Chapter XV of Luke, and is the end of the story of the Prodigal Son. Here it is first in a very recent translation, the New English Bible, published in 1961:

Now the elder son was out on the farm; and on his way back, as he approached the house, he heard music and dancing. He called one of the servants and asked what it meant. The servant told him, 'Your brother has come home, and your father has killed the fatted calf because he has him back safe and sound.' But he was angry and refused to go in. His father came out and pleaded with him; but he retorted, 'You know how I have slaved for you all these years; I never once disobeyed your orders; and you never gave me so much as a kid, for a feast with my friends. But now that this son of yours turns up, after running through your money with his women, you kill the fatted calf for him.' 'My boy,' said the father, 'you are always with me, and everything I have is yours. How could we help celebrating this happy day? Your brother here was dead and has come back to life, was lost and is found.'

There is perhaps a certain unevenness of manner in that, but at any rate it is twentieth-century English, with nothing archaic or affected about it. Now let us look at the same passage as it appeared in the famous Authorized Version of the year 1611:

Now his elder sonne was in the field, and as he came and drew nigh to the house, he heard musicke & dauncing, and he called one of the seruants, and asked what these things meant. And he said vnto him, Thy brother is come, and thy father hath killed the fatted calfe, because he hath receiued him safe and sound. And he was angry, and would not goe in: therefore came his father out, and intreated him. And he answering said to his father, Loe, these many yeeres doe I serue thee, neither transgressed I at any time thy commande-ment, and yet thou neuer gauest mee a kid, that I might make merry with my friends: but as soone as this thy sonne was come, which hath deuoured thy liuing with harlots, thou hast killed for him the fatted calfe. And he said vnto him, Sonne, thou art euer with me, and all that I haue is thine. It was meete that we should make merry, and be glad: for this thy brother was dead, and is aliue againe: and was lost, and is found.

That, you will probably agree, is not really very different from twentieth-century English. There are a number of words and expressions which strike us as old fashioned, like *drew nigh* ('came near'), *transgressed* ('disobeyed'), *meete* ('fitting'), and so on; but there is nothing in the vocabulary that is really puzzling. The passage differs from present-day English in using *thou* instead of *you* when one person is addressed, and after *thou* the verb has the ending -*est* ('thou neuer *gauest* mee a kid'). Other verbs too have endings different from those used today, for example *hath* where we say *has*. Another difference from present-day usage is the use of *which* where we should say *who* ('thy sonne . . . *which* hath deuoured'). There is also one place where the order of the words is different from twentieth century usage: 'therefore came his father out', where we should say 'and so his father came out'. These are small things in themselves, but taken all together they give the passage a distinctly old fashioned flavour.

The spellings are quite close to modern ones, though you have to get used to the interchangeability of *u* and *v* (*vnto*, *neuer*), which of course has nothing to do with pronunciation. But you may have been struck by the spelling *dauncing*, which does rather suggest a different pronunciation from *dancing*. As a matter of fact, there is plenty of evidence to show that pronunciation in 1611 differed in many ways from our pronunciation, even when the spellings are the same. The vowels especially were different, and if you could hear a Londoner of 1611 his speech would remind you in some ways of American, and in some ways of West Country speech.

As our third example we can take the same passage as rendered by John Wycliffe, the first man to translate the entire Bible into English. Wycliffe died in 1384, and his translation probably dates from the last few years of his life. In the original text, there are two different kinds of letter *g*: one corresponds to modern *g*; the other corresponds sometimes to modern *y*, and sometimes to modern *gh*, and I have transcribed it accordingly. Otherwise, the original spelling is preserved, but the punctuation is modernized.

Forsoth his eldere sone was in the feeld, and whanne he cam and neighede to the hous, he herde a symfonye and a croude. And he clepide oon of the seruauntis, and axide what thingis thes weren. And he seide to him, Thi brodir is comen, and thi fadir hath slayn a fat calf, for he resseyued him saf. Forsoth he was wroth, and wolde not entre: therfore his fadir yede out, bigan to preie him. And he answeringe to his fadir seide, Lo, so manye yeeris I serue to thee, and I brak neuere thi commaundement, thou hast neuere yovun a kyde to me, that I schulde ete largely with my frendis. But aftir that this thi sone, which deuouride his substaunce with hooris, cam, thou hast slayn to him a fat calf. And he seide to him, Sone, thou ert euere with me, and alle myne thingis ben thyne. Forsoth it bihofte to ete plenteuously, and for to ioye: for this thi brother was deed, and lyuede ayeyn: he peryschide, and he is founden.

This, plainly, is much more remote from modern English. There are many more words and phrases which, while perfectly comprehensible, sound archaic, like *forsoth* ('indeed') and *wroth* ('angry'). There are also words which are quite strange to the modern reader, like *neighede* ('approached'), *clepide* ('called'), and *yede* ('went'). There are familiar-looking words with unfamiliar meanings, like *symfonye* ('musical instrument'), *croude* ('fiddle'), and *largely* ('liberally, plenteously'). There are also distinctive endings to words, like *-is* in plural nouns (*thyngis* 'goods', *hooris* 'whores'), and *-n* in plural verbs (*weren* 'were', *ben* 'are'). As in the previous passage, *u* and *v* are used interchangeably, and so are *i* and *j* (*ioye*). But there are also many words where the spelling clearly shows a pronunciation very different from ours, like *whanne* ('when'), *oon* ('one'), *axide* ('asked'), *ert* ('art'), *brodir* ('brother'), *bihofte* ('behoved'), *ayeyn* ('again'), and *yovun* ('given'). The word order, however, is very close to that of modern English.

For our final example, we go back behind the Norman Conquest, to a manuscript of about the year 1000. As is customary in modern editions of texts from this period, I mark long vowels by putting a line over them, while short vowels are left unmarked. The symbol þ is equivalent to the modern *th*; the symbol æ is pronounced like the vowel of the word *man* in modern educated southeastern English. The punctuation is modernized. As the English of this period is difficult for the modern reader, I give only the opening of the passage.

> Sōþlīce his yldra sunu wæs on æcere; and hē cōm, and þā hē þām hūse genealǣhte, hē gehȳrde þæne swēg and þæt wered. þā clypode hē ānne þēow, and ācsode hine hwæt þæt wǣre. þā cwæþ hē, þīn brōþor cōm, and þī nfæder ofslōh ān fætt cealf, forþām þe hē hine hālne onfēng.

Part of the difficulty of this lies in the number of unfamiliar words: *þā* ('when, then'), *genealǣhte* ('approached'), *swēg* ('noise'), *wered* ('multitude, band'), *þēow* ('servant'), *ofslōh* ('killed'), *forþām þe* ('because'), *hine* ('him'), *onfēng* ('received') – these are all words that have died out from the language; in the later passages, some of them have been replaced by words borrowed from French after the Norman Conquest (*servant, approached*). Even words which have survived may be used in an unfamiliar sense: the word *æcere* is our *acre*, but means 'field', and *hālne* is our *whole*, but means 'well, safe'. Even words unchanged in meaning appear in unfamiliar spelling, like *yldra sunu* ('elder son'), and were obviously pronounced differently from their modern counterparts.

The passage also differs from modern English in the way words change their endings according to their grammatical function in the sentence. This could be demonstrated in very many words in the passage, but three brief examples will suffice. The word for 'field' is *æcer*, but after the preposition *on* it has to add the ending *-e* (pronounced as an extra syllable), and so we get the expression *on æcere*. The expression for 'the house' is *þæt hūs*, but 'to the house' is *þām hūse*, and this is the form that appears in the text. The normal word for 'was' is *wæs*, as in the first sentence of the passage; but there is also a form *wǣre* (the so-called 'subjunctive' form) which has to be used in certain constructions, like 'ācsode hine hwæt þæt *wǣre*' ('asked him what it was').

The passage also differs from modern English in its word

order. Translated literally word for word into modern English, it runs as follows:

> Indeed, his elder son was on field; and he came, and when he the house approached, he heard the noise and the band. Then called he a servant, and asked him what it was. Then said he, Your brother came, and your father killed a fat calf, because he him safe received.

Some parts of this have a word order familiar in modern English, like 'he heard the noise and the band'; but others would be impossible today, for example 'Then called he a servant' and 'When he the house approached'; they are however common in the earliest forms of English – and are normal in modern German.

The English language, then, has changed very considerably in the last thousand years. New words have appeared, and some old ones disappeared. Words have changed in meaning. The grammatical endings of words have changed. There have been changes in word order, in the ways in which words can be arranged to make meaningful utterances. Pronunciation has changed. Taken all together, these changes add up to a major transformation of the language.

It is also pretty clear, even from the four passages that I have quoted, that the rate of change has varied. Between the New English Bible and the Authorized Version there is a period of just three and a half centuries, but the differences between them are less than those between the Authorized Version and Wycliffe, which are separated by only about two and a quarter centuries. The differences between the Wycliffe and the pre-Conquest passage, too, are very great. If we were to study a larger number of passages to fill in the chronological gaps, we should find that the twelfth century and the fifteenth century were periods of particularly rapid change in English. The existence of such periods of more rapid change makes it convenient to divide the history of the English language into three broad periods, called Old English, Middle English, and Modern English (or New English). No exact boundaries can be drawn, but Old English covers from the first Anglo-Saxon settlements in England up to about 1100, Middle English from 1100 to about 1450, and Modern English from 1450 to the present day.

THE CAUSES OF LINGUISTIC CHANGE

All living languages undergo changes analogous to those we have just seen exemplified in English. What causes such changes? There is no single answer to this question: changes in a language are of various kinds, and there are various reasons for them.

The changes that have caused most dispute are those in pronunciation. We have various sources of evidence for the pronunciations of earlier times, like the evidence of spellings, the treatment of words borrowed from other languages or borrowed by them, the descriptions of contemporary grammarians, and the modern pronunciations in all the languages and dialects concerned. These, combined with a knowledge of the mechanism of speech production, can often give us a very good idea of the pronunciation of an earlier age, though absolute certainty is never possible. When we study the pronunciation of a language over any period of a few generations or more, we find that it is subject to change. Moreover, there are always large-scale regularities in the changes: for example, over a certain period of time, all the long *a* sounds in a language may change into long *o* sounds, or all the *b* sounds in a certain position (for example, at the end of a word) may change into *p* sounds. Such regular changes are often called 'sound laws'. There are no universal sound laws, but simply particular sound laws for one given language at one given period.

One cause which has been suggested for changes in pronunciation is geographic and climatic. It has been suggested that people living in mountain country are subject to certain changes in pronunciation compared with plainsmen, that a dry climate makes people speak nasally, that a hot climate causes drawling speech. But such theories must be considered unproven, since none of them has taken account of more than a small selection of the facts. Other people have suggested biological and racial factors: it has been said, for example, that races with thick lips have difficulty in producing certain sounds. Once again, no really convincing evidence has been produced for this; moreover, the theory is most obviously useful for explaining changes in a language when it is adopted by one people from another, and in these circumstances the theory is hardly necessary: the influence of one language on another is quite enough to explain such changes, without racial characteristics being invoked.

We learn our mother tongue very thoroughly, and acquire a whole set of speech habits which become second nature to us. When later we learn a foreign language, we inevitably carry over some of these speech habits into it, and so do not speak it exactly like a native. Consequently, in bilingual situations the second language tends to be modified. Such modifications may not persist, of course: an isolated Polish or German immigrant to Britain will usually have grandchildren who speak English like natives, because the influence of the general speech environment (playmates, school, work) is stronger than that of the home. But if a large and closely knit group of people adopt a new language, then the modifications that they make in it may persist among their descendants, even if the latter no longer speak the original language that caused the changes. This can be seen in Wales, where the influence of Welsh has affected the pronunciation of English, and the very characteristic melody of Welsh English has been carried over from Welsh. Many historical changes in languages may have been due to a linguistic substratum of this kind: a conquering minority that imposed its language on a conquered population must often have had its language modified by its victims.

It is also possible that fashion plays a part in the process of change. It certainly plays a part in the spread of change: one person imitates another, and people with the most prestige are most likely to be imitated, so that a change that takes place in one social group may be imitated (more or less accurately) by speakers in another group. When a social group goes up or down in the world, its pronunciation will gain or lose prestige. It is said that, after the Russian Revolution, the upper class pronunciation of Russian, which had formerly been considered desirable, became on the contrary an undesirable kind of speech to have, so that people tried to conceal it. Some of the changes in accepted English pronunciation in the sixteenth and seventeenth centuries have been shown to consist in the replacement of one style of pronunciation by another style already existing, and it is likely that such substitutions were a result of the great social changes of the period: the increased power and wealth of the middle classes, and their steady infiltration upwards into the ranks of the landed gentry, probably carried elements of middle class dialect into upper class speech.

However, besides spreading changes that have already taken place, fashion may actually cause changes in pronunciation. In a stratified society, the important thing about a fashion is that it is exclusive: as soon as the fashion has penetrated to a lower social group, it's time to move on. This can be seen in clothes: fashionable people may find it flattering to be imitated, but as soon as the new fashion has really caught on they must change to something else, to mark themselves off as different. It may be the same with language, for social groups use characteristic styles of language to mark themselves off from other groups. A group that has high prestige may find that its style of speech is being imitated by other groups, and then its members may (perhaps unconsciously) begin to change it, perhaps by exaggerating its distinguishing characteristics.

However, while interaction between different languages, and between the dialects of a single language, can explain some changes in pronunciation, it cannot explain them all. Another cause that has been suggested is the fact that children grow. The vocal organs of children, it is argued, are a different size from those of adults; they learn to mimic the noises their parents make, but on what is in effect a different instrument; as they grow up, they go on moving their vocal organs in the same way, but the sounds that they produce are now different,

THE FLUX OF LANGUAGE

because the organs have changed. However, if this were an important factor, we should expect all changes of pronunciation to be in the same direction, irrespective of language or period, and this is not in fact the case. The theory assumes that we stop using our ears and making corrections after we grow up, which is surely not true.

A less specific variant of the argument, and a more plausible one, is that the imitation of children is imperfect: they copy their parents' speech, but never reproduce it exactly. This seems to be true enough; and it moreover seems to be true that even adults show a certain amount of random variation in their pronunciation of a given phoneme, even if the phonetic context is kept unchanged. However, these facts cannot explain changes in pronunciation unless it can be shown that there is some systematic trend in the failures in imitation: if they are merely random deviations they will cancel one another out and there will be no nett change in the language. For some of these random variations to be selected at the expense of others, there must be further forces at work.

One such force which is often invoked is the principle of ease, or minimization of effort. We are all naturally lazy, it is argued, and so we tend to take short cuts in the movements of our speech organs, to replace movements calling for great accuracy or energy by less demanding ones, to omit sounds if they are not essential for understanding, and so on. This is certainly an important factor in linguistic change, though we have to add that what seems easy or difficult to a speaker will depend on the particular language he has learned. If we have a sequence of three sounds in which the first and the third are voiced, while the middle one is voiceless, the speaker has to carry out the operation of switching off his voice before the second sound and then switching it on again before the third. An economy of effort can be obtained by omitting these operations and allowing the voice to continue for all three sounds. Such a change would be seen if the pronunciation of *fussy* were changed to that of *fuzzy*, the voiceless *s* being replaced by the voiced *z* between the two vowels. Changes of this kind are common in the history of language, but nevertheless we cannot lay it down as a universal rule that *fuzzy* is easier to pronounce than *fussy*. In Swedish, for example, the *z* sound does not exist, and Swedes who learn English find it difficult to say *fuzzy*, which they very often mispronounce as *fussy*. For them, plainly, *fussy* is the easier of the two pronunciations, because it is more in accordance with the sound-system of their own language.

The change from *fussy* to *fuzzy* would be an example of *assimilation*, which is a very common kind of change. Assimilation is the changing of a sound under the influence of a neighbouring sound. For example, the word *scant* was once *skamt*, but the *m* has been changed to *n* under the influence of the following *t*. An economy of effort has hereby been achieved, because *n* and *t* are articulated in the same place (with the tip of the tongue against the teeth-ridge), whereas *m* is articulated elsewhere (with the two lips). What has happened, then, is that the place of articulation of the nasal consonant has been changed to conform with that of the following plosive consonant. A more recent example of the same kind of thing is the common pronunciation of *tenpence* as *tempence*. Sometimes it is the second of the two sounds that is changed by the assimilation. This can be seen in some changes that have taken place in English under the influence of the *w* sound: until about 1600, words like *swan* and *wash* rhymed with words like *man* and *rash*; the change in the vowel has given it the lip rounding and the retracted tongue position of the *w*, and so economized in effort.

Assimilation is not the only way in which we change our pronunciation in order to reduce effort. A sound may come to be pronounced less energetically, wherever it occurs: the English *r* and *h* sounds are undoubtedly pronounced much less vigorously now than they were a thousand years ago. In some positions a sound may disappear altogether: at one time the *t* was pronounced in words like *castle* and *Christmas*, and the *g* in words like *gnat* and *gnaw*. Sometimes, a whole syllable is dropped out if it occurs twice running: a modern example is *temporary*, which in Britain is often pronounced as if it were *tempory*. On the other hand, ease of pronunciation can lead to an extra sound being put in: in Old English, our *bramble* was *brēmel*, and *thunder* was *þunor*, but the pronunciations with *b* and *d* actually call for less precise movements: the *b* and *d* arose from slight mistimings in the transition from the nasal to the following consonant, the nasal passages being closed a little too early, before the tongue and lips had moved to the position for the following consonant. Sometimes, too, ease of pronunciation apparently leads us to reverse the order of two sounds: this has happened in the words *wasp* and *burn*, which would otherwise be *waps* and *brin* or *bren*.

The loss or slurring of sounds produced in pursuit of economy of effort can often be tolerated, because a language always provides more signals than the absolute minimum necessary for communication, to give a margin of safety. However, the necessities of communication, the urgent needs of man as a user of language, provide a counterforce to the principle of minimum effort. If, through excessive economy of effort, an utterance is not understood, or is misunderstood, the speaker is obliged to repeat it, making more effort, or recasting it. The necessities of communication, moreover, may be responsible for the selection of some of the random variations of a sound rather than others, so that a change in pronunciation occurs in a certain direction. This direction may be chosen because it makes the sound inherently more audible: for example, open nasal vowels are more distinctive in quality than close ones, and in languages which have such vowels it is not uncommon for a nasal *e* to develop into a nasal *a*.

However, in considering such changes we cannot look at the isolated phoneme: we have to consider the sound-system of the language as a whole. The 'safeness' or otherwise of a sound for communicative purposes does not only depend on its own inherent distinctiveness: it depends also on the other sounds in the language with which it can be contrasted, and the likelihood that it may be confused with them. Suppose that in the vowel system of a language there is a short *e* sound (as in *bed*); in one direction from it is a short *a* sound (as in *bat*), and in another direction a short *er* sound (as in the first syllable of *about*); but in the upward direction there is no short vowel, no kind of short *i* for example. Suppose now that random variations occur in speakers' pronunciation of these three vowels. When the variations of *e* go too far in the direction of *a* or *er*, the speaker will be forced to correct them, to avoid misunderstanding. But when the variations are in the direction of *i*, there is no such necessity for checking or correction. The result will be a shift in the centre of gravity of the *e* sound, which will drift up towards *i*. Moreover, the movement of *e* towards *i* will leave more scope for variations in *a*, which may tend to drift up towards *e*, especially if it is hemmed in on other sides by other short vowels. In this way, a whole chain of vowel changes may take place.

In this example I have assumed that the contrast between the three vowels is important enough in the functioning of the language for speakers to resist any changes which destroy this contrast. This will be the case if large numbers of words are distinguished from one another by these vowels, if the contrast between them does a lot of work in the language. The functional load carried by a contrast is an important factor when speakers decide whether to let a change take place or not. There may be forces in the system making for the amalgamation of two phonemes, and if there are very few words in the language which will be confused with one another as a result then there will not be much resistance to it; but if serious confusion will be caused by the amalgamation it will be resisted more strongly, and perhaps prevented.

This does not mean, on the other hand, that a phoneme with a small functional load will necessarily be thrown out of the system, either by being lost or by being amalgamated with another phoneme. It also depends on the degree of effort required to *retain* the phoneme, which may be quite small. For example, the contrast in English between the voiced and voiceless *th* sounds carries a very small load; there are a few pairs of words that are distinguished from one another solely by this difference, like *thigh* and *thy*, or *mouth* (noun) and *mouth* (verb), but not many. In practice the distinction between the two phonemes is of negligible importance, and it would cause no great inconvenience if they were amalgamated, for example by both evolving into some third sound. On the other hand, it takes very little effort to retain the distinction between them. They belong to a whole series of voiced and voiceless fricatives (*v* and *f*, *z* and *s*, *zh* and *sh*), and so fall into a familiar pattern; and if we abolished the distinction between them we should not economize in the number of *types* of contrast that we made: we should still have to distinguish fricatives from other kinds of consonant, and between voiced and voiceless fricatives.

The stability of the *th* sounds thus results from the fact that they are, in André Martinet's terminology, 'well integrated' in the consonant system of English. An even better integrated group of consonants in Modern English is the following:

Voiceless plosives	*p*	*t*	*k*
Voiced plosives	*b*	*d*	*g*
Nasals	*m*	*n*	*ng*

Each of these three series uses the same places of articulation: the two lips pressed together for *p*, *b*, *m*; the tip of the tongue pressed against the teeth-ridge for *t*, *d*, *n*; the back of the tongue pressed up against the soft palate for *k*, *g*, *ng*. So, using only three articulatory positions, and only three distinctive articulatory features (plosiveness, nasality, voice), we get no less than nine distinct phonemes. This group is very stable, because the loss of any one of the nine would produce negligible economy in the system: if, say, *ng* were to disappear, we should still have to be able to produce nasality for *m* and *n*, and we should still have to be able to articulate with the back of the tongue against the soft palate for *g* and *k*. So even if *ng* carried a very small load in the language we should still be unlikely to get rid of it. For the same reason, if there were a hole in the pattern, it would stand a good chance in time of getting filled. If there were no *ng* in Modern English, but there was some other consonant which was not very well integrated in any subsystem, then any variations of this consonant that moved it in the direction of *ng* would tend to be accepted, because they would represent an 'easier' pronunciation – easier, that is, in terms of the economy of the system as a whole.

Changes in grammar, syntax, vocabulary, and meaning, while they can be complicated enough, are less puzzling than changes in pronunciation. Many of the same causes can be seen at work. The influence of other languages, for example, is obvious enough: nations with high commercial, political, and cultural prestige often influence their neighbours: for centuries, French influenced all the languages of Europe, while today the influence of the English language is penetrating all over the world, largely because of the power and prestige of the United States. This influence is strongest in the field of vocabulary, but one language can also influence the grammar and syntax of another; this may happen, for example, when a religion spreads and its sacred books are translated: in the Old English period there were many translations from the Latin, and there is some evidence that Latin syntax influenced the structure of English.

In the realm of vocabulary and meaning, the influence of general social and cultural change is very obvious. As society changes, there are new things that need new names: physical objects, institutions, sets of attitudes, values, concepts; and new words are produced to handle them. Sentimentality, classicism, wave mechanics, parliaments, derequisitioning – these are human inventions just as much as steam engines or aeroplanes or nylon: and man inevitably also invented names for them. Moreover, because the world is constantly changing, words insensibly change their meanings. It is easy enough to see that the word *ship* does not mean the same to us as it did to the Anglo-Saxons; it is easier to overlook shifts of meaning in words that refer to values or to complexes of attitudes: for example, in Shakespeare's day, the word *gentle* meant a good deal more than 'kind, sweet natured', for it referred to high birth as well as to moral qualities, and had a whole social theory behind it.

As in pronunciation, so at the other levels of language, we

see the constant conflict between the principle of minimum effort and the demands of communication. Minimization of effort, for example, is seen in the way words are often shortened, as when *public house* becomes *pub*, or *television* becomes *telly*, and also in the laconic and elliptical expressions that we often use in colloquial and intimate discourse. We also see the constant interplay between the needs of the users and the inherent tendencies of the language system itself. One important way in which the language system promotes change is through the operation of *analogy*, which also tends to work in the direction of economy. Analogy is seen at work when children are learning their language. A child learns pairs like *dog / dogs*, *bed / beds*, *bag / bags*, and so on. Then it learns a new word, say *plug*, and quite correctly forms the plural *plugs* from it, on analogy with these other pairs. Analogy, then, is the process of inventing a new element in conformity with some part of the language system that you already know.

The way in which analogy can lead to change is seen when the child learns words like *man* and *mouse*, and forms the analogical plurals *mans* and *mouses*. Such childish errors are quickly corrected, but analogical formations of this kind also take place in adult speech, and often become accepted. In Britain, we say that a swimmer *dived* into the water, but in the northern United States it is common to say that he *dove* into the water. Here the American form is the traditional one, and the British *dived* is an analogical formation, which has arisen on the pattern of the enormous number of English verbs that form their past tense in this way in *-ed*. The rarer a word is, the more likely it is to be affected by analogy. You will notice that the unusual plural forms in English, which are the ones that have managed to resist the analogy of the common plural in *-s*, are mostly very common words, like *men*, *feet*, and *children*.

CHAPTER IV

LANGUAGE FAMILIES

THE PROCESS of change in a language often leads to divergent development. Imagine a language which is spoken only by the population of two small adjacent villages. In each village, the language will slowly change, but the changes will not be identical in both villages, because conditions are slightly different. Hence the speech used in one of the villages may gradually diverge from the speech used in the other. If there is rivalry between the villages, they may even pride themselves on such divergences, as a mark of local patriotism. Within the single village, speech will remain fairly uniform, because the speakers are in constant contact, and so influence one another. The rate at which the speech of one village diverges from that of the other will depend partly on the degree of difference between their ways of life, and partly on the intensity of communication between them. If the villages are close together and have a good deal of inter-village contact, so that many members of one village are constantly talking with members of the other, then divergence will be kept small, because the speech of one community will be constantly influencing the speech of the other. But if communications are bad, and members of one village seldom meet anybody from the other, then the rate of divergence may well be high. When a language has diverged into two forms like this, we say that it has two *dialects*.

Suppose now that the inhabitants of one of the villages pack up their belongings and migrate *en masse*. They go off to a distant country and live under conditions quite different from their old home, and completely lose contact with the other village. The rate at which the two dialects diverge will now increase, partly because of the difference of environment, partly because they no longer influence one another. After a few hundred years, the two dialects may have got so different that they are no longer mutually intelligible. We should now say that they were two different *languages*. Both have grown by a process of continuous change out of the single original language, but because of divergent development there are now two languages instead of one. When two languages have evolved in this way from some single earlier language, we say that they are *related*. The development of related languages from an earlier parent-language can be represented diagrammatically as a family tree, thus:

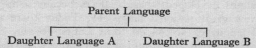

As we shall see later, this kind of diagram is in some ways inadequate, and we must certainly avoid thinking of languages as if they were people. But as long as we bear this in mind, we shall find that family trees are a convenient way of depicting the relationships between languages.

LANGUAGES DESCENDED FROM LATIN

There are numerous examples in history of divergent development leading to the formation of related languages. For example, when the Romans conquered a large part of Europe, North Africa, and the Near East, their language, Latin, became spoken over wide areas as the standard language of administration and government, especially in the western part of the Empire. Then, in the fourth century of our era, the Empire began to disintegrate, and, in the centuries which followed, was overrun by barbarian invasions – Huns, Slavs, Germans – and gradually broke up. In the new countries that eventually emerged from the ruins of the western Empire, various languages were spoken. In some places, both Latin and the local languages had been swept away and replaced by the language of an invader – in England, by Anglo-Saxon, in North Africa, by Arabic. But in other places Latin was firmly enough rooted to survive as the language of the new nation, as in France,

Italy, and Spain. But, because there was no longer a single unifying centre to hold the language together, divergent development took place, and Latin evolved into a number of different new languages. In general, the further a place was from Rome, the more the new language diverged from the original Latin.

In the early Middle Ages, there was a whole welter of local dialects developed from Latin; each region, with its own feudal court, would have its own local dialect. But, as the modern nation states developed, these dialects became consolidated into a few great national languages. Today there are five national languages descended from Latin: Italian, Spanish, Portuguese, French, and Roumanian. There are also other languages derived from Latin which have not become national languages, but which belong to some large group with a common culture: such are Romansch (spoken in parts of Switzerland and of Italy), Provençal (spoken in southern France), Catalan (spoken in Catalonia and the Balearic Isles), and Sardinian (spoken in southern Sardinia). Languages descended from Latin are called *Romance* languages. We can draw a family tree of the Romance languages, thus:

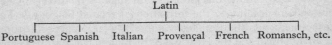

Latin

Portuguese Spanish Italian Provençal French Romansch, etc.

Each of the Romance languages has developed its own grammar and syntax, but they all bear signs of their common origin in Latin. The most obvious resemblances are in vocabulary; each language has undergone considerable changes in pronunciation, but the Latin origin of large numbers of words is quite evident. For example, the Latin word for 'good' is *bonus*; this has become Italian *buono*, Spanish *bueno*, French *bon*, Portuguese *bom*, and Roumanian *bun*. The Latin *homo* 'man', has become Italian *uomo*, Spanish *hombre*, French *homme*, Portuguese *homem*, and Roumanian *om*. Of course, not all words in the five languages correspond in this way: they have all borrowed words from their neighbours (the Roumanians from the Slavs, for example); and sometimes a Latin word has had a different fate in different languages. The Latin for 'head' is *caput*, which appears as Spanish *cabeza* and Portuguese *cabeça*. But the French word for 'head' is *tête*, and the Italian is *testa*; these come from the Latin *testa*, which meant 'brick, pot, pitcher'; clearly this was a slang word for head (like our *nut* and *block*), perhaps soldiers' slang. The word *caput* has however descended into French, as *chef*, and into Italian, as *capo*, both meaning 'chief, leader'.

SOME LANGUAGE FAMILIES

This process of divergent development leading to the formation of new languages has occurred many times in human history, which is why there are now over two thousand different languages in the world. An examination of these languages shows that many of them belong to some group of related languages, and some of these groups are very large, constituting what we can call language families. A language which has arisen by the process of divergent development may itself give rise to further languages by a continuation of the same process, until there is a whole complex family of languages with various branches, some more nearly and some more distantly related to one another.

An example of such a family is the Semitic group of languages. At the time of the earliest written records this was already a family with many members: in Mesopotamia were the East Semitic languages, Babylonian and Assyrian, while round the eastern shores of the Mediterranean were the West Semitic languages, such as Moabite, Phoenician, Aramaic, and Hebrew. The East Semitic languages have died out, and the most important surviving Semitic language is undoubtedly Arabic, a South Semitic language, which, with some dialectal variations, is spoken along the whole northern coast of Africa and round the eastern shores of the Mediterranean. Also surviving are Syriac, Ethiopian, and Hebrew, which is a remarkable example of a language being revived for everyday use after a long period during which it had been used only for religious purposes. The more important Semitic languages are shown in the following family tree:

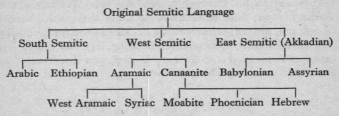

But the Semitic languages are themselves related to another family, the Hamitic languages, and at some time in the remote past (certainly long before 3000 BC) there must have been a single Hamito-Semitic language which was the common ancestor of all Semitic and Hamitic languages. The language of ancient Egypt belonged to the Hamitic group; today, of course, the language of Egypt is a form of Arabic, but a descendant of the old Hamitic language of Egypt, Coptic, is still used for religious purposes in some parts of the country. Surviving Hamitic languages are spoken across a large part of North Africa, and include Berber and Somali. We can now expand our family tree, as follows:

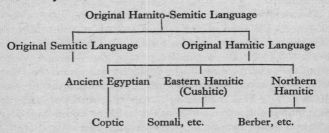

One characteristic of the Hamito-Semitic languages is their use of roots consisting of three consonants. By inserting different vowels into this consonant skeleton, and adding prefixes and suffixes, they produce words of different but related meaning. For example, in Arabic the group *ktb* is used for words that have to do with writing: in modern Egyptian Arabic, *kitaab* means 'book', *kutub* 'books', *katab* 'he wrote', *yiktib* 'he writes', *maktuub* 'written', *kitaaba* '(act of) writing', *kaatib* 'clerk', *maktab* 'office', *maktaba* 'library', and so on.

Another large language family is the Ural–Altaic. This has two main branches, the Ugro-Finnish and the Altaic (though some authorities deny that these branches are in fact related). The Ugro-Finnish branch includes Hungarian, Finnish, Estonian, and Lapp, while the Altaic includes Turkish and Mongol. A skeleton family-tree of the Ural–Altaic languages (assuming that the two branches really are related) would look something like this:

If you have ever visited Finland or Hungary, or seen newspapers from those countries, you may have been struck by the complete unfamiliarity of the language, whereas in most European countries there are many words that can be guessed, or which at any rate do not seem to be difficult to remember when once learnt. For example, the English numerals *one*, *two*, *three* are quite like German *eins*, *zwei*, *drei* and Swedish *en*, *två*, *tre* and even French *un*, *deux*, *trois*; but the Finnish words are *yksi*, *kaksi*, *kolme*, and the Hungarian *egy*, *kettö*, *három*, which are quite strange to us. The reason is, of course, that English and most other European languages belong to a family quite unrelated to the Ural–Altaic.

A family with an enormous number of speakers is the Sino-

Tibetan, which includes Thai, Burmese, Tibetan, and the various dialects of Chinese (not all of which are mutually intelligible). Japanese is not related to this group, but is probably related to Korean. In Southern India and Ceylon can be found Dravidian languages, which include Tamil and Telegu. In Malaya and the Pacific islands is the Malayo-Polynesian family, including Malayan, Melanesian, and Polynesian. In Africa, south of the Hamito-Semitic languages, are two large groups of languages, the Bantu and the Sudanese–Guinean, which may perhaps be branches of one family; the Sudanese–Guinean languages are mainly spoken north of the equator, the Bantu languages south of it; the former include Nubian and Hausa, and the latter Swahili and Zulu.

These are all important families with large numbers of speakers, but there are many smaller ones, like the Eskimo languages, various families of languages among the American Indians, the Papuan languages of Australia and New Guinea, and the Caucasian languages by the Caspian Sea, like Georgian (the mother tongue of the late Joseph Stalin). In addition, there are isolated languages which have no known family connexions; such is Basque, spoken by nearly a million people in the French and Spanish Pyrenees, which is unlike any other known language.

Convergent Development

The process of divergent development, then, has produced an enormous number of languages out of a smaller number of earlier ones (possibly out of one original one). However, there are forces that work the other way, that may even reduce a language family or branch to a single language again. For example, Latin was only one of a number of related languages, dialects of Italic, which were spoken in the city states of ancient Italy; at one time, some of these other Italic languages, such as Umbrian and Oscan, may have been at least as important as Latin. But as the Romans conquered Italy, their language conquered too, and eventually the other Italic languages died out.

So we have the differentiation of a language into a number of variants, and then, for political reasons, one of these variants becomes dominant and the others disappear. On the family tree, we can draw a line under the name to mean 'died without issue':

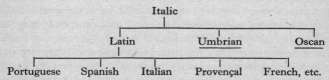

Something analogous has happened with the Semitic languages: many of these have died out, and one form, Arabic, has become the dominant one, because it was the language of the victorious expansionist armies of Islam.

The same centralizing tendency can often be seen at work even when there is no question of conquest. Within a single political unit, like a modern national state, there is usually one form of the language which has higher prestige than the others, and which acts as a brake on the divergent tendencies in the language. This prestige dialect may be the language of the ruling class, or it may simply be the educated speech of the capital, which is often the cultural as well as the administrative centre, and so exerts great influence on the rest of the country. Usually, such a prestige dialect underlies the standard literary form of the language, which influences the whole country through books and education. The existence of a standard language discourages further divergence, because many people try to make their usage more like the standard, especially if they wish to make their way in administration and government, or if they are social climbers. It may also lead to the actual dying out of other dialects. In Old English there were many dialects, but Modern English is very largely descended from just one of them, a dialect of the East Midland region; some features from the other dialects have survived, but most of them have disappeared.

A standard literary language may continue to be influential

even after the political decline of the group that made it important. An example of this is the Greek *koinē*, the standard literary language of the eastern Mediterranean from the time of Alexander the Great in the fourth century BC. This language was a modified form of the Attic dialect of Athens, which became the literary standard for the Greek-speaking world in the fifth century BC, when Athens was politically and culturally the dominant city of Greece. Athenian political dominance lasted less than a century, but the prestige of Athenian literature and of Athenian speech remained, and from it developed the koinē. This word means 'shared, common, popular', and it was indeed the common language of a large area for something like a thousand years. It is, for example, the language in which the New Testament was written. In the fourth century of our era, the sons of Constantine divided the Roman Empire, the younger son taking the eastern part and the elder son the western part, and this division became permanent. The administrative language of the Western Empire, ruled from Rome, was Latin; but the administrative language of the Eastern Empire, ruled from Constantinople, was the Greek koinē. This division is still reflected in the division between the Roman Catholic church and the Greek Orthodox church, which use Latin and Greek respectively as their liturgical languages.

CHAPTER V

THE INDO-EUROPEAN LANGUAGES

WE HAVE talked about related languages and language families. What languages is English related to? If you know any European languages, you may well have been struck by resemblances between them and English. For example, German *Vater*, *singen*, *leben*, *Stein* resemble their English translations *father*, *sing*, *live*, *stone*, and there are scores of such resemblances. However, resemblances alone do not prove relatedness: the resemblances must be systematic. Consider then the following table, showing a number of words of similar meaning in modern English, German, and Swedish:

English	German	Swedish
stone	Stein	sten
bone	Bein	ben
oak	Eiche	ek
home	Heim	hem
rope	Reif	rep
goat	Geiss	get
one	ein	en

The important thing here is not just that the words look alike, but that there are regular correspondences: words with English long *o* have German *ei* and Swedish *e*. Such correspondences arise when related languages are produced by divergent development, because, as we have seen, the changes in pronunciation in any one language or dialect follow regular sound laws.

There are indeed certain anomalies in the table. German *Bein* does not mean 'bone' but 'leg'; however, the Swedish *ben* means both 'bone' and 'leg', and the same was once true of the German word. German *Reif* means 'ring, hoop', but it did formerly mean also 'rope'. The English word *one* apparently does not fit the pattern, for it has the wrong pronunciation; however, if we go back a thousand years, we find that *one* is descended from an Old English word *ān* (pronounced with a long *ah* sound); and the words for stone, bone, oak, home, rope, and goat also have this long *ā* in Old English: *stān, bān, āc, hām, rāp, gāt*. Obviously we should expect *one* to rhyme with *stone* in Modern English, but something has gone wrong. In fact, our modern pronunciation of *one* has been taken over from one of the regional dialects (perhaps to avoid confusion with *own*); but the expected pronunciation is found in *alone* and *atone*, which historically are derived from *all one* and *at one*.

THE GERMANIC LANGUAGES

This last example suggests that, when we examine family relationships between languages, it may be important to go back to the earliest known forms of the languages. The following table shows the same seven words as they appear in Old English, Gothic, Old High German, and Old Norse. Gothic was the language of the Goths, who invaded the Roman Empire; Old High German was the ancestor of modern standard literary German; and Old Norse was the early form of the Scandinavian languages, as found for example in the medieval Icelandic sagas.

Old English	Gothic	Old High German	Old Norse
stān	stains	stein	steinn
bān	—	bein	bein
āc	—	eih	eik
hām	haims	heim	heimr
rāp	raip	reif	reip
gāt	gaits	geiz	geit
ān	ains	ein	einn

Here again there are regular correspondences: words which have *ā* in Old English have *ai* in Gothic, *ei* in Old Norse, and *ei* in Old High German. The spelling *ei* probably represents a pronunciation like that of *ay* in English *may*, while Gothic *ai* was probably pronounced rather like the *i* in *mine*. It seems likely that the original sound from which they all developed was similar to the Gothic one, though we cannot know exactly.

This is only one correspondence, but a full examination of

these languages shows regular correspondences for all their sounds, and confirms that they are indeed related. The correspondences are not always obvious, and there are difficulties and complications. One source of confusion is seen if we examine the word *boat*, which comes from Old English *bāt*. In this case, however, the other languages fail to correspond. The German word is *Boot*, where we might have expected **Beiss* (the asterisk shows that the form is a hypothetical one, and has not been recorded). The Swedish form is not **bet*, but *båt*, which would correspond to an Old Swedish *bāt*; and the usual Old Norse word is *bátr*. However, there is also a rarer Old Norse word *beitr*, found in poetry, and this does correspond to the English word, whereas the other forms make no kind of sense at all. What is the explanation? What happened, almost certainly, is that the Scanadinavians borrowed their *bátr* from the Old English *bāt*: it is an example of a *loan* word, a word taken over bodily from one language into another. And the German word *Boot* was also borrowed from English, but at a rather later date, after the Old English *ā* had changed into a long *o* sound. You may find it rather surprising that the Scandinavians, a famous seafaring race, should borrow such a word as *boat* from the English; but you must remember that the Anglo-Saxons and their cousins the Frisians were famous as deep-sea sailors and pirates before the Scandinavian Vikings had been heard of: the Saxons were the terror of the seas in the days of the late Roman Empire, at a time when the ancestors of the Danes and Norwegians were still probably only longshoremen.

Another source of complication can be illustrated by the word for a waste place. This is German *Heide*, Old High German *heida*, Swedish *hed*, Old Norse *heiðr*, and Gothic *haiþi*. (The Old Norse letter *ð* is pronounced like *th* in *this*, and the Gothic letter *þ* like *th* in *thing*.) From this we might expect to find an English word **hoath*, but of course the word is in fact *heath*, which is quite regularly descended from Old English *hǽþ*. In this case the clue to the difference is given by the *-i* at the end of the Gothic word. It can be shown that, in prehistoric Old English, the sound *i* caused a change in the vowel of the preceding syllable, provided it was in the same word. The prehistoric Old English form of *heath* was something like **hāpi*; the *i* caused the *ā* to change to *ǣ*, and was later itself lost by a regular sound law. Dependent sound changes of this kind (often called 'combinative changes') greatly complicate the task of establishing correspondences.

However, though complicated, it can be done, and has been done for this group of languages. In addition to the languages I have mentioned, the group contains others, such as Dutch, Danish, and Norwegian. The languages of this group are called *Germanic* languages. Besides the regular correspondences in sounds, they resemble one another closely in structure: they have the same or similar features of grammar and syntax. For example, in English there are two main ways of putting a verb into the past tense: in one group of verbs we change the vowel, as in *I sing, I sang*, in another we add an ending containing a *d* or *t* sound, as in *I live, I lived*. Exactly the same is true in the other Germanic languages: in German we have *ich singe, ich sang*, and *ich lebe, ich lebte*; in Swedish, *jag sjunger, jag sjöng*, and *jag lever, jag levde*.

ENGLISH AND FRENCH

English, then, belongs to the group of Germanic languages. But does this group form part of any larger family of languages? One possibility which may have occurred to you, if you know French, is a close relationship between French and English. Enormous numbers of English words closely resemble French words of similar meaning; to English *people* corresponds French *peuple*; *battle* is *bataille*; *to change* is *changer*; and one could easily give a whole string of French words of this kind – *musique, art, palais, collaboration, collision, combattant, danger, danse, machine*, and so on. This, however, is a false trail. You will remember that it is important to look at the earliest known forms of a language when determining its family relationships. If we go back to the earliest known forms of English, all these words that resemble French words simply do not exist. As we go back in time their number gets less and less, and when we get back to the period before the Norman Conquest they have disappeared entirely. They are in fact loan words, taken over bodily from French, or in some cases direct from Latin. There are many such borrowed words in English, but they have not destroyed the essentially Germanic character of English, which retains typical Germanic structural features and a central core of Germanic words. Such are the everyday words for the closest members of the family (father, mother, brother, son), for the parts of the body (head, foot, arm, hand), and for the numerals (one, two, three). Such words are seldom borrowed from other languages, and are a good guide to family relationships.

THE INDO-EUROPEAN LANGUAGES

We see, then, that our attempt to compare Modern English with Modern French was misguided. We should instead have gone back to the ancestor of French, which is Latin, and compared it with the earliest known forms of the Germanic languages; and we should have looked especially at grammatical features, and at words from the central part of the vocabulary, like *father* and *mother* and the numerals. Let us try a comparison of this kind, throwing in a couple of other ancient languages for good measure. We can begin with the numerals from one to ten; these are given in the table below for classical Latin, classical Greek, and Sanskrit, an ancient language of northern India. To represent the Germanic languages I give Old English and Gothic.

	Latin	*Greek*	*Sanskrit*	*Gothic*	*Old English*
1.	ūnus	heis	ēka	ains	ān
2.	duo	duō	dvā	twai	twēgen, twā
3.	tres	treis	trayas	þri	þrī
4.	quattuor	tettares	catvāras	fidwor	feower
5.	quinque	pente	panca	fimf	fīf
6.	sex	hex	sas	saihs	siex
7.	septem	hepta	sapta	sibun	seofon
8.	octō	oktō	astau	ahtau	eahta
9.	nouem	ennea	nava	niun	nigon
10.	decem	deka	dasa	taihun	tīen

The resemblances between the Latin, Greek, and Sanskrit are quite striking. Moreover, there are things that suggest regular correspondences: where Latin and Sanskrit begin a word with *s*, Greek begins it with *h*; where Latin and Greek have *o*, Sanskrit has *a*. The resemblances to the Germanic languages are less close, but nevertheless clear enough; and they would be even clearer if we took into account certain related words and variant forms: for example, in Greek there is a word *oinē*, which means 'the one-spot on a dice', and this corresponds more closely than *heis* to the Latin and Germanic words for 'one'. There are also signs of regular correspondences between the Germanic forms and the others. For example, at the beginning of a word Germanic has *t* for their *d*, and it has *h* where they have *k* or *c*. Let us follow up just one possible correspondence. In the words for *five*, Greek and Sanskrit have *p* (*pente*, *panca*) where the Germanic languages have *f* (*fimf*, *fif*). Can we find further evidence for this relationship? Consider the following table:

Old English	Gothic	Latin	Greek	Sanskrit
fæder ('father')	fadar	pater	pater	pitar
nefa ('nephew')	—	nepos	—	napat
feor ('far')	fairra	—	pera	paras
faran ('go, fare')	faran	(ex)-perior	peraein	parayati
full ('full')	fulls	plenus	pleres	purnas
fearh ('pig')	—	porcus	—	—
feþer ('feather')	—	penna	pteron	patra
fell ('skin')	fill	pellis	pella	—

The words have the same or closely related meanings in the different languages; there are small variations: Sanskrit *napat* means 'grandson', not 'nephew'; but as a matter of fact Old English *nefa* could also mean 'grandson'. And in all these words we have Germanic *f* corresponding to *p* in the other three languages. Similar series of correspondences can be established for the other sounds of these languages. And the correspondences are not confined to sounds: the Germanic languages also show resemblances in detail to Latin, Greek, and Sanskrit in grammar and syntax, for example in the grammatical endings of words. It is certain that all these languages are related.

But the family does not end here. Similar detailed resemblances, both in sounds and in grammar, can be demonstrated with a large number of other languages, including Russian, Lithuanian, Welsh, Albanian, and Persian. In fact English belongs to a very extensive family of languages, with many branches. This family includes most of the languages of Europe and of India, and so is usually called *Indo-European*.

THE BRANCHES OF INDO-EUROPEAN

One branch of Indo-European is Indo-Iranian, or Aryan, so called because the ancient peoples who spoke it called themselves Aryas ('noble ones'). This branch has two groups, the Indian and the Iranian. To the Indian group belongs the language of the ancient Vedic hymns from northwest India, which go back by oral tradition to a very remote past, perhaps to about 1400 BC, though the first written texts are much later. A later form of this language is classical Sanskrit, which was standardized round about 300 BC, and has since been the learned language of India (rather like Latin in Europe). Modern representatives of the group are Bengali, Hindi, and other languages of northern India, together with some from farther south, like Sinhalese. The other Aryan group, Iranian, includes modern Persian and neighbouring languages such as Ossetian and Kurdish. An ancient form of this language, Old Persian, is found in inscriptions, like those of King Darius dating from about 500 BC; a different form of ancient Persian is found in the Avesta, the sacred writings of the Zoroastrians, parts of which go back to perhaps 600 BC. The ancient writings of the Aryan branch preserve many archaic features of Indo-European, and so are of great value for comparative study.

Another branch with ancient texts is Greek, which has a literature from the seventh century BC. The Homeric epics, which were long handed down by oral tradition, go back even earlier, to the ninth or tenth century BC (though not to the time of the Trojan war itself, which was about 1200 BC). A few years ago, tablets from Crete in a script called Minoan Linear B were

deciphered by the late Michael Ventris, and revealed a form of
Greek in use there way back in 1450 BC or thereabouts; not all
the experts, however, accept Ventris's decipherment. The
Greek branch includes all the various ancient Hellenic dialects,
from one of which, Attic, is descended modern Greek.

Two branches which have some things in common are the
Italic and the Celtic. Italic consisted of a number of dialects of
ancient Italy, including Oscan, Umbrian, and Latin. The
earliest Latin texts date from the third century BC; of the other
Italic languages we have only fragments. Celtic, once widely
diffused over Europe, can be divided into three groups,
Gaulish, Britannic, and Gaelic. Gaulish was spoken in France
and northern Italy in the time of the Roman Republic, and was
spread abroad by Celtic military expeditions to central Europe
and as far as Asia Minor; it died out during the early centuries
of the Christian era, and is known only from a few inscriptions
and from names of people and places preserved in Latin texts.
Britannic was the branch of Celtic spoken in Britain before the
Anglo-Saxon invasions. It survived into modern times in three
languages: Cornish, which is known in texts from the fifteenth
century and which died out in the eighteenth; Welsh, which
has literary texts going back to the eleventh century; and
Breton, which has literary texts from the fourteenth century.
Breton, it should be noticed, is not a descendant of Gaulish: it
was taken across to Brittany by refugees from Britain at the
time of the Anglo-Saxon conquest. The third branch, Gaelic,
includes Scottish Gaelic, Irish Gaelic, and Manx; its earliest
records are inscriptions from the fourth or fifth century AD; in
Irish, there is a rich literature, with written records going back
to the eighth century AD.

Another two branches of Indo-European that have things in
common are Baltic and Slavonic. The Baltic languages include
Lithuanian, Lettish, and Old Prussian (which died out in the
seventeenth century). The Slavonic branch has many members,
including Serbian, Croatian, Bulgarian, Czech, Polish, and
the various types of Russian. The earliest recorded Slavonic,
called Old Slavonic, is the language of certain religious writings

of the tenth and eleventh centuries AD, emanating from Bulgaria.

There are still three minor branches unmentioned: Albanian, Armenian, and Tocharian (an extinct language of Chinese Turkestan, which has some affinities with Italic and Celtic). Then there is the large and important Germanic branch. And finally we have to add Hittite, one of the languages of the Hittite empire in Anatolia round about 1500 BC, which is recorded in numerous texts in a cuneiform writing. Hittite is certainly related to Indo-European, though much of its vocabulary is non-Indo-European; it perhaps represents a very early branching-off from the parent language, so that its relation to the other branches of Indo-European is that of cousin rather than sister.

Even from this brief survey, it will be seen what an enormous and complicated family the Indo-European languages are. It will also be seen how important they are in the modern world – more important than any other group of languages. Altogether, well over a thousand million people speak an Indo-European language as their mother tongue; of these, well over three hundred million speak a Germanic language, nearly three hundred million a Romance language, about two hundred and fifty million an Indian language, and about two hundred million a Slavonic language; the other branches are all small. No other language family can compare with this in size; the Hamito-Semitic, Japanese–Korean, Dravidian, African Negro, and Malayo-Polynesian families have roughly one hundred million speakers each – about one tenth the size of Indo-European; and even the enormous Sino-Tibetan family, with about five hundred million speakers, is still only half the size.

WHO WERE THE INDO-EUROPEANS?

This great complex of languages with its millions of speakers has developed, if we are right, out of some single language, which must have been spoken thousands of years ago by some comparatively small body of people in a relatively restricted geographical area. This language we can call Proto-Indo-European. The people who spoke it or who spoke languages evolved from it we can for convenience call Indo-Europeans, but we must remember that this does not imply anything about race or culture, only about language: people of very different races and cultures can come to be native speakers of Indo-European languages; such speakers today for example include Indians, Greeks, American Negroes, Russians, Mexicans, and Englishmen. It is highly probable, of course, that the speakers of Proto-Indo-European, living together in a limited area, had a common culture, whatever race or races they consisted of. But who were they? Where did they live? And how did they come to spread over the world?

It is plain, for a start, that, immediately before their dispersal, the Indo-Europeans were not living in any of the advanced cultural centres of the ancient world, such as Mesopotamia, the Mediterranean basin, or the Indus and Ganges valleys. When they appear in such places it is as intruders from outside. They appear on the fringes of the Mesopotamian area around 1500 BC, when a dynasty with Indo-European names are found ruling a non-Indo-European people, the Mitanni, who lived on the upper Euphrates. At about the same time, Hittite was being used in Anatolia, and the Aryas were in northwest India: their earliest records, the Vedas, suggest that at this time they were in the Punjab, and were in conflict with earlier inhabitants of India; it seems, therefore, that they had invaded India from the northwest, from Afghanistan or Iran; and since the Indian branch of Indo-European is closely related to the Iranian branch, it seems likely that the Indians and the Iranians had lived together for some time, perhaps on the Iranian Plateau, before the Indian group moved on to invade India. At this date, however, we know nothing about the Iranians, who do not impinge on the histories of other peoples until the invasion of Mesopotamia by the Medes and the Persians many centuries later.

In Europe, we have no very early records of the Indo-Europeans, except for the Greeks. If Ventris's decipherment of

Minoan Linear B is accepted, then we know that a form of Greek, Mycenean, was in use on Crete and the Greek mainland by 1500 BC. We do not know what direction Mycenean Greek came from, but later Greek arrivals, like the Dorians, came from the north; the ancestors of the Greeks may very well have come, therefore, from the valley of the Danube. The records of Italic are later, but here the archaeologist can help us, for we can fairly confidently equate the Italic-speaking peoples with a culture that appeared in northern Italy in about 1500 BC, and spread southwards; some elements in this culture suggest that it was an offshoot of a lake-dwelling people in the Alps. For the early history of the Celts we also depend on the archaeologists; these peoples also first appear in the region of the Alps, and their great period of expansion began in about 500 BC. The Germans we first hear about from the Romans, not long before the beginning of our era; they were then living in northern Germany and Scandinavia. At the same period, the Slavs were living north of the Carpathians, mainly between the Vistula and the Dnieper; they appear to have been living there for many centuries before they began to expand in the early years of the Christian era.

The Indo-European languages of which we have early records had already diverged markedly from one another. It seems likely, therefore, that the dispersal of the Indo-Europeans must have begun by 2000 BC, and that it may have begun a good deal earlier. Obviously, however, the place from which the dispersal started is still very much anybody's guess. But there are further sources of evidence. One is that of the languages themselves.

One line of argument is that the languages which preserve most fully the features of Proto-Indo-European will belong to peoples who have stayed near the original Indo-European home, and not moved away to changed conditions and to contacts with other peoples. It is doubtful, however, whether this will get us far. The modern language which is most archaic, and which has preserved a large number of features believed to be typical of the original language, is Lithuanian. But the

Lithuanians live next door to the Germanic peoples, whose language underwent profound modifications, for example in pronunciation, in the prehistoric period. Lithuanian has probably been so static because its speakers lived for a long period in a region surrounded by thick forest, cut off from outside influences and from change; but it does not follow that this region was the cradle of the Indo-European peoples. A similar conservatism is seen in modern Icelandic, which is the most archaic of the Scandinavian languages: but we know perfectly well that Iceland was not the cradle of the Scandinavian languages, because Scandinavian speech was first taken there in the ninth century AD, by Norwegian colonists.

Another line of approach is to examine the family relationships of the Indo-European languages, to try to see which belong most closely together. From this we might hope to work out which branches migrated together, in what order different groups broke away, and so on. One possible family tree would be as follows. First we divide into two main branches:

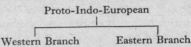

The western branch divides as follows:

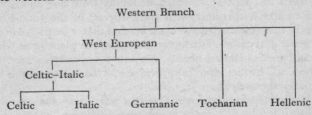

And the eastern branch as follows:

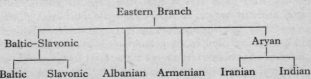

The first division into two main groups is important; the groups are marked by a number of differences in grammar, pronunciation, and vocabulary, which suggests that there was an early division of the Indo-Europeans into two main areas, perhaps representing migrations in different directions. One of the distinctive differences in pronunciation between the two groups is the treatment of Indo-European palatal *k*, which becomes a velar *k* in the Western languages, but is changed to some kind of palatal fricative (*s* or *sh*) in the Eastern languages. Thus the word for 'hundred' is Greek *he-katon*, Latin *centum*, Old Irish *cet*, and Welsh *cant* (the *c* in each case representing a *k* sound); but in Sanskrit it is *satam*, in Avestan *satem*, in Lithuanian *szimtas*, and in Old Slavonic *seto*. For this reason, the two groups are often referred to as the *kentum* languages and the *satem* languages. On the whole, the kentum languages are in the west and the satem languages in the east, but a puzzling anomaly is Tocharian, right across in Western China, which is a kentum language. The division into kentum and satem languages had already taken place when we get our first glimpses of Indo-European round about 1500 BC.

However, although our family tree has some value, it is not entirely satisfactory, because there are always some points on which a language shows the closest resemblance to a language which is *remote* from it on the tree. Greek and Sanskrit are in different major branches, but nevertheless resemble one another a good deal in syntax, and to some extent in vocabulary. Greek and Iranian belong to different major branches, but they agree in changing Indo-European *s-* at the beginning of a word into *h-*; the word for 'old' is Latin *senex*, Sanskrit *sanas*, and Old Irish *sen*, but in Greek it is *henos* and in Old Iranian *hana*. Moreover, no amount of juggling with the family tree can completely remove discrepancies of this kind. In fact, it is impossible to depict the relationships of the Indo-European languages in an entirely satisfactory way by means of a model in which branches divide and subdivide.

These facts make sense if we envisage Proto-Indo-European as having broken up into a number of dialects *before* the dispersal began (which is what we might have expected anyway). For, under such conditions, changes will spread from various centres within the region, and the boundaries of one change will not necessarily coincide with those of another. The

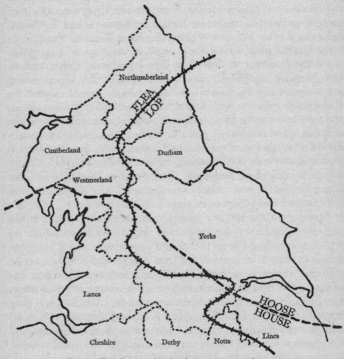

FIG. 9. Two intersecting isoglosses, see opposite page.

speakers in a given area may pick up one new pronunciation from their neighbours to the east, and another from their neighbours to the west, so that their speech combines features of different dialect regions. At the same time, another change may spread down from the north, and stop halfway across their area, so that some of them have it and some not. In this way, dialect features will appear in various permutations and combinations throughout the whole region.

In fact, this is the kind of situation which is often found in studies of modern dialects. One small example of this is given in Figure 9, which shows the dividing lines, or *isoglosses*, for two pairs of features in the traditional rural dialects of Northern England. One line shows the boundary between two pronunciations of the vowel of the word *house*: north of the line, it is a pure vowel (*hoose*), while south of the line it is a diphthong (*house*). The second line shows the limit of occurrence of one particular word, namely *lop*, meaning 'flea': this word is found only east of the line, not to the west of it; it is in fact a loan from Scandinavian, and has obviously spread across the region from the east. The important point is that these two lines run in quite different directions, and cut one another, so that all possible combinations of the four features occur. To return to Proto-Indo-European, it is clear enough that, if this kind of thing went on before the dispersal, the family resemblances between the various branches have only a limited value as a guide to their prehistoric migrations.

THE PROTO-INDO-EUROPEAN VOCABULARY

There is, however, another kind of linguistic evidence that may help us. Words which occur in a large number of Indo-European languages, and which cannot be shown to be loan words, were presumably a part of the vocabulary of Proto-Indo-European. But if the words existed, then the things denoted by the words existed too, and must have been familiar to the people that spoke the language. In this way, it is argued, we can deduce what kinds of animals and plants the Indo-Europeans were familiar with (and hence what part of the world they lived in), what stage of culture they had reached, and so on.

The method, indeed, has dangers. For example, it is hardly safe to argue too strongly from the *absence* of a word from the majority of languages: loss of words is a common happening in all languages, and when peoples have been widely dispersed and met widely different conditions, we must expect that many of them will lose large numbers of words. A people who migrated from the arctic to the tropics might well be expected to lose the words for snow and ice. On the other hand, the absence of some whole group of words, covering an entire field of activity, may well be given some weight. Moreover, in changed conditions a word may not be lost, but may instead change its meaning: the Indo-European word for 'snow' survived on the burning plains of India, as the Sanskrit *snehas*, but meant 'grease' or 'slipperiness'.

Another danger is that we may be deceived by loan words. When a people learns a new technique or becomes familiar with new objects, it often takes over the appropriate names from the people from whom it learns the technique or acquires the objects. So several branches of the Indo-Europeans may well have borrowed the vocabulary of, for example, agriculture from the same people, or from peoples speaking similar languages. However, while it is obviously likely that the Celts and the Germans might borrow the same words while on their travels, it is not really very likely that they would also borrow the same words as the Indians and Iranians. Indeed, if we seriously thought that a large part of the common vocabulary of the Indo-European languages was due to borrowing from a common source after their dispersal, then our whole concept of them as related languages would collapse. We can guard against the danger of loan words by giving most weight to words that are found both in European and in Asiatic languages; and only such words are counted as original Indo-European in what follows.

The common vocabulary thus obtained suggests that the Indo-Europeans before their dispersal were a nomadic or semi-nomadic pastoral people. They had cattle and sheep, for there are common words for both of these: for example, our *ox* is Welsh *ych* and Sanskrit *uksan*, and our *ewe* is related to Latin *ouis* and Sanskrit *avis*. Cattle were obviously highly prized: the

Old English word *feoh*, corresponding to Latin *pecu*, meant both 'cattle' and 'wealth'; and the Latin word for 'money, wealth' was *pecunia*; and cattle figure prominently in the early writings of the Indo-Europeans. They also had other domestic animals, including the dog and possibly the pig, the goat, and the goose, but there is no common word for the ass. They certainly had horses, for which a rich vocabulary has survived, and they also had vehicles, for there are words for wheel, axle, nave, and yoke. They had cheese and butter, but no common word for milk has survived, which shows how chancy the evidence is. No large common vocabulary has survived for agriculture; such a vocabulary is found in the European languages, but this may obviously date from after the dispersal. There are, however, common words for grain, and Greek and Sanskrit have cognate words for plough and for furrow, so perhaps the Proto-Indo-Europeans had at least some acquaintance with agriculture; it may have been practised in certain regions, for example. We might indeed expect on other grounds that the Indo-Europeans would be pastoralists or hunters rather than farmers, for it is the former rather than the latter who tend to become migrants and invade settled civilizations: pure agriculturalists tend to be earthbound. We may also note that there is a common word for mead, but not for beer (which is an agriculturalist's product). There is, however, no common vocabulary for hunting or fishing.

There are a number of common words for tools and weapons, including arrows. There is evidence that stone was used for these: for example, the Latin verb *secare*, 'to cut', is related to the word *saxum*, 'a stone, rock', and the latter is identical with the Old English *seax*, which meant 'knife', and which is also related to *scythe* and *saw*. Originally, it seems, a stone and a cutting implement were the same thing. However, the Proto-Indo-Europeans also knew metal, for there are two common words for copper or bronze, one of which survives as our word *ore* (Latin *aes*, Sanskrit *ayas*), and there are also words for gold and silver. There is, however, no common terminology for the techniques of metallurgy. They were probably in the transitional stage when stone is still the predominant material for tools and weapons, but metal is beginning to be used. As one would expect at this stage, their vocabulary shows a familiarity with pottery and probably also with weaving. There are also words for house and for door, suggesting something more substantial than a tent, but no word for window.

They knew both rain and snow, but their summer seems to have been hot, which suggests a continental climate. The wild animals they knew included wolves, bears, otters, mice, hares, and beavers, but apparently not lions, tigers, elephants, or camels; so presumably they lived in a cool temperate zone. Great play has been made with the Indo-European words for the beech tree, the eel, and the salmon. The beech does not grow in northeast Europe, or anywhere east of the Caspian, so it has been argued that the original home of the Indo-Europeans must have been farther west. The eel and the salmon are not found in the rivers that flow into the Black Sea, so it has been argued that this region must be ruled out. However, it is not certain that these words originally referred to the species in question. For example, the word for 'salmon' (German *Lachs*, Swedish *lax*, Russian *lososi* 'salmon', Tocharian *laks* 'fish') may not originally have referred to the true salmon, but to a species of *salmo* found north of the Black Sea, or may even have meant 'fish' in general.

It seems that rivers and streams were common, but there is no word for the sea or the ocean, so they were apparently an inland people. There is a word for ship, seen for example in Latin *nauis* and Sanskrit *naus*, but originally this may well have been the name of a vessel used for crossing rivers.

There is a large common Indo-European vocabulary for family relationships, and it would seem that the family played an important part in their social organization. The linguistic evidence suggests that this family went by male descent, and that when a woman married she went to live with her husband's family. For example, there is a widespread Indo-European word for daughter-in-law (seen in Latin *nurus*), but no such widespread word for son-in-law; and there are common words for husband's brother, husband's sister, and husband's brothers' wives, but no such common words for the wife's relatives.

This view of the Indo-European family is supported by the Indo-European names of Gods. There are a few common to the European and Asiatic languages, and they seem to be personifications of natural forces; they do not, however, include a Great Mother goddess or Earth Goddess of the type common in matriarchal societies. Prominent among them, however, is a Sky God – the Greek Zeus, the Sanskrit Dyaus, the Old English Tiw (whose name survives in the word *Tuesday*); and this god was a Father God, as we can see from his Latin name, Jupiter, which means 'Sky Father'. In historical times we sometimes find societies with Indo-European languages which have a Great Mother goddess, for example Minoan Crete; in such cases it is to be presumed that Indo-European speakers have invaded the culture from outside and taken over its religion.

THE HOME OF THE INDO-EUROPEANS

A certain amount has emerged from this about Proto-Indo-European culture, but not enough to pin it down with certainty to a particular locality. At one time it was assumed that the Indo-Europeans had come from Asia; partly this was just a traditional idea – all migrations came from Asia – but there were also some serious arguments for it. Today, however, this view is not in favour. The linguistic evidence is against it; for example the complete absence of an Indo-European word for 'camel' (our word being borrowed from Semitic). And the archaeological evidence fails to reveal the requisite wave after wave of invaders coming from the east. The general view today, therefore, is that the original home of the Indo-Europeans was somewhere in Europe. Three main areas in Europe have especially been championed: (1) Scandinavia and the adjacent part of northern Germany; (2) the Danube valley, especially the Hungarian Plain; and (3) the steppes of the southern Ukraine, north of the Black Sea.

The Scandinavian theory has found a good deal of support in Germany, and one cannot help suspecting interested motives in this. The Germans have always adopted a slightly proprietary air towards the Indo-European languages (they call them the Indo-*Germanic* languages); and a belief in a Scandinavian homeland for the Indo-Europeans often goes with a belief that the Indo-Europeans were of a certain racial type – that they belonged to the 'Nordic race', tall, fair, long-headed. The Germanic-speaking peoples are then seen as the 'pure' and 'original' Indo-Europeans, who have elsewhere been diluted by other races. At its crudest, this kind of view becomes the arrogant racialism of the Nazis, who see themselves as the master race of 'pure Aryan stock', destined to rule or destroy other (and of course inferior) races. In this form, the theory is sheer nonsense, though nonsense of a very dangerous kind. But there are more sophisticated versions of it; and, for almost any European, there is a certain insidious appeal in the suggestion that Indo-European was the invention of the so-called white races, by whose intrinsic superiority it was spread over the world. But the theory that Proto-Indo-European was spoken by a 'pure Nordic race' will not stand up to serious examination.

This is not to say that we have no evidence about some of the physical characteristics of early speakers of Indo-European languages. There is some evidence in the early texts to suggest that many such speakers were relatively fair, and perhaps that they were tall. There is such evidence, for example, about the Indo-Europeans who invaded India, Italy, and Greece, where such racial types have since disappeared, presumably absorbed by the indigenous population. Moreover, in countries that were invaded by Indo-Europeans, fair colouring has tended to remain a mark of aristocratic birth, and dark colouring the mark of the peasant. Even in modern India, fairness is socially desirable, at any rate in the north, and an Indian woman advertising for a husband will often emphasize the fairness of her complexion. It might be thought that this is merely a hangover from the days of British rule and the white man's prestige; but in pictorial art of pre-British times we often find the same emphasis on fairness, and it is easy to find paintings where aristocratic ladies are shown as relatively fair, while their attendants are dark (as for example in the rock paintings at Sigiriya in Ceylon, dating from about AD 500). Moreover, there can be no doubt that the inhabitants of northern India are fairer than those of the south; indeed, the Tamil nationalist movement in southern India, which wants to break away from the Hindi-speaking north, now proclaims darkness of skin as one of its national marks.

It is facts like these that have been seized on by those who believe that the Indo-Europeans were of the Nordic race. And, the argument continues, the central region for tall long-headed skeletons in prehistoric times is the North European plain, so that is where the Indo-Europeans came from.

But the conclusion goes far beyond the evidence. For one thing, the early literary evidence by no means proves that the Indo-Europeans had very fair hair. Colour words are very shifty things, and phrases commonly translated as 'yellow haired' may equally probably have meant 'auburn haired' or 'brown haired'. It does seem probable that the Indo-European invaders were lighter in colouring than some of the peoples they overran, as in India, but this does not prove that they were blonde. Moreover, we have to bear in mind that members of an aristocracy are not obliged to work long hours in the sun and the wind, as peasants are, and that peasants therefore tend to have darker complexions; this no doubt plays a large part in the prestige of fairness in many different cultures in later times, irrespective of any racial characters.

Moreover, there is no firm evidence that the original Indo-Europeans were long-headed: skeletons definitely identified as belonging to early Indo-European-speaking cultures are in fact of various types: some, for example, are tall but round-headed. But we have no very early evidence anyway. The supporters of the Nordic theory have in fact made a leap in their argument: from evidence for a certain (arguable) degree of fairness to a conclusion of tall, blonde, long-headed. This leap has commonly been made under the influence of a myth and of an unspoken assumption. The myth is that there are 'pure races', when in fact all human groups for whom we have accurate information turn out to have a mixture of characters. The unspoken assumption is that this 'pure race' in its purest form is found in the early Germanic-speaking peoples. But in fact we have no reason to believe that the early Germanic peoples were 'pure Indo-Europeans': their particular physical characteristics (the homogeneity of which has no doubt been exaggerated in any case) may perfectly well have been those of another people who were conquered by Indo-Europeans.

The 'racial' evidence, therefore, can be dismissed: it really gives us no firm reasons for locating the original Indo-Europeans in northern Germany, or Scandinavia, or anywhere else. And in other respects the Scandinavian theory has serious weaknesses. For example, Scandinavia does not tally very well with the kind of evidence we have looked at from comparative philology: it is a maritime region (whereas there is no common Indo-European word for sea or ocean or fishing), and it is not very suitable terrain for horse-drawn vehicles, which belong rather to the steppes. Nor is there an Indo-European word for amber, which was one of the most sought-after products of the Baltic. Moreover, the great changes in pronunciation that the Germanic languages underwent in prehistoric times make one suspect that they had been learnt by some conquered people: if they are 'pure' forms of Indo-European, the Germanic languages have evolved a susprisingly long way from their original. There also seem to be difficulties in the archaeological evidence.

Archaeological evidence also plays a large part in the arguments about the other possible regions in Europe. There seems to be a good deal of support at present for the view that Indo-European expansion began from the Hungarian plain, but the claims of the Ukraine have also been strongly argued. These two areas seem the most plausible at present, but the discussion is still unconcluded, and there may yet be evidence to come which will one day settle the issue.

It does seem likely, however, that in prehistoric times the peoples speaking the Proto-Indo-European language were living somewhere on the plains of central or eastern Europe, forming a loosely linked group of communities with common gods and similar social organization. In about 2500 BC, after the language had developed into a number of dialects, they began to expand in different directions. A large group went south-eastwards, either over the Caucasus or through Asia Minor; some of these stayed in Armenia, while others pressed on to north Mesopotamia and conquered the Mitanni, but the majority continued to the Iranian plateau and settled there, and later expanded into northwest India. Meanwhile, other groups spread southwards to the Balkans and to Crete; others went westwards to the Alps, whence they later emerged to spread over Italy, France, and Spain; and others again moved northwards to the Baltic. Naturally, many details are obscure, but the general lines of the expansion are fairly clear.

In the course of their expansion, the Indo-Europeans over-ran countries which had reached a higher level of civilization than they had themselves: the Aryas, for example, conquered the civilizations of India, and the Persians those of Meso-potamia. This need not surprise us: primitive nomadic peoples have often overrun more advanced urban civilizations, and there is no need to postulate (as some people have done) some special intellectual or physical prowess in the Indo-Europeans that set them apart from other peoples. It merely shows that they had cultivated the art of war rather successfully (perhaps having profited from the technical advances of neighbouring urban civilizations), and that they were under some kind of environmental pressure (like change of climate or exhaustion of pastures) that made them need to migrate or expand. More-over, the urban civilization that is overrun may have internal weaknesses of a social or political kind, just as, much later, the Roman Empire had when it was overrun by the technically more backward Germanic peoples.

Perhaps, however, there is one technical factor which played an important part in the expansions and conquests of the Indo-

Europeans. This is the use of horse-drawn vehicles, which we have seen to be characteristic of Proto-Indo-European society. When the Aryas invaded India, they were fighting in horse-drawn chariots, and similar vehicles were used by other Indo-European peoples, like the Celts and the Hellenes. The horse was a late introduction into the river valleys of the great early urban civilizations, in which the normal draught animal was the ass; and when the horse did come to them, it came from the north. It seems likely that in this respect the Indo-Europeans were ahead of their time, and that it was their use of the horse chariot that enabled them to overrun such a large part of the Eurasian continent. The Englishman's sentimental attachment to horses may have a deeper historical justification than he realizes.

CHAPTER VI

THE GERMANIC LANGUAGES

THE BRANCH of Indo-European that English belongs to is called Germanic, and includes German, Dutch, Flemish, Frisian, Danish, Swedish, Norwegian, and Icelandic. All these languages are descended from one parent language, a dialect of Indo-European, which we can call Proto-Germanic. Round about the beginning of the Christian era, the speakers of Proto-Germanic still formed a relatively homogeneous cultural and linguistic group, living in the north of Europe. We have no records of the language in this period, but we know something about the people who spoke it, because they are described by Roman authors, who called them the *Germani*. One of the best known of these descriptions is that written by Tacitus in AD 98, called *Germania*.

PRIMITIVE GERMANIC SOCIETY

Tacitus describes the Germans as a tribal society living in scattered settlements in the woody and marshy country of northern Europe. They hate cities, he says, and keep their houses far apart, living in wooden buildings, or sometimes, in winter, in pits dug in the ground and covered over with rubbish. They keep flocks, and grow grain crops, but their agriculture is not very advanced, and they do not practise horticulture. Because of the large amount of open ground, they change their plough lands yearly, allotting areas to whole villages, and distributing land to cultivators in order of rank. The family plays a large part in their social organization, and the more relatives a man has the greater is his influence in his old age. They have kings, chosen for their birth, and chiefs, chosen for their valour, but in major affairs the whole community consults together; and the freedom of the Germans is a greater danger to Rome than the despotism of the Parthian kings. Chiefs are attended by companions, who fight for them in battle, and who in return are rewarded by the chiefs with gifts of weapons, horses, treasure, and land. In battle, it is disgraceful for a chief to be outshone by his companions, and disgraceful for the companions to be less brave than their chief; the greatest disgrace is to come back from a battle alive after your chief has been killed: this means lifelong infamy. The Germans dislike peace, for it is only in war that renown and booty can be won. In peacetime, the warriors idle about at home, eating, drinking, and gambling, and leaving the work of the house and of the fields to women, weaklings, and slaves. They are extremely hospitable, to strangers as well as to acquaintances, but their love of drinking often leads to quarrels. They are monogamous, and their women are held in high esteem. The physical type is everywhere the same: fierce blue eyes, fair hair, and huge bodies. The normal dress is the short cloak, though the skins of animals are also worn; the women often wear linen undergarments. Very few of the men have breastplates or helmets, and they have very little iron. They worship above all Mercury (i.e. Woden), and sacrifice animals to Hercules and Mars (i.e. Thor and Tiw). They set very great store by auspices and the casting of lots. Their only form of recorded history is their ancient songs, in which they tell of the earth-born god Tuisto and his son Mannus, ancestor of the whole German race; the various sons of Mannus are the ancestors of the different German tribes. And Tacitus goes on to give an account of each of these tribes, its location and peculiarities.

To some extent, Tacitus is undoubtedly using the Germans as a means of attacking the corruptions of Rome in his own day: they are the noble savages whose customs are in many ways a criticism of Roman life. But at the same time he obviously has access to a great deal of genuine information about the Germans, and many of the details of his account are confirmed by what we know about the Germanic peoples in later times. When he wrote, they were already pressing on the borders of the Roman Empire, and Tacitus recognized them as a danger to Rome. Earlier, they had probably been confined to a small area in southern Scandinavia and northern Germany between the Elbe and the Oder, but round about 300 BC they had begun to expand in all directions, perhaps because of overpopulation and the poverty of their natural resources. In the course of a few centuries they pushed northwards up the Scandinavian peninsula into territory occupied by Finns; they expanded westwards beyond the Elbe, into northwest Germany and the Netherlands, overrunning areas occupied by Celtic-speaking peoples; they expanded eastwards round the shores of the Baltic Sea, into Finnish or Baltic-speaking regions; and they pressed southwards into Bohemia, and later into southwest Germany. At the same time, the territory to their south ruled by Rome was also expanding, and by the time of Tacitus there was a considerable area of contact between Romans and Germans along the northern frontiers of the Empire. There was a good deal of trade, with a number of recognized routes up through German territory to the Baltic; there was considerable cultural influence by the Romans on the Germans (many of whom served their time in the Roman legions); and of course there were frequent clashes.

THE BRANCHES OF GERMANIC

As a result of this expansion of the Germanic peoples, dialect differences within Proto-Germanic became more marked, and we can distinguish three main branches or groups of dialects, which are called North Germanic, East Germanic, and West Germanic.

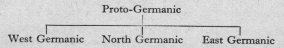

To North Germanic belong the modern Scandinavian languages – Norwegian, Swedish, Danish, Icelandic, and Gutnish (the language of the island of Gotland). The earliest recorded form of North Germanic (Old Norse) is found in runic inscriptions from about AD 300; at this period it shows very little trace of dialectal variations, and it is not until the Viking Age, from about AD 800 onwards, that it begins to break up into the dialects which have developed into the modern Scandinavian languages. Here is a family tree for the North Germanic languages:

The East Germanic dialects were spoken by the tribes that expanded east of the Oder around the shores of the Baltic. They included the Goths, and Gothic is the only East Germanic language of which we have any records. Round about AD 200 the Goths migrated southeastwards, and settled in the plains north of the Black Sea, where they divided into two branches, the Ostrogoths east of the Dnieper, and the Visigoths west of it. The main record of Gothic is the fragmentary remains of a translation of the Bible into Visigothic, made by the bishop Wulfila or Ulfilas in the middle of the fourth century. The Goths were later overrun by the Huns, but a form of Gothic was being spoken in the Crimea as late as the seventeenth century; however, it has since died out, and no East Germanic language has survived into our own times. Here is a family tree for the East Germanic languages:

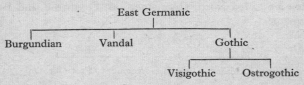

To West Germanic belong the High German dialects of southern Germany, the Low German dialects of northern Germany (which in their earliest recorded form are called Old Saxon), Dutch, Flemish, Frisian, and English. The language most nearly related to English is Frisian, which was once spoken along the coast of the North Sea from northern Holland to central Denmark, but which is now heard only in a few coastal regions and on some of the Dutch islands. Before the migration of the Anglo-Saxons to England, they must have been near neighbours of the Frisians, and we can postulate a prehistoric Anglo-Frisian dialect, out of which evolved Old English and Old Frisian. Here is a family tree for the West Germanic languages:

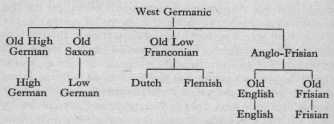

The expansion of the Germanic peoples did not, of course, end in the time of Tacitus. During the break-up of the Roman Empire, Germanic military expeditions were made all over Europe and the Mediterranean: Goths swept through Spain and Italy, Vandals invaded North Africa, Franks and Burgundians settled in France, Anglo-Saxons occupied England. Later still, Scandinavian Vikings harried the whole of Europe, and established kingdoms in England, Ireland, Normandy, Sicily, and Russia. Often, however, such conquests were made by relatively small groups, whose language ultimately disappeared: Gothic, we have seen, did not survive anywhere; Frankish disappeared in France, and French is a Romance language; the Vikings established their language permanently nowhere except in Iceland and the Faroes. Of course, the Germanic languages often left traces on the language that conquered them: French has a few hundred loan words from Germanic, including such a highly characteristic Germanic word as *guerre*, 'war'; the Langobards, or 'long beards', left their name in *Lombardy* when they invaded Italy in the sixth century

AD; and the very name of *Russia* is a Scandinavian loan word. And, even though so many dialects died out, there were in earlier times a vast number of Germanic dialects spoken in Europe. Their consolidation into a small number of national languages was due to the rise of the modern nation states; as we have seen, the existence of a coherent political unit favours the triumph of a single dialect (a prestige dialect or standard literary language) within its area.

We have no records of the Proto-Germanic language from which all these languages are descended. However, we can reconstruct it to quite a considerable extent by comparing the various daughter languages; especially valuable are the languages with early literary records, like Gothic, Old Norse, Old English, Old High German, and Old Saxon. We can also learn a good deal by comparing our reconstructions with the forms found in other branches of Indo-European. Further minor sources of information are the Germanic names recorded by Latin and Greek authors, and the words borrowed from Proto-Germanic by other languages. For example, the Finnish word *kuningas*, meaning 'king', is plainly borrowed from Germanic, and it preserves a more archaic form of the word than any of the Germanic languages themselves (Old Norse *konungr*, Old High German *kuning*, Old English *cyning*); the Proto-Germanic form was probably **kuningaz*.

The Inflexional System of Proto-Germanic

The Proto-Germanic language, reconstructed in this way, has close structural and phonological affinities with the other Indo-European languages, together with certain peculiar developments of its own. Like the postulated Proto-Indo-European language, Proto-Germanic is a highly *inflected* language: that is to say, it makes great use in its grammar of variations in the *endings* of words. Not much of the Indo-European system of inflexions is left in Modern English, which prefers other grammatical devices, but there is enough at any rate to show what an inflexion is. For example, when we change *cup* to *cups*, we are using an inflexion, the -*s* used to mark the plural in nouns. When we change *I walk* to *he walks*, we use a different -*s* inflexion, the one that marks the third person singular of the verb; we could also change it to *I walked*, and here we are using the -*ed* inflexion which marks pastness in verbs. Other inflexions in Modern English are the -*m* of *whom*, and the -*er*, -*est* in *blacker*, *blackest*.

Inflexions do not, however, play a very big part in Modern English grammar. To get a better idea of what an inflected language is like, you need to look at something like classical Latin, or modern German. The English sentence *The master beat the servant* could be rendered in Latin, word for word, as *Dominus uerberauit seruum*, though classical Latin would normally prefer the order *Dominus seruum uerberauit*. The important point is, however, that altering the order of the Latin words cannot alter the basic meaning of the sentence: if we write *Seruum uerberauit dominus*, we are adopting a rather unusual word order, and giving special emphasis to the word 'servant', but it still means 'The master beat the servant'. English uses word order to indicate who is the beater and who the beaten, but in Latin this information is conveyed by the inflexions -*us* and -*um*. If we wish to say that the servant beat the master, we must change these endings, and write *Seruus dominum uerberauit*. In grammatical terminology, we are inflecting the nouns *seruus* and *dominus* for case: the ending -*us* shows the nominative case, used for the subject of the sentence, and the ending -*um* the accusative case, used for the object of the sentence.

Latin nouns, moreover, have other inflexions, which to some extent do the work which in Modern English is performed by prepositions (words like *of* and *with*). Thus the noun *dominus* has the following set of inflexions:

	Singular	*Plural*
Nominative	dominus 'a master'	domini 'masters'
Vocative	domine 'master!'	domini 'masters!'
Accusative	dominum 'a master'	dominos 'masters'
Genitive	domini 'of a master'	dominorum 'of masters'
Dative	domino 'to, for a master'	dominis 'to, for masters'
Ablative	domino 'by, with, from a master'	dominis 'by, with, from masters'

The Latin noun, it will be seen, has six different cases, and there are separate inflexions for the singular and the plural.

Latin inherited its system of case inflexions from Proto-Indo-European, and a somewhat similar system was inherited by Proto-Germanic, though both Latin and Proto-Germanic reduced the number of case distinctions: for all practical purposes, they had only five or six cases, whereas Proto-Indo-European had at least eight. The cases preserved in Proto-Germanic were the nominative (showing the 'beater' relationship), the accusative (the 'beaten' relationship), the genitive ('of'), the dative ('to' or 'for'), and the instrumental ('by'). There are also traces of a vocative case (used in addressing somebody) and of a locative (corresponding to 'at'). As in Latin, there were separate inflexions for the singular and the plural. In Proto-Indo-European, there had also been inflexions for the *dual* number, i.e. to indicate that there were *two* of a thing, but this distinction was largely discarded in Proto-Germanic. It probably arose because of the paired organs of the human body (hands, eyes, etc.), but it has not proved to be a distinction with a high survival value.

In Proto-Germanic, as in the other Indo-European languages, there was no single set of case inflexions used for all nouns alike, but several different sets, some nouns following one pattern, and others another. That is, there were various *declensions* of nouns. All nouns, moreover, had grammatical gender (see GENDER in the glossary, p. 272): every noun had to be either masculine, or feminine, or neuter. This grammatical gender had no necessary connexion with sex, for the names of inanimate objects could be masculine or feminine, and the names of sexed creatures could be neuter. The words for *he*, *she*, and *it* had to be used in accordance with grammatical gender, not in accordance with sex (or 'natural gender'). This is still the case in modern German, where for example *das Mädchen* ('the girl') is neuter and must be referred to as 'it', while *die Polizei* ('the police') is feminine and must be referred to as 'she'.

So far we have been dealing with nouns, i.e. the names of

people, places, or things, but similar considerations apply to adjectives, i.e. words like *good*, *happy*, *green*, *beautiful*. These were also inflected in Proto-Indo-European, and had to be put in the same case and number as the noun they were attached to. Moreover, the adjectives had different inflexions for different genders, and had to agree with the noun in gender. So in Latin the noun *dominus* 'master' is masculine, and 'a great master' is *magnus dominus*; but *domus* 'house' is feminine, and 'a great house' is *magna domus*; while *opus* 'work' is neuter, and 'a great work' is *magnum opus*. In Proto-Indo-European, the adjective inflexions had been essentially the same as the noun inflexions, but in many of the daughter languages they became distinguished from them in various ways. This happened in Proto-Germanic, which developed two distinct sets of inflexions for the adjectives, called the strong and the weak declension of the adjective. The distinction between the strong and the weak forms of the adjective has not survived in Modern English, but it can still be found in many of the other Germanic languages. In modern Swedish, for example, 'a good man' is *en god man*, but 'the good man' is *den goda mannen*; in the first phrase, the strong form of the adjective is used (*god*); in the second, the weak form (*goda*). In Swedish, the weak form is used after the definite article *the*, after words like *this* and *that*, and after possessive words like *my* and *your*; otherwise the strong form is used. In Old English, similarly, the strong form of the adjective was used in *gōd mann* ('a good man'), and the weak form in *sē gōda mann* ('the good man').

Proto-Germanic, like Proto-Indo-European, also had a system of cases for the pronouns, articles, and similar words. Where modern English has the one form *the*, Proto-Germanic had a whole series of forms according to the case, number, and gender of the noun that followed; this was still so in Old English, where for example 'the man' is *sē mann* (masculine), 'the gift' is *sēo giefu* (feminine), and 'the woman' is *þæt wīf* (neuter). The declension of the definite article is still found in modern German, where the foreign learner is all too familiar with *der*, *die*, *das*. Similarly with the personal pronouns (*I*, *you*, *he*, etc.), which had different forms for different cases. Here, moreover, Proto-Germanic preserved dual forms as well as plurals, and these are found in some of the daughter languages. In early Old English, for example, there is a form *ic* meaning 'I', and a form *wē* meaning 'we', but also a form *wit*, meaning 'we two'; similarly, *þū* is singular 'thou', *gē* is plural 'you', and *git* is dual 'you two'.

Proto-Indo-European also had a great array of inflexions for its verbs. Proto-Germanic retained many of these, but it simplified the system. For example, it had only two tenses of the verb, a present tense and a past tense: there were forms corresponding to *I sing* and *I sang*, but no forms corresponding to *I shall sing*, *I am singing*, *I have sung*, and so on. Within these two tenses, however, Proto-Germanic had different endings for different persons, like Latin, in which 'I sing' is *canto*, 'he sings' is *cantat*, 'they sing' is *cantant*, and so on. Like Latin, too, Proto-Germanic had two sets of inflexions for the verbs, one indicative and one subjunctive. This distinction has been largely lost in Modern English, but a relic of it can be seen in the difference between *he was* (indicative) and *he were* (subjunctive): as for example in the sentences 'If *he was* there he will tell us about it' and 'If *he were* here he would tell us about it'. Like Latin, too, Proto-Germanic had inflexions to mark the passive; these did not survive in Old English, but are found in Gothic, where *haita* means 'I call', while *haitada* means 'I am called'.

It was in the verbs that Proto-Germanic made one of its own distinctive developments. From Proto-Indo-European it had inherited a whole series of verbs which showed change of tense by changing the vowel of their stem, like Modern English *I sing*, *I sang*, or *I bind*, *I bound*; these are called *strong* verbs. This alternation of vowels for grammatical purposes is highly characteristic of the Indo-European languages, and there were large numbers of strong verbs in Proto-Germanic. However, beside the strong verbs, Proto-Germanic invented a new type, called weak verbs. In these, the past tense is formed by adding an inflexion to the verb, as in *I walk, I walked.* This inflexion had various forms; in Gothic, 'I seek' is *sokja,* 'I sought' *sokida;* 'I anoint' is *salbo,* 'I anointed' *salboda;* 'I have' is *haba,* 'I had' *habaida.* There we have the endings *-ida, -oda,* and *-aida.* However, they all have the consonant *d,* and either this or some other dental consonant appears in the weak past tense in all the Germanic languages; in Proto-Germanic, the inflexions must have contained either a *d* or a voiced *th.* The origin of the weak conjugation of verbs is uncertain; one theory is that the ending was originally a part of the verb 'to do', rather as though 'he walked' had developed out of 'he walk did'; but no single theory seems able to explain all the facts. What is certain is that the weak verbs have become of very great importance in the Germanic languages. In Old English, for example, the weak verbs are already the majority; since then, many strong verbs have changed over to weak, like the verb 'to help', which formerly had the past tense *healp,* but now has *helped;* and all new verbs formed or borrowed by the language are made weak. So that today the strong verbs, which were the original type, are a small minority, and indeed are often popularly called 'irregular verbs', which is really adding insult to injury.

The Phonology of Proto-Germanic

In pronunciation, Proto-Indo-European underwent considerable changes in developing into Proto-Germanic. The history of pronunciation in any language is full of detail and complication, so I shall merely pick out a few of the more prominent developments. One important change was in the matter of accent. The accent on a syllable depends partly on stress (acoustic loudness), partly on musical pitch, but some languages rely more on one than on the other. Proto-Indo-European probably made great use of musical accent, but in Proto-Germanic the stress accent became predominant. At the same time, there was a strong tendency in Proto-Germanic to adopt a uniform position for the stress in a word, by putting it on the first syllable. This was not the case in Proto-Indo-European, where the accent could fall on any syllable of a word, whether prefix, stem, suffix, or inflexion. This so-called 'free' accent can still be seen in classical Greek: for example, the Greek word for 'mother' is *mḗtēr*, with the accent on the first syllable, but the genitive case, 'of a mother', is *mētéros*, with the accent on the second syllable, or *mētrós* (a contracted form) with the accent on the final syllable. The tendency in Proto-Germanic to stabilize the accent on the first syllable of the word, together with the adoption of a predominantly stress type of accent (and perhaps too a tendency towards the even spacing of strong stresses), had important consequences. Above all, it led to a weakening and often to a loss of unstressed syllables, especially at the end of a word, and this is a trend which has continued in the Germanic languages throughout their history. For example, the Proto-Indo-European form of the infinitive of the verb 'to bear' was something like *bheronom, which in Proto-Germanic became *beranan. In prehistoric Old English, the final -an was weakened and then lost, and the recorded Old English form is *beran*. Then the final -an was weakened to -en, giving early Middle English *beren*; in the course of the Middle English period the final -n was lost, and the word became *bere*, which was still a two-syllable word (with the final -e perhaps pronounced like short -er). Finally, at the end of the Middle English period, the final -e was lost in its turn, and the modern form has simply the single syllable *bear*. Similar processes of attrition, though not always as drastic as this, have taken place in the other Germanic languages.

The consonant system of Proto-Indo-European had a rich array of stop consonants. This system underwent great changes in Proto-Germanic. The most important series of changes is called 'the first sound shifting', or sometimes 'Grimm's Law', after the early nineteenth-century philologist Jakob Grimm, who analysed it. The main features of the first sound shifting are shown in slightly simplified form in the following table:

Aspirated voiced stops		Voiced stops		Voiceless stops		Voiceless fricatives
bh	→	b	→	p	→	f
dh	→	d	→	t	→	th
gh	→	g	→	k	→	h

A few examples will show what is meant. Proto-Indo-European *p* became Germanic *f*:

Latin	Greek	Sanskrit	Gothic	English
pedem	poda	padam	fotus	foot
pecus	—	pacu	faihu	fee
piscis	—	—	fisks	fish

Proto-Indo-European *t* became Germanic voiceless *th*; in some cases this has become voiced *th* in Modern English, as in the word *thou*, but there can be no doubt that it was voiceless in Old English. Examples:

Latin	Greek	Sanskrit	Old Norse	English
tres	treis	trayas	þrir	three
tenuis	tanaos	tanu	þunnr	thin
tu	tu	tvam	þu	thou

Proto-Indo-European *k* became in Germanic the sound heard in Modern German *ach* or Scots *loch*; it is convenient to represent this sound by the letter *h*, since this was its spelling in Old English and other early Germanic languages. Between vowels, this *h* was lost in prehistoric Old English, but can be seen in other Germanic languages. Examples:

Latin	Greek	Welsh	Gothic	O.H. German	English
cordem	kardia	craidd	hairto	herza	heart
centum	-katon	cant	hund	hunt	hund(red)
decem	deka	deg	taihun	zehan	ten

The Indo-European voiced stops *b*, *d*, and *g* became in Germanic the corresponding voiceless stops *p*, *t*, and *k*. The *b* was not very common, but examples of its development to Germanic *p* can be seen in the English words *deep* (Lithuanian *dubs*), *thorp* (Lithuanian *troba* 'house', Latin *trabs* 'beam'), and *sleep* (related to Old Slavonic *slabu*, 'weak'). The following are examples of the change from *d* to *t*:

Latin	Greek	Sanskrit	Gothic	English
edo	edo	admi	itan	eat
decem	deka	daca	taihun	ten
uidere	oida	veda	witan	to wit

In this last example, the Latin word means 'to see', and the remainder mean 'to know' or 'I know'; in Old English there was a verb *witan* 'to know', and it is from this that we get the expression *to wit*, meaning 'namely'; the same root is seen in *witness* and *unwittingly*.

The change of Indo-European *g* to Germanic *k* is seen in the following examples:

Latin	Greek	Gothic	English
ager	agros	akrs	acre
genus	genos	kuni	kin
gelidus	—	kalds	cold

Proto-Indo-European had a series of phonemes which in Sanskrit became *bh*, *dh*, and *gh*, and in Greek *ph*, *th*, and *ch*. The exact nature of the original sounds is disputed, but traditionally they have been called aspirated voiced stops, and represented by the symbols *bh*, *dh*, and *gh*. In my table of the first sound shifting they are shown as changing into Proto-Germanic *b*, *d*, and *g*; this is not quite accurate, for almost certainly they in fact became voiced fricatives; but in most positions these developed in the various Germanic languages into the voiced stops *b*, *d*, and *g*. The English verb *to bear* corresponds to Sanskrit *bharami* and Greek *phero*; *brother* corresponds to Sanskrit *bhratar* and Greek *phrater*; and *red* is related to Sanskrit *rudhiras*.

We do not know the exact dates of these consonant changes in Proto-Germanic, but they probably began around 1000 BC, and took many centuries to complete – perhaps a whole millenium. They were followed by a smaller series of changes called 'Verner's Law', in which certain voiceless consonants became voiced if they preceded the main stress in the word, but otherwise remained unchanged; this probably took place in the first century of the Christian era. Finally came the fixing of the stress on the first syllable of the word, which cannot have taken place until after Verner's Law had operated. These changes in the consonant system gave Proto-Germanic an entirely new look, and conceal from the casual gaze the relationship of the Germanic languages with the rest of the Indo-European family.

Proto-Germanic also made changes in the Indo-European vowel system, though these were less extensive than the consonant changes. The three most important vowels in Proto-Indo-European were *a*, *e*, and *o*, each of which could be either long or short. There were also short *i* and *u*, which could operate either as unstressed vowels or as consonants, according to their position, and could also be combined with any of the three main vowels, long or short, to form diphthongs. There were also other vowels used only in unstressed syllables, and a number of syllabic consonants.

In tracing vowel changes in Proto-Germanic, or in any of the later Germanic languages, we always have to distinguish between stressed and unstressed syllables, since these give different results. Henceforward, when I talk about vowel changes I shall be referring to stressed syllables unless I specify otherwise. For Proto-Germanic, let us look at examples of just two vowel changes in stressed syllables: short *o* became *a*, and long *ā* became *ō*. Examples of the first:

Latin	Greek	O. Irish	Gothic.	O.H. German	
octō	oktō	ochtn	ahtau	ahto	'eight'
hortus	chortos	gort	gards	gart	'yard, garden, enclosure'
hostis	—	—	gasts	gast	'stranger, guest, enemy'

The stressed syllable in Germanic is of course the first, and it is there that the change is seen. Examples of the change of *ā* to *ō*:

Latin	Greek	O. Irish	Gothic	O. Norse	O. English	
frāter	phrātēr	brāthir	brōþar	brōþer	brōþor	'brother'
māter	mātēr	māthir	—	mōþer	mōdor	'mother'

The Greek *mātēr* is from the Doric dialect, other dialects having *mētēr*.

As I mentioned earlier, the vowels played an important part in the grammar of Proto-Indo-European, because of the way they alternated in related forms (as in our *sing*, *sang*, *sung*), and this system descended to Proto-Germanic. There were several series of vowels which alternated in this way; each member of such a series is called a grade, and the whole phenomenon is known as gradation (or ablaut). One such series in Proto-Indo-European, for example, was short *e*, short *o*, and zero (the zero grade occurring if the syllable was unstressed). This series was used in some of the strong verbs, the *e* grade appearing in the present tense, the *o* grade in the past singular, and the zero grade in the past plural and the past participle (in which the stress was originally on the ending, not on the stem). As a matter of fact, this is the series that was used in *sing*, *sang*, *sung*, though this fact has been obscured by the vowel changes that took place in Proto-Germanic. The original Proto-Indo-European stems of these words were something like *sengw- (*e* grade), *songw- (*o* grade), and *sngw- (zero grade). In Proto-Germanic these became *sing-, *sang-, *sung-, as seen for example in Old English *singan* ('to sing'), *sang* ('he sang'), *sungon* ('they sang'), *gesungen* ('sung'). The *e* changed to *i* because of the following *ng*, a normal combinative change in Proto-Germanic. The short *o* changed to short *a* in all positions, as we have already seen. The *u* appeared in the zero-grade form through the influence of the following syllabic *n*; in Proto-Germanic, the Proto-Indo-European syllabic consonants *m*, *n*, *l*, and *r* became *um*, *un*, *ul*, and *ur*, so that a syllable that originally had no vowel often appears in the Germanic languages with *u*.

Gradation is not confined to verbs, however. We see the alternation of *e* and *o* grades in the Greek verb *lego* 'I speak' and the related noun *logos* 'speech'; and this same alternation, ultimately, lies behind the modern English pairs *bind* and *band*, *ride* and *road*, *learn* and *lore*. In some cases, related words appear with different grades in different languages; these must

go back to variant forms in Proto-Indo-European, which probably arose in varying conditions of stress and intonation. For
example, the word for 'knee' had in Proto-Indo-European the
variant forms *gen-, *gon-, and *gn-. The e grade appears in
Latin genu and the o grade in Greek gonu. In the Germanic
languages it is the zero grade *gn- that appears; by Grimm's
law this becomes kn-, as in Gothic kniu and old English cnēo.

These, then, are some of the main developments in Proto-
Germanic: simplification of the inflexional system of Proto-
Indo-European; the introduction of the weak declension of the
adjective; the introduction of the weak verbs; the great consonant change known as Grimm's Law, and the smaller change
known as Verner's Law; the change from predominantly pitch
to predominantly stress accent; the fixing of the accent on the
first syllable of the word; and of course a host of lesser changes,
both in grammar and in pronunciation.

THE VOCABULARY OF PROTO-GERMANIC

Some of the vocabulary of Proto-Germanic also seems to be
peculiar to it, since it is not paralleled in the other Indo-
European languages. In some cases this may be pure chance, a
word having been preserved by Germanic and lost by the other
branches, but no doubt some of the words were invented or
acquired by the Germanic peoples after the dispersal of the
Indo-Europeans. Among the words peculiar to Germanic are a
number that have to do with ships and seafaring; words to
which there are no certain correspondences in other Indo-
European languages include ship, sail, boat, keel, sheet, stay
('rope supporting a mast'), possibly float, and sea itself. This
tallies with the view that the Indo-Europeans originally lived
inland: nautical vocabularies would then be developed independently by those peoples that reached the coast and took to
the sea.

The Proto-Germans borrowed a number of words from
neighbouring peoples, especially the Celts and the Romans,
who were on a higher cultural level and so had things to teach

them. The Celts were skilled in metallurgy, and the Germanic words *iron* and *lead* were probably borrowed from them. From the Romans were borrowed quite a number of words, many of them to do with war, trade, building, horticulture, and food – all fields where the Germans had much to learn from their southern neighbours. The word *pile*, 'pointed stake', is from Latin *pilum*, 'javelin', and goes back to these early days, as does the word *street*, taken from the Latin (*uia*) *strata*, a tribute to the impression made on the Germans by Roman military roads. Tacitus described the Germans as living in ugly wooden houses, or even in pits covered with rubbish, but they learnt a good deal about building from the Romans, and borrowed the words, *wall*, *tile*, *chalk*, *mill*, and *pit* (from Latin *puteus*, 'a well'). As could be expected, they also learnt Roman trading terms, for there was a good deal of traffic between the two areas; the loans include *pound*, *mile*, *cheap*, *monger*, and *mint* (originally meaning 'coin, money', from Latin *moneta*). Tacitus said that the Germans did not grow fruit trees or cultivate gardens, but again they seem to have been willing to learn, for they borrowed the words *apple*, *plum*, *cherry*, and *pear*, not to mention *wine*. As has happened so often since, culinary refinements also came to the north of Europe from the Mediterranean; the very word *kitchen* was borrowed from Latin, and so were *pepper*, *peas*, *mint* (the herb), *cheese*, *butter*, *kettle*, and *dish*. To judge from the linguistic evidence, the Germans were not so much impressed by Roman law, ideals of order, and so on, as by more concrete manifestations of Roman civilization – roads, buildings, food.

CHAPTER VII

OLD ENGLISH

DURING THE three or four centuries after Tacitus wrote his *Germania*, the Germanic peoples were in a state of flux and movement. We know little of their history in this turbulent period of migration and expansion; but we do know that, towards the end of these centuries of flux, our Germanic ancestors settled in England.

Saxon pirates were a threat to Britain as early as the third century AD, and the Romans built an extensive system of defences against them around the southern and eastern coasts of England, called The Forts of the Saxon Shore. There is even some archaeological evidence to suggest that Saxons may have settled in East Anglia and the Vale of York while Britain was still a Roman province. The main Germanic settlements, however, were made after the Roman legions had withdrawn from Britain in AD 410, and the traditional accounts of the landing of Hengest and Horsa in Kent place it in the year 449. The Anglo-Saxon settlement of Britain must not be thought of, however, as the arrival of a unified invading army, but rather as the arrival and penetration of various unco-ordinated bands of adventurers in different parts of the country, beginning in the second half of the fifth century and going on all through the sixth. The struggle with the Romano-Celtic population was a long one, and Anglo-Saxon domination in England was not assured until late in the sixth century. We know little about this struggle: it was the age of King Arthur, and there are more legends than hard facts. But by about 700, the Anglo-Saxons had occupied the whole of England except Cornwall, and parts of the Scottish lowlands too; Wales, of course, remained a British stronghold.

ANGLO-SAXONS AND CELTS

The Anglo-Saxon conquest was not just the arrival of a ruling minority, but the settlement of a whole people. Their language remained the dominant one, and there are few traces of Celtic influence on Old English; indeed, the number of Celtic words taken into English in the whole of its history has been very small. The names of some English towns were taken over from the Celts, for example London and Leeds. Rivers often retain Celtic names: Avon and Ouse are simply Celtic words for 'water' or 'stream'; Derwent, Darent, and Dart are all forms of the British name for 'oak river'; the Thames is the 'dark river'; while Trent apparently means 'a river liable to flooding'. Among county names, Kent and Devon are Celtic, and so are the first elements in Cornwall and Cumberland; the latter means 'the land of the Cymry (i.e. the Welsh)', and testifies to the long continuance of Celtic power in the north-west.

Names for topographical features that entered Old English from Celtic include *coomb* and *down* (in the sense of 'upland', as in *the South Downs*). This *down* is the Celtic equivalent of our *town*, which shows the change of *d* to *t* in accordance with Grimm's Law. The old Celtic word was *dūn*, which meant 'hill, fortified hill, fort, town', and occurs as an element in ancient Celtic place names, like Camulodunon, the British name for Colchester. The cognate Old English word was *tūn*, which originally meant 'enclosure', and so came to mean 'homestead', 'estate', 'village', and finally 'town'. The Anglo-Saxons borrowed the Celtic *dūn* simply in the sense of 'hill, upland'. The phrase *of dūne* meant 'from the hill', and so 'in a descending direction'. In Middle English this became *adowne*, then *adown*; then the first syllable was lost, and we arrived at the modern adverb and preposition *down*; which explains the apparently paradoxical fact that in Modern English *down* means both 'upland' and 'in a descending direction'.

These few Celtic words in Old English were merely a drop

in the ocean, however. Even in English place names, where Celtic left its biggest mark, Celtic words are far outnumbered by English ones, and only in areas where the Anglo-Saxons penetrated late are Celtic names at all common for villages. There are an enormous number of place-names elements of English derivation. Among the common ones are *ton* (Old English *tūn*), *ham* (Old English *hām* 'homestead' and *hamm* 'meadow'), *ley* (Old English *lēah*, meaning both 'glade' and 'wood'), *worth* (Old English *worþ*, 'enclosure, homestead'), *field* (Old English *feld*, 'open country'), and *ing* (Old English *-ingas*, 'the people of'). Thus Buckingham was 'the meadow of Bucca's people', Chorley was 'the glade (or wood) of the churls', and Brighton was 'the homestead of Beorhthelm'.

The failure of Celtic to influence Old English to any great extent does not necessarily mean that the Britons were all killed or driven out. There is in fact evidence that quite a number of Britons lived among the Anglo-Saxons, but they were a defeated people, whose language had no prestige compared with that of the conquerors, and the Anglo-Saxons had settled in such large numbers that there could be no question of their absorption by the Celts. The Old English word *wealh* meant both 'Welshman' and 'slave', which nicely illustrates both the survival of the Britons among the Anglo-Saxons, and their low status.

Angles, Saxons, and Jutes

The piecemeal way in which the Anglo-Saxons conquered England led to a profusion of small kingdoms, and no doubt to dialect differentiation. There were probably dialect differences from the start anyway, for the invaders came from more than one Germanic tribe. Bede, writing about 730, has this to say:

They were from three very powerful races of the Germans, namely the Saxons, the Angles, and the Jutes. From the Jutes are descended the people of Kent and the Victuarii (that is, the race which lives in the Isle of Wight, and in those parts of Wessex opposite the Isle of Wight, who are still called Jutes). From the Saxons (that is, from the land now called Old Saxony) came the East Saxons, the South Saxons, and the West Saxons. From the Angles (that is, from the country called Angulus, between the countries of the Jutes and of the Saxons, which is said to have remained unpopulated to the present day) are sprung the East Anglians, the Middle Anglians, the Mercians, all the Northumbrian peoples (that is, those to the north of the River Humber), and the other Anglian peoples.

The land of the Old Saxons was in northwest Germany (in Schleswig-Holstein, and perhaps farther west too along the North Sea coast), and it is safe to assume that the Saxons who invaded England came from this region. The Angles probably came from slightly farther north, from the Danish mainland and islands. The Jutes are more obscure; they may have come from Jutland, which is what Bede's account would suggest, but their culture seems to have had affinities with that of the Franks farther south, and some people believe that they came from the Rhineland.

Whatever their exact origins, these three groups were in any case closely related in language and culture, and regarded themselves as one people: for example, they tended to apply the word *English* to all groups, not just to the Angles. However, political unity came slowly. In the early days there was a medley of petty kingdoms; the names of some of these are preserved in our modern counties: Essex, Middlesex, and Sussex were the realms of the East, Middle, and South Saxons, while Norfolk and Suffolk were the north and south folk of the East Angles; the names of others survive only in the history books, like the kingdoms of the Bernice in Yorkshire and the Dere in Northumberland. By a process of conquest and amalgamation, this medley of kingdoms was eventually reduced to seven: Northumbria (north of the Humber), Mercia (in the Midlands), East Anglia, Essex, Sussex, Kent, and Wessex (based on central southern England).[1] Different kings managed to establish their overlordship over other kingdoms at various times, but these dominations were often personal and tem-

FIG. 10. England before the Vikings, showing Anglo-Saxon and British Kingdoms. Farther North were Scots and Picts.

porary. In very broad terms, we can see a gradual shift of the centres of power and civilization southwards. In the seventh century, Northumbria was very powerful, and was a great

[1] The approximate positions of these seven kingdoms are shown in *Figure 10*.

centre of learning. In the eighth century this leadership passed to Mercia, and in the ninth century to Wessex; and it was the kings of Wessex who finally succeeded in unifying the country. In the late ninth century the West Saxon kings, notably King Alfred, saved the south and west of England from the Danes, and in the tenth century Alfred's successors carried out the reconquest of the north and east. At the end of the tenth century, Edgar not only ruled all England, but was recognized as overlord of Wales and Scotland as well. From this time, the unity of England was durable; the king might be Danish, like Knut, or English, like Edward the Confessor, or Norman French, like William the Conqueror, but in any case he ruled a single country.

The West Saxon Literary Language

The unification of England under the West Saxon kings led to the recognition of the West Saxon dialect as a literary standard. The texts from the Old English period are in four main dialects: West Saxon, Kentish, Mercian, and Northumbrian (the last two often being grouped together as Anglian); and there were certainly other dialects of which we have no records.[1] The bulk of our records, however, are in the West Saxon dialect. Many of the earlier manuscripts were destroyed in the Viking conquests of the north and midlands, in which the burning of monasteries was part of the fun; and in the later part of the period there was a tendency for the manuscripts to be copied by West Saxon scribes and so put into the West Saxon dialect. For example, the Old English epic poem *Beowulf* was certainly written in an Anglian dialect, but the only surviving manuscript is in West Saxon, though there are stray forms which betray its original dialect.

The interesting thing is that, although West Saxon became the literary standard of a united England in the late Anglo-Saxon period, it is not the direct ancestor of modern standard

[1] The approximate boundaries of the four main dialect-areas are shown in *Figure 11*.

English, which is mainly derived from an Anglian dialect. One difference between West Saxon and Anglian is preserved in the modern words *weald* (from West Saxon) and *wold* (from Anglian): before certain consonant groups a vowel became diphthongized in West Saxon but not in Anglian, the Old Eng-

FIG. 11. The main dialect-areas of Old English.

lish forms being Anglian *wald* and West Saxon *weald*, both meaning 'forest'. The same difference is seen in the words for 'cold': Anglian *cald*, West Saxon *ceald*. The modern word is quite regularly descended from the Anglian form; the West Saxon form would have produced a modern word **cheald*. Another West Saxon characteristic was the use of the diphthongs *ie* and *īe*, which did not exist in the other dialects. The West

Saxon verb 'to hear' was *hīeran*, which could be expected to develop into a modern form **hire*; our word *hear* is in fact quite regularly descended from the Anglian form, *hēran*.

CHRISTIANITY AND WRITING

We know little about the Anglo-Saxons until after their conversion to Christianity, which brought them into the main stream of European history, and (most important) introduced writing. As elsewhere in medieval Europe, writing was in the hands of clerics, who often had strong views about what it was proper to record, so that we learn little about the ways of the heathen English from their writings. Some pagan lore has, however, remained fossilized in the language. The heathen gods Tiw, Woden, and Thunor ('thunder', corresponding to the Scandinavian Thor) have given their names to Tuesday, Wednesday, and Thursday. Woden's wife Frig has given her name to Friday, and, more remarkably, the heathen goddess Eostre has given her name to the Christian festival of Easter. These pagan deities are also commemorated in place names like Tuesley, Wednesbury, and Thunderfield, and pagan practices are attested by place names like Harrow (Old English *hearh*, 'temple') and Wye in Kent (Old English *wēoh*, 'idol, shrine').

The conversion of the English to Christianity began in about the year 600, and took a century to complete. It was carried out from two directions, the Celtic church penetrating from the northwest, and the Roman church from the southeast.

With Christianity came writing. The English indeed already had one form of writing, runes, but these were suitable only for short inscriptions, not for texts of any length. Runes had been used by the Germanic peoples from at least the third century AD, for carving or scratching inscriptions on stone, metal work, or wood (the word *book* originally meant 'beech'). The word *rune* also meant 'mystery, secret', and the inscriptions were evidently thought to have magical power (as often among early peoples). Runes go back ultimately to some form of the Greek alphabet, but, because of their use for inscriptions, have acquired a decidedly angular form. The best known inscriptions are the Scandinavian ones, but the English also used a form of the runic alphabet which, from its first six letters, is known as the 'futhorc'. When the clerics introduced writing to England, they used a Celtic version of the Roman alphabet, but eked it out with runic symbols from the futhorc; for example, the runic symbol 'wynn' was used for the Old English *w* sound.

In modern editions of Old English texts, it is customary to give the Latin letters their modern form, and to use special symbols only for some of the letters that represent a departure from the Latin alphabet. It is also common in modern editions to mark long vowels by putting a horizontal line over them, while leaving the short vowels unmarked ($\bar{e}$ long, *e* short). I shall follow modern conventions in these matters.

The Pronunciation of Old English

Old English script used the six vowel symbols *a*, *e*, *i*, *o*, *u*, and *y*, and a seventh one, *æ*, called 'ash', made by combining two symbols. All these could represent either long or short sounds. The short *a* was a sound somewhat like that of *Mann* in modern German, or of *hat* in northern English dialect, while the short *æ* was like the vowel of *hat* in modern educated south-eastern English. The long $\bar{a}$ was like that in *father*, while the long $\bar{æ}$ was like the long vowel now often heard in educated London speech in words like *bad*. The short *u* was like that in *put*, not like that in *cut*; the long $\bar{u}$ was like the vowel of *food*. The *y* symbol represented an *i* sound made with the lips rounded, like the vowel of French *plume* or German *grün*. All the symbols represented pure vowels, not diphthongs: the long *i* was like that in *machine* (not like that in *fine*), while $\bar{o}$ and $\bar{e}$ were like the vowels of German *wo* and *weh* (not like the diphthongs in modern English *rose* and *make*). To represent diphthongs, the Anglo-Saxons used digraphs: *ea*, *eo*, *io*, *ie*; these too could be either short or long.

Of the consonant symbols, many were used very much as

today, but some call for comment. Old English did not use the letter *v*; the symbol *f* represented both the *f* sound and the *v* sound. The reason for this is that, in Old English, *f* and *v* were both members of the same phoneme: when this phoneme occurred in the middle of a word before a voiced sound, and was not doubled, it was pronounced *v*; in all other positions it was pronounced *f*. So the *f* sound was used in *fæder* ('father'), *fíf* ('five'), *hæft* ('haft, handle'), and *pyffan* ('to puff'), and the *v* sound in *giefan* ('to give'), *seofon* ('seven'), *hræfn* ('raven'), and *lifde* ('he lived'). Often, you will notice, the pronunciation corresponds to modern usage, but not always, since *five* now ends with a *v* sound.

There are two other similar pairs in Old English. There was a symbol *s*, but not normally a symbol *z*, and once again for the same reason: *s* and *z* were members of the same phoneme, and the rules for their distribution were exactly the same as for *f* and *v*. So the *s* sound occurred in *sǽ* ('sea'), *hūs* ('house'), *stānas* ('stones'), *west* ('west'), and *cyssan* ('to kiss'), and the *z* sound in *nosu* ('nose') and *bōsm* ('bosom'). The third pair that behaved in this way were the voiceless and voiced *th* sound (as in *thing* and *this*). Here the Old English scribes confused matters a little by using two symbols, the runic symbol þ, called 'thorn', and a symbol called 'eth', formed by crossing a *d*, thus ð. However, they did not use one of these symbols for the voiced sound and the other for the voiceless, but used them both indiscriminately. For simplicity, I shall use only thorn in my transcriptions from Old English. The distribution of the two sounds was exactly as for *s* and *z*; thus the voiceless sound was used in *þegn* ('thane, attendant'), *trēowþ* ('good faith'), *þes* ('this'), and *moþþe* ('moth'), and the voiced sound in *baþian* ('to bathe') and *fæþm* ('embrace, fathom'). In all three cases, Old English has a single phoneme consisting of a pair of voiced and voiceless sounds, where Modern English has two separate phonemes. The Old English arrangement does not go back to Proto-Germanic, but arose in Old English itself by a process of assimilation.

The letter *k* was not normally used. The *k* sound was represented by *c*, but where it preceded a front vowel in prehistoric English it had developed into a palatal stop instead of a velar one (i.e. it was articulated farther forward in the mouth, somewhere between *k* and *t*). This palatal stop has become Modern English *ch* (as in *church*); it may not have developed as far as this in the Old English period, but it is convenient to use the *ch* pronunciation when reading Old English. It is not always possible to tell by looking at an Old English word whether the *c* is palatal or velar, since the vowel which caused the palatalization may well have changed since prehistoric Old English times; thus *cēlan* ('to cool') and *cynn* ('kin') have the velar stop, even though they have front vowels, because they derive from prehistoric Old English forms **cōljan* and **kunni*. Often, the modern pronunciation is a guide: thus the velar pronunciation belongs to *cyssan* ('to kiss'), *cǣg* ('key'), *þancian* ('to thank'), and *cæppe* ('cap, hood'), while the palatal pronunciation belongs to *cinn* ('chin'), *cēosan* ('choose'), and *cīdan* ('quarrel, chide'). Originally, it is plain, the two sounds were merely variants of a single phoneme, but by the end of the Old English period they had become two separate phonemes. This can be seen if we consider two words already given as examples, *cinn* with palatal *c* and *cynn* with velar *c*. In late Old English, the *y* of *cynn* lost its lip rounding and became *i*, so that the word was then *cinn* (pronounced *kinn*). At that stage, therefore, there was a pair of words, which we can call 'kin' and 'chin', which were distinguished from one another solely by the difference between *k* and *ch*; and this means, by definition, that *k* and *ch* belong to different phonemes.

The combination *sc* also became palatalized in Old English, and has developed into modern English *sh*. It is therefore convenient to use the *sh* pronunciation when reading Old English, as in *scip* ('ship') and *biscop* ('bishop'). The combination *cg* represented a sound like the *j* of *judge*, as in *ecg* ('edge'), *secgan* ('to say'), *brycg* ('bridge').

The letter *g* in Old English is more difficult to interpret, since it not only represents both velar and palatal sounds (in rather the same way as *c*), but also represents both fricatives and stops. Once again, it is best to be guided by the modern pronunciation. Sometimes it is a palatal fricative (somewhat like the semivowel *y* in Modern English *yes*), as in the words *gēar* ('year'), *cǣg* ('key'), and *geong* ('young'). Sometimes it is a velar stop (like the *g* in Modern English *go*), as in the words *gōd* ('good'), *gēs* ('geese'), and *dogga* ('dog'). And sometimes it is a voiced velar fricative, made by narrowing the passage between the back of the tongue and the soft palate, as in the words *fugol* ('bird') and *lagu* ('law'); in Middle English this sound usually became *w*, and in Modern English is the second half of a diphthong (*fowl, law*).

The letter *h* represented a stronger sound than it does today; sometimes it was like the *ch* of German *ach*, and sometimes like the *ch* of German *ich*, according to the neighbouring vowel. The *ng* sound (as in modern *sing*) existed in Old English, but not as a separate phoneme: it was simply a variant of the *n* phoneme, used before *k* and *g*; in such words as *singan*, therefore, the *n* and the *g* were pronounced separately (as in our word *finger*, not as in *singer*).

When you read Old English, remember that every symbol must be pronounced: the *h* must be pronounced in *niht* ('night'), the *c* in *cnēo* ('knee'), the *r* in *wæter* ('water') and in *bearn* ('child'), the *e* at the end of *moþþe* ('moth') and of *cwene* ('woman'), both the *n* and the *g* in *sang* ('song'), both *s* sounds in *cyssan* ('kiss'), and so on. You should also try to avoid carrying over habits of pronunciation that are due to relatively recent sound changes in English. The qualities of vowels are not altered by a following *r* or *l* as they often are in Modern English (e.g. *burn, ball*). The first vowel in words like *cwene* must be kept short. And unstressed vowels must be given their full value, so that for example *bera* ('a bear') is distinguished from *bere* ('barley'). In the matter of stress, be guided by Modern English.

SOUND-CHANGES IN OLD ENGLISH

Old English, of course, shows certain developments of its own compared with the other Germanic languages. We have

already seen that the Proto-Germanic diphthong *ai* became
Old English *ā*, so that Old English has *stān* and *hām* where
Gothic has *stains* ('stone') and *haims* ('village'). The other Germanic diphthongs were also changed in Old English; for
example *au* became *ēa*, so that Old English has *drēam* where
Old Norse has *draumr* ('dream'), and *bēam* where German
has *Baum* ('tree, pole'), and *ēare* where Gothic has *auso*
('ear').

In prehistoric Old English a number of combinative sound
changes took place. The most important was the one called
'front mutation' or 'i-umlaut'. This was a series of changes in
vowels; it took place when there was an *i, ī,* or *j* in the following
syllable (where *j* represents a sound rather like the *y* in our
yes). Subsequently, the *i, ī,* or *j* which had caused the change
itself disappeared, or changed to *e*, but its original presence can
be established by an examination of the corresponding words
in related languages. Front mutation, for example, accounts
for the difference in vowel between the related words *dole* and
deal. In Old English they are *dāl* ('a portion') and *dǣlan* ('to
divide'), in which the *ǣ* is due to front mutation; this is clear
if we look at the equivalent Gothic words, which are *dails* and
dailjan. The same vowel change accounts for the differences in
vowel between *whole* and *heal*, *load* and *to lead*, *broad* and
breadth, *one* and *any*, and *hot* and *heat*; these all have *ā* and *ǣ*
in Old English, though they have various developments in
Modern English.

The change from *ā* to *ǣ* was a movement to a closer and
more frontal vowel, and this is the general direction of the
change caused by front mutation. Thus *ū* became fronted to
ȳ, a change which accounts for the different vowels of *mouse*
and *mice*; in Old English, the singular was *mūs*; the original
plural form was **mūsiz*, but the *i* caused the *ū* to change to *ȳ*,
and then the ending *-iz* was lost, giving the Old English
plural *mȳs*. Another example of the mutation of *ū* to *ȳ* is provided by the Old English words (*fūl* ('impure') and *fȳlþ*
('impurity'), corresponding to Old Saxon *fūl* and *fūlitha*; but
in this case the *ȳ* was shortened to *y* in late Old English or early

Middle English, while the *ū* remained long, so that the modern words are *foul* and *filth*.

Similarly, front mutation changed short *u* to *y*; this change is reflected in the different vowels of *full* and *fill*, which in Old English are *full* and *fyllan* (from an earlier form **fulljan*). In some positions, an unmutated *u* developed into an Old English *o*; sometimes, therefore, we get a contrast between unmutated *o* and mutated *y*, as in the words *gold* ('gold') and *gyldan* ('to gild'). Other pairs of modern words illustrating the front mutation of *u* to *y* are *knot* and *knit*, *fox* and *vixen*, *lust* and *to list* ('desire, please').

Front mutation also changed *ō* to *ē*, and this accounts for the different vowels of *food* (Old English *fōd*) and *to feed* (Old English *fēdan*). Other such pairs in Modern English are *doom* and *deem*, *goose* and *geese*, *tooth* and *teeth*, *foot* and *feet*, *blood* and *bleed*, *book* and *beech*. Even where the *ō* has been shortened since Old English times, you will notice that we still have the spelling with *oo*, which shows that the vowel was once long. And, finally, front mutation changed short *a*, *æ*, and *o*, which all became *e*; modern pairs illustrating these changes include *man* and *men*, *wander* and *wend*, *Canterbury* and *Kent*, *long* and *length*, *strong* and *strength*, *tale* and *tell*, *straight* and *stretch*.

Even from these few examples, you will see that front mutation made considerable changes in the pronunciation of English. Notice that you must not confuse pairs like *foot* and *feet*, where the vowel difference is caused by front mutation in Old English, with pairs like *sing* and *sang*, where the difference goes right back to the system of vowel gradation in Proto-Indo-European.

THE GRAMMAR OF OLD ENGLISH

In grammar, Old English carried out some simplifications of the Proto-Germanic system. Old English nouns have only four cases, the nominative, accusative, genitive, and dative. Moreover, the number of commonly used declensions begins to be reduced, the vast majority of nouns tending to be attracted into three or four large declensions. At the same time, the total number of distinctive case endings is less than in Proto-Germanic, because of the weakening and loss of sounds in unstressed syllables in prehistoric Old English. A few distinctive endings remained: all nouns have the ending *-um* for the dative plural, and most have *-a* for the genitive plural; and many masculine nouns have a genitive singular in *-es* and a nominative and accusative plural in *-as*. But the extent to which distinctions were already being obliterated can be illustrated from the feminine noun *giefu* 'a gift', which has the one form *giefe* for its accusative, genitive, and dative singular, and sometimes for its nominative and accusative plural too. Again, the masculine noun *guma* 'a man' has the one form *guman* for its accusative, genitive, and dative singular and its nominative and accusative plural. Old English in fact relied a good deal for its case distinctions on the adjectives, which had preserved more distinctive endings than the nouns, and on the definite article *sē* ('the'), which still had a large number of forms for different cases and genders. Old English did still, however, make great use of its inflexional system, and to a great extent it still preserved grammatical gender.

The Vocabulary of Old English

To enlarge its vocabulary, Old English depended mainly on its own resources, not on borrowings from other languages. From Indo-European, the Germanic languages had inherited a whole set of ways for forming new words, which especially made use of prefixes and suffixes which could be added to stems to form words of specific types. For example, there was a Proto-Germanic suffix **-iþō*, which could be added to adjectives to form abstract nouns; hence such modern English pairs as *true* and *truth*, *foul* and *filth*, *merry* and *mirth*, *strong* and *strength*, *slow* and *sloth*.

However, Old English did borrow a certain number of words from other languages, especially names for the concepts and institutions of Christianity. The word *church* (Old English *cirica*) is derived from the Greek *kuriakon*, and goes back to heathen days; it is found in all the Germanic languages, whereas the Romance languages have words derived from Latin *ecclesia*, like the French *église*. Another early loan is *devil* (Old English *deofol*), from Greek *diabolos* via Latin *diabolus*. Most of the words connected with Christianity, however, date from after the Conversion, and are from Latin (though Latin itself had borrowed many of them from Greek). They include the Old English words *apostol* 'apostle', *biscop* 'bishop' (Latin *episcopus*), *munuc* 'monk' (Latin *monachus*), *mynster* 'monastery, cathedral' (Latin *monasterium*), and a number of others, including words for abbot, disciple, nun, pope, pilgrim, and school.

But even in this field Old English made considerable use of its native language material. Sometimes it simply transferred existing words to a Christian use, like *hell*, *holy*, and *Easter*. Sometimes it coined new words from native elements: thus Latin *evangelium* was rendered as *gōdspell*, 'good message', which has become our *gospel*, and 'trinity' was rendered as *prines*, 'threeness'. Old English, indeed, was very fond of compounds of this kind; thus literature, arithmetic, grammar, and astronomy were called *bōccrǽft*, *rīmcrǽft*, *stǽfcrǽft*, and *tungolcrǽft*, i.e. book skill, number skill, letter skill, and star skill. Homelier compounds have survived to our own times, in words like *homestead*, *woman* (Old English *wīfmann*), *sunbeam*, and *earwig*.

Specimens of Old English

We can end this chapter with brief examples of Old English prose and verse. First a few lines from the opening of the *Colloquy* of Aelfric, abbot of Eynsham, who was writing from about 990. Aelfric was the classic of Old English prose writers, and wrote homilies and lives of the saints for the instruction of parish clergy. The Colloquy is a slighter work, a dialogue in Latin, with an English translation (probably not by Aelfric himself), for use in the teaching of Latin. After each speech, I give a literal translation into Modern English. The master is talking with his pupils:

> *Pupil*: Wē cildra biddaþ þē, ēalā lārēow, þæt þū tǣce ūs sprecan rihte, forþām ungelǣrede wē sindon, and gewæmmodlīce we sprecaþ. (We children beg thee, oh teacher, that thou teach us to speak correctly, because ignorant we are and corruptly we speak.)
>
> *Master*: Hwæt wille gē sprecan? (What wish ye to say?)
>
> *Pupil*: Hwæt rēce wē hwæt wē sprecan, būton hit riht sprǣc sȳ and behēfe, næs īdel oþþe fracod? (What care we what we say, except it correct speech be and seemly, not idle or worthless?)
>
> *Master*: Wille gē bēon beswungen on leornunge? (Wish ye to be beaten in learning?)
>
> *Pupil*: Lēofre is ūs bēon beswungen for lāre þænne hit ne cunnan; ac wē witan þē bilewitne wesan, and nellan onbelǣdan swincgla ūs, būton þū bī tōgenȳdd fram ūs. (Dearer is to us – i.e. We prefer – to be beaten for the sake of learning than it not to know; but we know thee kindly to be, and not to wish to inflict blows on us, unless thou be compelled by us.)

Notice that the pupils address their teacher as *thou* (singular), but he addresses them as *ye* (plural), because there are a number of them; whereas today we use *you* in both cases. In Old English, *thou* and *thee* were singular, and *ye* and *you* plural, but in Middle English times the custom arose of using *ye* and *you* as polite or deferential ways of addressing a single person; by early Modern English times, *thou* and *thee* were used mainly for addressing intimates, children, and inferiors, until they dropped out of everyday speech (except in some local dialects) round about 1700. The difference between *ye* and *you* was the same as that between *he* and *him*: *ye* was the nominative, and *you* the accusative. This distinction is still observed in the King Edward VI prayer book and the 1611 Bible: for example, 'And if any man say ought unto *you*, *ye* shall say, The Lord hath need of them'; but in everyday speech at that period the two forms were already being confused and used indiscriminately, and ultimately *ye* dropped out of use.

Originally, *you* was not the accusative form, but the dative: Old English *ēow*, 'to you'. The accusative form was *ēowic*, but this fell out of use during the Old English period, and the dative *ēow* was used in its place. This in fact has happened with all the personal pronouns: our words *him*, *me*, *us*, *her*, and *thee* originally meant 'to him', 'to me', 'to us', and so on. The accusative forms were *hine*, *mec*, *ūsic*, *hīe*, and *þec*, but these fell out of use during the Old and Middle English periods, and were replaced by the dative forms. The Aelfric passage, which is late Old English, uses *þē*, not *þec*.

Notice that the word *wille* in the passage means 'wish', and is not part of a future tense. Questions are formed without using *do*: Aelfric writes *Hwæt rēce wē?* ('What do we care?'); similarly, negatives were expressed by putting *ne* or some similar particle in front of the verb, not by using *doesn't* or *don't*.

A little later in the Colloquy, the master is talking to a ploughman, who has been describing the hardness of his life and the amount of work he has to do:

Master: Hæfst þū ænigne gefēran? (Hast thou any companion?)

Pupil: Ic hæbbe sumne cnapan þȳwende oxan mid gādīsene, þe ēac swilce nū hās is for cylde and hrēame. (I have a certain boy driving oxen with goad-iron, who likewise now hoarse is on account of cold and shouting.)

Master: Hwæt māre dēst þū on dæg? (What more dost thou daily?)

Pupil: Gewyslice þænne māre ic dō. Ic sceal fyllan binnan oxan mid hig, and wæterian hī, and scearn heora beran ūt. (Indeed then more I do. I must fill mangers for oxen with hay, and water them, and dung of them carry out – i.e. carry out their dung.)

Master: Hig, hig! Micel gedeorf is hit. (Hey, hey! Great labour is it.)

Pupil: Geleof, micel gedeorf hit is forþām ic neom frēoh.
(Sir, great labour it is, because I not am free.)

The phrase *ǣnigne gefēran* at the beginning of that extract illustrates the importance of the adjective in the Old English inflexional system. The word *gefēran* could equally well mean 'companion' or 'companions', but the ending -*ne* added to *ǣnig* can only be accusative singular masculine, and shows that the right translation is 'companion'. The same is true of *sumne cnapan*, 'a certain boy'. Just as, in the first extract, *wille* did not correspond exactly to modern *will*, so in this one the word *sceal* does not correspond in meaning to modern *shall*: for *ic sceal* means 'I must, I have to', and originally meant 'I owe, I am in debt'. In the pupil's first speech occurs the word *þe*, which I have translated 'who'; the words *who* and *which* did exist in Old English (*hwā, hwilc*), but were used mainly for asking questions; for the relative function, Old English used *þe*, or the definite article *sē*, or the two together. In Middle English, *which* and *that* were used as relatives, but *who* was not used in this way until early Modern English, and even then not always; in the 1611 Bible, the Lord's Prayer begins 'Our Father, *which* art in heaven'. You may also have been struck in the extract by the word *neom*, 'am not'; as we have seen, a sentence could be negated by putting *ne* in front of the verb, but in some cases the *ne* amalgamated with the verb, giving words like *nill* 'will not' and *nis* 'is not'. A survival of this in Modern English is the phrase *willy nilly*, meaning 'will he, nill he', i.e. 'whether he likes it or not'. You will also have noticed that both passages show a greater freedom in word order than Modern English: for example, the master said 'Great labour is it', and the pupil, agreeing, said 'Great labour it is'.

Finally, a few lines of Old English poetry. Like early Germanic poetry in general, this did not use rhyme, but alliteration. Two stressed words in the first half of the line, and one word (sometimes two) in the second half of the line all had to begin with the same letter; all vowels, however, were allowed to alliterate together. There were also quite complicated rules about the permissible patterns of syllable length and stress in a line, though these became laxer in the course of the Old English period, as did the rules about alliteration. I have chosen a famous passage from a late Old English poem which celebrates an actual historical event. In 991 the men of Essex, led by Byrhtnoth their 'ealdormann' (i.e. the king's deputy and the chief executive for the county), fought a battle at Maldon against an invading army of Norwegian vikings, who had sailed up the Blackwater. After a bitter struggle, the English were defeated and Byrhtnoth killed, and the end of the poem, from which my extract comes, tells how his 'companions', in traditional Germanic style, remained on the battlefield to die with their lord.

> Byrhtwold maþelode,   bord hafenode,
> sē wæs eald geneat,   æsc ācwehte,
> hē full baldlīce   beornas lǣrde:
> 'Hige sceal þē heardra,   heorte þē cēnre,
> mōd sceal þē māre,   þē ūre mægen lȳtlaþ.
> Hēr līþ ūre ealdor   eall forhēawen,
> gōd on grēote;   ā mæg gnornian
> sē þe nū fram þīs wīgplegan   wendan þenceþ.
> Ic eom frōd fēores: fram ic ne wille,
> ac ic mē be healfe   mīnum hlāforde
> be swā leofan men   licgan þence.'

This can be rendered as follows:

> Byrhtwold spoke, lifted his shield,
> he was an old retainer, shook his ash (spear),
> he full boldly exhorted the warriors:
> 'Mind must be the tougher, heart the bolder,
> Courage must be the greater, as our strength diminishes.
> Here lies our lord, all hewn in pieces,
> the noble man in the dust; ever will have cause to mourn
> who now from this battle thinks to depart.
> I am old of life: hence I will not,
> but by the side of my lord,
> by the man so dear, I intend to lie.'

There, nine hundred years after Tacitus, and nearly four hundred years after the conversion of the English to Christianity, still speaks the authentic voice of the Germanic heroic age, when the greatest shame was for the companion to return alive when his lord was slain. Like much heroic poetry, it is highly formal, moving forward with parallel phrases and near-repetitions, and has a very marked diction of its own. The passage quoted, for example, opens with a standard epic tag, 'so-and-so spoke'. The stock of conventional diction was very large, because of the need for alliteration; thus there are many poetic words for warrior (like *beorn* in the passage), horse, weapon, ship, prince, and so on. Some of these are descriptive compounds: the sea, for example, may be called 'the swan road'. And some are decorative periphrases, so that a king is called 'giver of rings' or 'giver of treasure'. An example in the passage is *wigplega*, which I have translated 'battle', but which literally means 'war play'.

CHAPTER VIII

THE VIKINGS IN ENGLAND

THE HARRYING of Europe by the Scandinavian Vikings, which took place between about 750 and 1050, was the last phase of the expansion of the early Germanic peoples; if it is better known than the earlier phases, that is simply because it was later, and took place in the full light of history. Its basic cause was perhaps overpopulation in a region of poor natural resources, but there were other contributory causes. The custom of leaving the inheritance to the eldest son meant that there were always younger sons wanting to carve out inheritances for themselves. Political changes drove many noblemen into exile. And, finally, in the late eighth century, Charlemagne destroyed the power of the Frisians, who had hitherto been the greatest maritime power of northwest Europe, and thereby left open the sea route southward for the Vikings.

The scale of Viking attacks varied from the piratical expedition by the single ship to the invasion of a country by enormous fleets and armies. The word *viking* means 'creek dweller', and hence 'pirate', and is not confined to the Scandinavian languages: it is found in Old English, in the form *wīcing*, before the days of the Scandinavian raids. It points, however, to the greatest asset of the Scandinavian raiders – their skill and daring as sailors and navigators, which had carried them to North America ('Wineland') long before Columbus, perhaps as early as 1000.

The Vikings consisted of Swedes, Norwegians, and Danes. The Swedes mostly went eastwards, to the Baltic countries and Russia, while the Norwegians and Danes tended to go westwards and southwards. The Vikings who attacked England were referred to by the Anglo-Saxons as *Dene*, 'Danes', but in fact there were also Norwegians among them. The first attacks probably took place round about 800, and by 838 they had become really serious. At first they were mere piratical raids in search of plunder; then large groups took to spending the winter in England, as happened in 850 and again in 854; then large armies stayed for longer periods, like the one which

FIG. 12. The division of England between King Alfred and the Danes in AD 886. Alfred held England south and west of the hatched line.

landed in East Anglia in 865 and operated as a single unit for no less than nine years; and finally came conquest and settlement, which began in the last few decades of the ninth century. The Vikings came very near to conquering the whole of England, but King Alfred held the south and west against them: the boundary between his territories and the Danelaw ran roughly along a line from London to Chester (see Figure 12). In the tenth century the West Saxon kings reconquered the north and east, but in the meantime the Vikings established kingdoms in those areas, notably in Yorkshire, East Anglia, and the North Midlands, and there was massive Scandinavian settlement.

The Scandinavian influx has left its mark on English place names, especially of course in the Danelaw. Common Scandinavian place-name elements are *by*, meaning 'village, homestead', as in *Grimsby* ('Grim's village'); *thorp*, meaning 'secondary settlement, outlying farmstead', as in *Grimsthorpe*; *toft*, meaning 'site, plot of land on which buildings stand', as in *Langtoft* (where the first element means 'long'); and *thwaite*, meaning 'woodland clearing, meadow', as in *Micklethwaite* ('large clearing'). Some place names are more distinctively Norwegian, some more Danish; the element *thorp*, for example, was rarely used by the Norwegians in England, and is a good sign of Danish settlement (though it also occurs in Anglo-Saxon place names). The main areas of Norwegian settlement were in the northwest – in Lancashire, Westmorland, and Cumberland; elsewhere in the Danelaw there were Danes, the densest settlements being in Yorkshire, Derbyshire, Nottinghamshire, Lincolnshire, Leicestershire, and Norfolk.

However, Scandinavian influence on English went a good deal farther than place names. The English were not exterminated by the Scandinavian settlers, but the latter were sufficiently important and numerous to influence English speech. Old English and Old Norse were still very similar, and Englishmen and Danes could probably understand each other, and pick up each other's language, without too much difficulty. We must visualize in the later Old English period various bilingual situations. There would be Englishmen speaking Old Norse, and Danes speaking Old English, and when they didn't know a word in the other language they would use a word from their own language, perhaps giving it inflexions and a pronunciation that they thought appropriate to the other language. Sometimes they would use a word in the other language but give it the meaning of the corresponding form in their own language. And no doubt there were children of mixed marriages who spoke an intermediate dialect. Thus great mixing took place between the two languages. In the end, Old Norse died out in England (it was already dying under King Knut, at whose court English was spoken), and English triumphed, but not before a good deal of Scandinavian had got mixed in with it. The final fusion of the English and Scandinavian peoples and cultures took place in the century following the Norman Conquest.

There are various ways of recognizing Scandinavian words in English, though in fact many words were practically identical in Old English and Old Norse, and would give the same result in Modern English. Some words, however, can be identified as of Scandinavian origin, because phonologically their form is different from what would be expected in a native English word. Thus the word *awe* is certainly of Scandinavian origin: the Old English form is *ege*, the first vowel having been changed by front mutation and the *g* palatalized by the following vowel, and it could be expected to produce a modern form *ey* (just as Old English *legen* has produced our word *lain*); but neither the front mutation nor the palatalization occurred in Old Norse, where the word was *agi*: and this, if borrowed in late Old English, would lead quite regularly to the modern *awe*. Another word where Old English had a palatal *g* and Old Norse a velar *g* was the word for 'egg', which was Old English *ǣg* and Old Norse *egg*; the Old English word became Middle English *ey*, a form found in Chaucer; our word *egg*, of course, comes from the Scandinavian. Similarly, Old English sometimes has palatal *c* where Old Norse retains velar *k*, so that *church* is English and *kirk* Scandinavian, *ditch* English and *dike* Scandinavian. Again, Germanic *sk* did not become palatalized in Old Norse as it did in Old English, so that a word of Scandinavian origin will have *sk* where one of English origin has *sh*: thus *shirt* is English and *skirt* Scandinavian (both words meaning originally 'a *short* garment'); and similarly with *shrub* and *scrub*.

Among the vowels, one difference is that Proto-Germanic *ai* becomes *ei* in Scandinavian but *ā* in Old English; thus Old Norse *nei* corresponds to Old English *nā*, the first giving Modern English *nay*, the second *no*. The Proto-Germanic diphthong *au* became *ēa* in Old English, but remained *au* in Old Norse, so that *lēas* corresponds to *lauss*; our word *loose* is descended from the Scandinavian form, but the Old English form is preserved as the suffix -*less*, in words like *homeless* (Old English *hāmlēas*). Such phonological tests are not foolproof, for in some cases a dialectal variant in Old English can produce the same result as Scandinavian influence, but on the whole they are the most reliable guide.

But even when phonological evidence is lacking or doubtful, we can sometimes be confident that a word comes from the Scandinavian. Often, for example, a word does not occur in Old English but does occur in Old Norse. An example is the verb 'to take', which is Old Norse *taka*; this is not found in Old English, which uses the verb *niman*. In Middle English, we find both *take* and *nime*, but *take* is found in areas where there was Scandinavian influence, and *nime* in areas free from such influence. The verb *to nim* survived into early Modern English, and is responsible for Shakespeare's Corporal Nym, who was very good at *nimming* other peoples' property; the past participle has survived as the word *numb*, which originally meant 'taken, seized'. Other examples include *anger*, *to cast*, and *ill*, from Old Norse *angr*, *kasta*, and *illr*; Old English used instead the words *wræþþ*, *weorpan*, and *yfel*, which have become *wrath*, *warp*, and *evil*.

Sometimes the Old Norse and Old English words would produce the same modern English word, but had different meanings. An example is the word *dwell*: Old Norse *dvelja* meant 'dwell', but Old English *dwellan* meant 'lead astray'. In other cases the form of the modern word may come from one language and the meaning from the other: thus Old English *brēad* usually meant 'fragment', while Old Norse *brauð* meant 'bread'; the modern word has its form from English and its meaning from Scandinavian. Odder is the word *dream*. Old

English *drēam* means 'joy, mirth, revelry', and is commonly used of the pleasures of the warriors relaxing in the hall over their beer or mead, and of the music accompanying those pleasures; it is never used in Old English in the sense of 'dream'. This, however, was the meaning of the Old Norse word *draumr*, and it might seem that here again the modern word has the English form and the Scandinavian meaning. This is by no means certain, however, because this time the Middle English dialects in which *dream* is first recorded in its modern sense are *not* ones which were subject to Scandinavian influence. Perhaps the true explanation is that the Old English word did have the meaning 'dream' in everyday speech, but that it was not used in this sense in the literary language; it is noteworthy that the Old Saxon word, *drōm*, means both 'joy' and 'dream'.

Most of the Scandinavian loan words first appear in writing in the Middle English period, but their form shows that they had been taken into English in the late Old English period, for they have undergone the sound changes that mark the transition from Old to Middle English. They do not appear earlier in writing because at that time there was no literary tradition in the Danelaw, and most surviving texts are in the West Saxon dialect, which was not under Scandinavian influence. A few loans, however, do occur in Old English texts. In the early days of the Viking raids there was obviously not much opportunity for conversation between Englishmen and Vikings; the only loans from this period are a few words for Viking ships and weapons, which have not survived into the modern language. Later, when the Vikings had begun to settle in England, a number of words were borrowed relating to law and administration, for the Danes had a highly developed legal sense; they include *thrall*, and the word *law* itself.

However, Middle English texts, especially those from the north and the east midlands, contain large numbers of Scandinavian loan words. Many of these have since died out from the language, but quite a number remain. To the legal and administrative terms borrowed can be added *by-law* (meaning 'village law' or 'town law'), *crave*, *wapentake*, and *Riding* (originally *thriding*, 'a third part').

But what is most striking about the Scandinavian loan words as a whole is that they are such *ordinary* words. The English and the Scandinavians were accustomed to much the same kind of rural life, having a similar Germanic background, and the fusion of the two peoples was a very close one; many of the words taken over, in consequence, were homely everyday ones. Thus the word *sister* is from Scandinavian (the Old English is *sweoster*), and the names of such close family relationships are very much part of the central core of vocabulary. So are the names of parts of the body, yet the words *leg* and *neck* are Scandinavian. Other common nouns include *window*, *sky*, *knife*, *skin*, *dirt*, *skill*, *bag*, *cake*, *fog*, and *fellow*. Everyday adjectives include *wrong*, *low*, *loose*, *odd*, *flat*, and *ugly*, and among the everyday verbs are *get*, *give*, *call*, *want*, *take*, *drag*, *smile*, and *raise*. The conjunction *though* is also from Scandinavian. So, even more remarkably, are the pronouns *they*, *them*, and *their*, which in Old English were *hie*, *him*, and *hiera*. The Scandinavian forms no doubt had an advantage because they were less likely to be confused with the words for *him* and *her*; they were first used in the northern dialects, and spread southwards during the Middle English period; *they* spread faster than the other two, and Chaucer and his contemporaries in southeast England in the fourteenth century used *they* for the nominative but English forms like *him* and *hire* for 'them' and 'their'. The form *him* meaning 'them' still survives in the unstressed form *'em*. The borrowing of such central grammatical words as personal pronouns shows the strength of the Scandinavian influence.

When the Scandinavian words appear in English texts they are of course given English inflexions. Occasionally, however, a Scandinavian inflexion was mistakenly apprehended as part of the stem, and incorporated in the English word. Thus there was an Old Norse ending -*t* which was added to adjectives to mark the neuter gender, and also to form adverbs; so the adjective *þverr* had the neuter form *þvert*, and this has been taken over into English as *thwart*; the same ending has survived in *want* and *scant*. The Old Norse reflexive ending -*sk*, meaning 'himself, oneself', has been preserved in *bask* ('to bathe oneself') and the archaic *busk* ('to prepare oneself').

Scandinavian influence on English was almost entirely confined to vocabulary, and there is no marked influence on grammar or syntax. In vocabulary, however, Old Norse made a considerable impact. In number, indeed, the surviving Scandinavian loan words are very few compared with the words later borrowed from French or from Latin; many of them, on the other hand, are words in frequent use, and there is a Scandinavian enclave in the very central regions of the English vocabulary. In the areas of densest Viking settlement, a larger vocabulary of Scandinavian loan words is preserved in regional dialects, so that there are still parts of England where you can hear good Scandinavian words like *big* ('build'), *laik* ('play'), *lait* ('search'), *hoast* ('cough'), *lie* ('scythe'), and *lathe* ('barn').

CHAPTER IX

THE NORMAN CONQUEST

THE NORMAN CONQUEST of 1066 was not such a violent break in English history as people sometimes imagine. There was already strong French influence in England before the Conquest: Edward the Confessor was himself half Norman, and his court had close relations with France. It is certainly true, however, that the Conquest had a profound influence on the English language. For some centuries, English ceased to be the language of the governing classes, and no such thing as standard literary English existed; and when English did once again become the language of the whole country it had changed a good deal under the influence of the language of the conquerors.

The rulers of Normandy had originally been Scandinavian Vikings, who occupied parts of northern France, and in the early tenth century were recognized by the French crown: in 912, Rollo became first Duke of Normandy, and accepted the king of France as his overlord. By the middle of the eleventh century, however, the Normans had long lost their Scandinavian speech: they spoke French, and were essentially French in culture. People sometimes talk, therefore, as though the Norman Conquest were the coming of a higher civilization to the backward and barbaric Anglo-Saxons. This, however, is absurd. Six hundred years had passed since the Anglo-Saxon invasion of England, and in that time the English had developed a sophisticated civilization. The Normans demonstrated their superiority in military techniques, for they had the new heavy cavalry that had been developed on the continent by the Franks, while the Anglo-Saxons still fought on foot in the old Germanic style, behind a wall of round shields. They also showed themselves superior at the construction of castles, and after the Conquest they built some fine churches and cathedrals. But it is difficult to see in what other ways they were superior to the people they conquered.

The Anglo-Saxons had a fine literature, both in verse and in prose. They had a tradition of scholarship which went back to the seventh century, and when Charlemagne, at the end of the eighth century, wanted to reform his educational system, he imported an Englishman to do it for him. This tradition had been badly disrupted by the Viking invasions, but there was a revival under West Saxon leadership in the second half of the tenth century. Of their works of art enough have survived to show that they were not backward in this field either: there are beautiful carved crosses, and jeweller's work, and illuminated manuscripts to compare with any in the world. They were also famous for their needlework, and the celebrated Bayeux tapestry was no doubt a piece of cultural loot, for it was almost certainly made in England.

These people did not need William of Normandy and his adventurers to bring them civilization. French became the language of the upper classes in England, not because of any cultural superiority in the conquerors, but simply because they *were* conquerors, and spoke French. What happened, in fact, was that the native aristocracy were very largely destroyed, and their lands were distributed to William's Norman followers, who became the new ruling class. Many key positions, such as bishoprics and abbacies, were also given to Normans in the years following the Conquest, so that the Church and education were dominated by them. French, therefore, was the language of the upper classes and the court, and it remained so for a full two centuries. So anybody whose native tongue was English, and who wanted to get on in the world, would have to learn French, and many people did so. The following comment on the situation was made in the late thirteenth century in a long history of England written in verse, usually known as the chronicle of Robert of Gloucester:

þus com, lo, Engelond in-to Normandies hond:
And þe Normans ne couþe speke þo bote hor owe speche,

And speke French as hii dude atom, and hor children dude also
  teche,
So þat heiemen of þis lond, þat of hor blod come,
Holdeþ alle þulke speche þat hii of hom nome;
Vor bote a man conne Frenss me telþ of him lute.
Ac lowe men holdeþ to Engliss, and to hor owe speche yute.
Ich wene þer ne beþ in al þe world contreyes none
þat ne holdeþ to hor owe speche, bote Engelond one.
Ac wel me wote uor to conne boþe wel it is,
Vor þe more þat a mon can, þe more wurþe he is.

This can be translated as follows:

> Thus came, lo, England into Normandy's hand: and the
> Normans then knew how to speak only their own language,
> and spoke French as they did at home, and also had their
> children taught (it), so that noblemen of this land, that come
> of their stock, all keep to the same speech that they received
> from them; for unless a man knows French, people make
> little account of him. But low men keep to English, and to
> their own language still. I think that in the whole world there
> are no countries that do not keep to their own language,
> except England alone. But people know well that it is good
> to master both, because the more a man knows the more
> honoured he is.

This bears witness to the prestige of French, but also to the
fact that English continued to be spoken by the majority
('lowe men'). However, now that English was no longer the
language of upper class culture and administration, West Saxon
lost its place as a standard literary language. For three centuries there was no single form of English recognized as a norm,
and every man wrote in his own dialect. Early Middle English
texts give the impression of a chaos of dialects, without many
common conventions in pronunciation or spelling, and with
wide divergences in grammar and vocabulary.

MIDDLE ENGLISH DIALECTS

The major dialects of Middle English, the approximate
boundaries of which are shown in Figure 13, are Northern

FIG. 13. Main dialect areas of Middle English. These are imprecise, but work
in progress at Edinburgh University will yield more information.

(divisible into Scots and Northern English), East Midland,
West Midland, South Eastern, and Southern (divisible into
Central Southern and South Western). These correspond fairly
closely to the Old English dialects; the fact that they are subdivided more is partly due to the fact that we know more about

them than about Old English dialects, but partly too it is due to substantial changes in the linguistic situation. The separation of the Northumbrian dialect of Old English into the Scottish and Northern English dialects of Middle English is plainly due to the political separation of the two regions, which led to the emergence of a Scots literary language in the course of the Middle English period. The marked difference between the East Midland and West Midland dialects of Middle English, which are both descended from the Mercian dialect of Old English, is due to the fact that the East Midlands were in the Danelaw, whereas the West Midlands were in the part of England held by King Alfred, so that the two areas were subjected to different influences. The South Eastern dialect, of course, is descended from the Kentish dialect of Old English, and the Southern Dialect from West Saxon.

There are many differences between these various Middle English dialects, and I shall merely pick out a few examples of various kinds. First, a few differences in pronunciation. The Old English *ā* remained north of the Humber, but south of the Humber it changed in the twelfth century into an open rounded sound, like the vowel of the present-day words *law* and *bought*; we can call this the *oa* sound of Middle English. In Modern English, the Middle English *oa* has developed into the diphthong that we use in words like *boat*, whereas Middle English *ā* has developed into the diphthong that we use in *dame*. Hence Old English *hām* has become *home* in southern England, but the form *haim* can still be heard in Scots dialects. The southern forms are of course normal in Modern English, both British and American, but there are a few words where a northern form has been retained: thus the word *raid* is merely a northern dialectal variant of the word *road*; both come from the Old English *rād*, which originally meant 'a riding, a journey'; the difference in meaning between the northern and southern forms is a telling comment on the life of the turbulent north in the Middle Ages, when a riding of Scots into England or of Englishmen into Scotland normally carried the implications of a *raid*. Another such doublet is the pair *whole* and *hale*, both descended from Old English *hāl*; the word *hail* (as a greeting) is from the Scandinavian version of the same word.

Another example of dialectal variation is the Middle English treatment of the Old English front rounded vowel *y*; in the North, in the East Midlands, and in Devon, Dorset, and Wilts, it was unrounded to *i*, so that Old English *cynn* ('kin') became *kinn*; in Kent, and in parts of Essex, Middlesex, Sussex, and Suffolk, it became *e*, so that we find *kenn*; and elsewhere (mainly, that is, in the old West Saxon areas) it remained *y*, usually spelt *u*, so that we find *kunn*. Similarly, Old English long *ȳ* became Middle English *i* or *ē*, or remained *ȳ*, in the same areas. Standard Modern English is descended from a dialect where *y* and *ȳ* normally developed into *i* and *ī*, the *i* having since become the diphthong that we use in words like *hide*; so Old English *cynn* and *mȳs* have become our *kin* and *mice*. But we have inherited stray forms from other dialects: thus *merry* and *left* (opposite of right) come from the southeastern dialect, for the Old English forms are *myrige* and *lyft*; and *bury* (Old English *byrgan*) has its pronunciation from Kentish but its spelling from the old West Saxon area; while *busy* (Old English *bysig*) also has the Southern spelling, but has its pronunciation from the East Midlands or North.

There were also differences in inflexions, and in the forms of the personal pronouns. During the Middle English period, there was a tendency for the northern forms to permeate southwards. The following examples will show the kind of differences that were typical in the late thirteenth century:

	'she comes'	'they come'
Northern	scho comis	thai come *or* comis
East Midland	sche comes *or* cometh	thei comen
West Midland	hue cometh *or* comes	hi comen
South Eastern	hi cometh	hi cometh
Southern	heo cometh	he cometh

The differences in vocabulary between the different regions are most striking in the matter of loan words. In the Northern and East Midland dialects there are large numbers of Scandinavian words; some of these permeated into the other dialects during the Middle English period, but many of them never became accepted outside the old Danelaw. French loan words, on the contrary, first appeared most densely around London, the centre of fashion and of administration, and permeated northwards and westwards from there; by the fourteenth century they were being used freely all over the country.

ENGLISH VERSUS FRENCH

While English was thus left without a standard literary dialect, the prestige languages in England were Latin and French. Latin was the language of the Church, of scholarship, and of international communication; after the Conquest it was also important in administration, but in this field it gradually gave way to French. The invaders of 1066 spoke Norman French, a northern dialect of the language, and in England this developed characteristics of its own, and is then called Anglo-Norman. In the thirteenth century, however, when the Central French dialect of Paris had begun to exert a strong influence on the rest of France, the Anglo-Norman dialect lost some of its prestige in England: it became rather old fashioned and rustic, and the courtly language was Central French.

In the thirteenth century, French was still being spoken at the English court, and literature was being written in French for the nobility of England; but it is this century that sees the tipping of the balance away from French and back to English. Although French was for a long time the prestige language in England, it was never the mother tongue of the majority of the population; a considerable number of Normans settled in England after the Conquest, but they never outnumbered the English in the way the Anglo-Saxon settlers had outnumbered the Britons; and ultimately French died out in England. An event which contributed to the triumph of English was King John's loss of Normandy to the French crown in the opening years of the thirteenth century. As a result of this, the English nobility, most of whom had estates in Normandy as well as in

England, had to decide which of the two they belonged to. A common solution was for one son to inherit the English estates, and another son the Norman estates, and this can be seen going on in the first half of the thirteenth century. Thus the ties with Normandy were severed, and the ex-Norman nobility gradually became English. The English crown, indeed, continued to hold lands in France, especially in southern Aquitaine, and also went on importing Frenchmen to its court; but the English nobility were jealous of such royal favourites, and in the Barons' Wars against Henry III in the middle of the century there was a good deal of anti-foreigner propaganda. National feeling was beginning to arise in England, as in other countries of western Europe, and this must have raised the prestige of the English language.

The fourteenth century sees the definitive triumph of English. French was now rapidly ceasing to be the mother tongue even of the nobility, and those who wanted to speak French had to learn it. Literature, even the most courtly literature, was written more and more in English, and in the second half of the century there was a great literary upsurge in English, with Chaucer as its major figure. In administration, English came to be used more and more. In 1362 the king's speech at the opening of Parliament was made in English, and in the same year an Act was passed making English the official language of the law courts instead of French, though their records were to be kept in Latin.

The fourteenth century also saw the switch from French to English as the medium of grammar school education. Here we have an interesting piece of contemporary evidence. During the first half of the century a monk of Chester called Ranulph Higden wrote in Latin a long work called *Polychronicon*; this was a universal history (a favourite medieval form), beginning at the Creation and coming down to Higden's own time. In 1385–87 this work was translated into English by John of Trevisa, writing in a southwestern dialect. In Book I of the work, Higden gives an account of the languages of Britain; the English, he says, have had Danes and Normans mixed in with them, and this has led to a corruption of the native language. He then continues (in Trevisa's translation):

> þis apeyring of þe burþtonge ys bycause of twey þinges. On ys for chyldern in scole, ayenes þe vsage and manere of al oþer nacions, buþ compelled for to leue here oune longage, and for to construe here lessons and here þinges a Freynsh, and habbeþ suþthe þe Normans come furst into Engelond. Also gentil men children buþ ytaught for to speke Freynsh fram tyme þat a buþ yrokked in here cradel, and conneþ speke and playe wiþ a child hys brouch; and oplondysch men wol lykne hamsylf to gentil men, and fondeþ wiþ gret bysynes for to speke Freynsh, for to be more ytold of.

This can be translated as follows:

> This corruption of the mother tongue is because of two things. One is because children in school, contrary to the usage and customs of all other nations, are compelled to abandon their own language, and to construe their lessons and their tasks in French, and have since the Normans first came to England. Moreover, gentlemen's children are taught to speak French from the time that they are rocked in their cradle and are able to speak and to play with a child's trinket; and rustic men want to make themselves like gentlemen, and strive with great industry to speak French, in order to be more highly thought of.

This passage testifies to the high prestige that French still enjoyed when it was written (perhaps around 1330), and to the continued use of French in education (though it is no doubt significant that Higden protests against this). But when John of Trevisa translated this passage in 1385, he added a piece of his own, which was not in the original. It begins as follows:

> þys manere was moche y-used tofore þe furste moreyn, and ys seþthe somdel ychaunged. For Iohan Cornwal, a mayster of gramere, chayngede þe lore in gramerscole and construccion of Freynsh into Englysch; and Richard Pencrych

lurnede þat manere techyng of hym, and oþer men of
Pencrych, so þat now, þe yer of oure Lord a þousond þre
hondred foure score and fyue, of the secunde kyng Richard
after þe Conquest nyne, in al þe gramerscoles of Engelond
childern leueþ Frensch, and construeþ and lurneþ an
Englysch.

This can be rendered:

This custom was much in use before the first plague (i.e.
the Black Death of 1349), and since then is somewhat
changed. For John Cornwall, a licensed teacher of grammar,
changed the teaching in grammar school and the construing
from French into English; and Richard Pencrich learnt that
method of teaching from him, and other men from Pencrich,
so that now, in the year of Our Lord 1385, in the ninth year
of Richard II, in all the grammar schools of England children
are abandoning French, and are construing and learning in
English.

Trevisa goes on to say that this has the advantage that the children learn quicker, but the disadvantage that they know no
more French than their left heel, which is bad for them if they
have to go abroad. And he adds that gentlemen have now to a
great extent given up teaching their children French.

The greatest stronghold of French in England was perhaps
the king's court; but when Henry IV seized the throne in 1399,
England, for the first time since the Norman Conquest, acquired a king whose mother tongue was English. In the
fifteenth century the retreat of French became a rout; not only
was it no longer a native language in England, but now there
were actually members of the nobility who could not speak
French at all; henceforth, a fluent command of French was to
be regarded as an accomplishment.

THE NEW STANDARD ENGLISH

With the re-establishment of English as the language of
administration and culture came the re-establishment of an

English literary language, a standard form of the language which could be regarded as a norm. As we have already seen, this language was not descended from the West Saxon literary language. The new standard language that arose in the late Middle Ages was based on the East Midland dialect. This was because of the importance of the East Midland dialect area in English cultural, economic, and administrative life. One of the universities, Cambridge, was in this area, and the other not too remote from its borders. It was perhaps the most important commercial area of England, as well as being one of the rich agricultural areas; you have to remember that, before the Industrial Revolution, the north of England lacked the economic importance that it has today: it was a primitive region, backward economically and socially compared with the south; and Norwich was one of the great cities of England at a time when Manchester, Liverpool, Leeds, and Sheffield were comparatively insignificant. Above all, an East Midland dialect was the basis of London speech, and London was the seat of government and the cultural centre of the nation. The London dialect was in fact rather a mixed one, but in the fourteenth century it seems to have been basically East Midland in type, with influences from the neighbouring Kentish and Southern dialects. These border influences on London speech explain some of the non-East-Midland forms in modern standard English, like the Kentish *merry* and *left* which we have already noticed. Mostly, however, Modern English has forms descended from the East Midland dialect of Middle English, itself mainly descended from the Mercian dialect of Old English.

The establishment of a standard language did not, of course, take place overnight. In the fourteenth century, while Chaucer was writing in what was to become standard English, Langland was writing in a Southwest Midland dialect, while up in the Northwest Midlands there was a school of poets writing in that local dialect, the most famous of their products being *Sir Gawayne and the Green Knight*. But gradually the prestige of the London language grew, and in the fifteenth century its influence was increased by the introduction of printing. In the sixteenth century there was wide recognition of the language of the court as the 'best' English, but even then it was no disgrace for a courtier to speak a regional dialect, and Sir Walter Raleigh had a Devon accent to his dying day. Nevertheless the *literary* language had been largely standardized by the end of the fifteenth century, and in the Modern English period you cannot tell what dialect a man speaks by examining his *writings*, as you could in the Middle English period.

FRENCH LOAN WORDS IN MIDDLE ENGLISH

Although French died out in England, it left its marks on English. Its main effect was on the vocabulary, and an enormous number of French loan words came into the language during the Middle English period. They came in fastest when French was dying out. In the eleventh and twelfth centuries, when French was the unchallenged language of the upper classes, the number of words borrowed by English was not enormous; but in the thirteenth, and still more the fourteenth century, there was a flood of loan words. This is not surprising: when bilingual speakers were changing over to English for such purposes as government and literature they felt the need for the specialized terms that they were accustomed to in those fields, and brought them over from French. It was not that English was deficient in such vocabulary: in almost every case there was already an English word for the concept, which was displaced by the French one; this is why so much of the Old English vocabulary now seems so unfamiliar to us.

The influx of French words differed in several ways from the influx of Scandinavian words. We have already seen that Scandinavian words spread down from the Danelaw, whereas French words spread from London and the court. Moreover, the French words were on the whole not such homely ones as the Scandinavian words: the Vikings had mixed in with the English on more or less equal terms, but the Normans formed a separate caste that imposed much of their culture on their subordinates. Many of the French loan words reflect this cultural and political dominance: they are often words to do with war, with ecclesiastical matters, with the law, with hunting, with heraldry, with the arts, with fashion. For the same reason, French words tended to penetrate *downwards* in society, whereas the Scandinavian words came in on the ground floor. And, finally, the French words were entirely new ones, with no obvious resemblance to anything in English, whereas many of the Scandinavian loans were merely dialectal variants of their English counterparts.

As might be expected, titles of rank were mostly taken from the French; these include (in their modern spelling) *sovereign*, *prince*, *peer*, *duke*, *marquis*, *count*, and *baron*; however, we did retain the English words *king*, *queen*, *lord*, *lady*, and *knight*. Words to do with administration include *government*, *crown*, *state*, *parliament*, *council*, *chancellor*, *nation*, *people*, and *country*. The law courts were long conducted in French, and we have borrowed the words *justice*, *court*, *judge*, *prison*, *verdict*, *sentence*, *attorney*, *plea*, *accuse*, *crime*, and *punish*. Many ecclesiastical posts were given to Frenchmen, and we have borrowed words like *religion*, *service*, *saviour*, *virgin*, *saint*, *relic*, *abbey*, *friar*, *clergy*, *parish*, *prayer*, and *sermon*. The military terms that were borrowed include many that are now obsolete, but there are also *armour*, *battle*, *castle*, *tower*, and *war* (itself originally taken into French from Germanic). There are many words that reflect French dominance in the arts and fashion; they include *fashion*, *dress*, *costume*, *apparel*; and *art*, *beauty*, *colour*, *column*, *paint*, *music*, *chant*, *poem*, and *romance*. Also borrowed were many abstract nouns, especially the names of mental and moral qualities: *cruelty*, *obedience*, *courtesy*, *mercy*, *charity*, and so on.

There are other indications of the aristocratic stamp of medieval French loan words. Things of the people usually retain their English names, whereas upper-class objects often have French names. Thus we have English *house*, but French *manor* and *palace*; English *man* and *maid*, but French *butler* and *servant*; and, as Scott pointed out in *Ivanhoe*, the domestic animals kept their English names while the English were looking after them in the fields (*calf*, *ox*, *swine*, *sheep*), but were given French names when they appeared on the Norman lord's table (*veal, beef, pork, mutton*). In Modern English we often have French and Germanic words surviving side by side with similar meanings; in such cases the Germanic word tends to be more popular, and perhaps more emotionally charged, while the French word is often more formal, or refined, or official; thus we have English *folk, hearty, holy, doom,* and *stench,* beside French *people, cordial, saint, judgement,* and *perfume.*

If you know modern French, you may sometimes be puzzled by the difference between an English word and the modern French word corresponding to it. Sometimes these differences are due to the changes that have taken place in the pronunciation of both languages since medieval times. Thus our word *chief* is a Middle English borrowing from Old French *chef,* but is pronounced differently. The initial consonant sound in our word is akin to the Old French one, whereas in Modern French this sound has become *sh*: on the other hand, Modern French has retained the original short *e* vowel, whereas *chief* has developed a long vowel. Our word *chef* is a more recent borrowing of the same word, and so has the Modern French pronunciation.

However, some of the discrepancies between Middle English loan words and Modern French words have other explanations. One cause is dialectal variation in Old French itself. Standard Modern French is descended from a Central French dialect of Old French, but the Normans spoke a Northern French dialect, which differed from it in a number of ways. For example, the Old French diphthong *ei* became *oi* in Central French, but in Anglo-Norman it remained *ei*. Hence we have English *prey, veil,* and *strait* (from Anglo-Norman *preie, veile, estreit*), where French has *proie, voile,* and *étroit*. In Modern French, of course, the *oi* has remained in the spelling but the pronunciation has become a kind of *wa*. Again, in Central French the groups *ka* and *ga* became *cha* and *ja,* but this change did not take place in Norman French: this accounts for English *garden* and *catch* beside French *jardin* and *chasser*. This last word illustrates another difference: in Normandy, Old French *s* became *ch*, so that Norman had *cachier* 'to chase' and *lanchier* 'to throw' where Central French had *chacier* and *lancier* (Modern French *chasser*, *lancer*); the Norman words have of course become our *catch* and *launch*. And, as a final example, there was a difference in the treatment of *w* in Old French loan words from Germanic; this *w* was retained in Norman, but changed to *g* in Central French, so that we have *war*, *wage*, and *wardrobe*, while Modern French has *guerre*, *gage*, and *garderobe*.

On the whole, however, only the *early* French loan words were taken from Norman; in the thirteenth and fourteenth centuries, when the great bulk of the borrowings were made, it was Central French that was fashionable, and it was from this dialect that the words were taken. But the borrowings from Norman are very thoroughly assimilated into English, and moreover include more ordinary everyday words than the later borrowings from Central French, presumably because they were in many cases introduced by the Norman rank and file who came over at the Conquest. Thus the early loans include words like *people*, *garden*, *market*, *hour*, and *wages*. In some cases, a word was borrowed in its Norman form, and then borrowed again later in its Central French form, so that we have both forms in Modern English, usually with different meanings. Thus from Anglo-Norman we have *catch*, *cattle*, *warden*, and *wage*, and from Central French the corresponding forms *chase*, *chattle*, *guardian*, and *gage* ('pledge').

When the words were first borrowed they may have been given a French pronunciation, especially among bilingual speakers. But very soon they were adapted to the English phonological system, and given the English sounds which to the speakers seemed nearest to the French ones. This of course is normal when a word is borrowed from another language. In recent times, for example, the word *garage* has been borrowed into English from French, but even a speaker who knows French pronounces the word in an English way: he does not, for example, use a French uvular *r*, or a French *a* sound. Moreover, the word *garage* (at any rate in British speech) has now been given an English kind of stress pattern, being stressed on the first syllable. The same kind of thing happened with many French loan words in Middle English: at first, a word like *nature* was stressed on the second syllable, as this seemed most like the French way of saying it, but after a time the stress was moved to the first syllable, as this was more in conformity with English speech habits. In Chaucer's poetry, such words can often be seen fluctuating, being sometimes stressed one way, sometimes the other. In words of more than two syllables, the stress has not always moved all the way to the first syllable, and the final stressing arrived at has been influenced by several different factors: compare *melody* with *melodious*, *advertise* with *advertisement*. Moreover, there are sometimes variant stressings in Modern English, as in *controversy*.

The early French loan words were so well assimilated into English that they were soon felt as not in any way foreign. This made it easier for the language to accept later Romance and Latin loan words; indeed, one of the results of the influx of French loans was to make English more hospitable to foreign words and less prone to use its own resources for word creation. Where Old English invented words like *tungolcræft* ('star skill') or *prines* ('threeness'), Middle and Modern English tend to borrow or adapt a word from abroad, like *astronomy* (from French from Latin from Greek) and *trinity* (from French from Latin). But once they have been taken into English, such loan words can be combined with native elements to form further words. French–English hybrids appear quite soon after the Conquest, the earliest types being French stems with English prefixes or suffixes, like *ungracious*, *preaching*, *gentleness*, *faithless*, and *beautiful*.

The dominance of French for so many centuries naturally had a great influence too on English literary traditions. Some of these were quite disrupted. The tradition of Old English historical writing in prose was lost, for example, and when people like Robert of Gloucester begin writing history in English again, they write verse chronicles in the French manner. However, there must have been places where some English literary traditions were preserved, and in the second half of the fourteenth century there was a flourishing school of poets using the alliterative line descended from Old English poetry. Chaucer, however, with his system of versification on continental models, makes such poetry look a little old-fashioned, for it was Chaucer's kind of poetry that was to triumph. Here, as in so many fields, the centuries of French linguistic domination made a deep impression on English culture.

CHAPTER X

MIDDLE ENGLISH

OLD ENGLISH did not disappear overnight at the Norman Conquest, nor did it immediately stop being written, for the West Saxon literary tradition was continued for a time in some of the great monasteries. But, in the years following the Conquest, the changes which had already begun to show themselves in pre-Conquest Old English continued at an increased speed, and in less than a century we can say that the Old English period is over, and that Middle English has begun.

The Conquest as a matter of fact made the change from Old to Middle English look more sudden than it really was, by introducing new spelling conventions. An established literary language like late West Saxon tends to be conservative in its spelling: changes occur in pronunciation, but the scribes go on writing the words in the traditional way. But the Norman scribes disregarded traditional English spelling, and simply spelt the language as they heard it, using the conventions of Norman French. Consequently, many changes that had not been reflected in Old English spelling, or that had only appeared in occasional spellings, now emerged clearly.

NEW SPELLING CONVENTIONS

Quite apart from revealing hidden changes, the new orthography gave English quite a new look. A number of new consonant symbols were introduced. A new *g* symbol was introduced for the stops represented by the Old English *g*, and the Old English symbol was retained only for the fricatives; in my transcriptions of Middle English texts I have used *y* for the old symbol and *g* for the new one. Where Old English had used *f* to represent both voiced and voiceless sounds, Middle English scribes used *u* or *v* for the voiced sound; and similarly *z* was introduced beside *s*, though not consistently; in Middle English, both these pairs represented two separate phonemes, where there had been only one phoneme in Old English. The combination *th* gradually replaced ð and þ, but ð is found up to about 1300, and þ remained quite common until about 1400; indeed, a debased form of þ survives even today in the initial Y of expressions like 'Ye Olde Tea Shoppe', in which *Ye* is simply a way of writing *þe*.

Some of the remaining differences in orthography between Old and Middle English are shown in the following table. We are not of course discussing changes in *pronunciation*, but the different *spellings* used to represent the same sound.

Old English	Middle English	Examples in Middle English
cw	qu	queen
sc	ss, sch, sh	fiss, fisch, fish
cg	i, j, g	iuge, juge ('judge')
c (velar)	k, c	kinn ('kin'), col ('cool')
c (palatal)	ch	chinn ('chin')
i	i, y	king, kyng, bodi, body
y	u	kunn ('kin'), busi ('busy')
ȳ	u, ui	fur, fuir ('fire')
ē	ee, ie, e	queen, quen, field
ō	oo, o	food, fod
ū	ou, ow	hous, hows ('house')

It is particularly important to notice that the letter *y* was no longer used for a front rounded sound, but was simply used as an alternative form of *i*, so that Middle English *king* and *kyng* represent exactly the same pronunciation; the dialects that preserved the front rounded sound of Old English *y* usually spelt it *u*.

Not all these changes were improvements: the *q* and the *y* were superfluous; and *ou* was not a very satisfactory spelling for the long *ū* sound, because it also represented two different Middle English diphthongs.

One oddity of Middle English spelling that is still with us was the result of a change of script. In place of the Celtic script of Old English, the Norman scribes introduced a continental style of handwriting. In this style it was difficult to tell how

many strokes had been made when letters like *m, n, v, w,*
and *u* occurred together, and groups like *wu, un, uv,* and *um*
are difficult to distinguish from one another. For this reason,
the scribes took to writing *o* instead of *u* when it occurred in
groups of this kind: so for Old English *sunu, cuman,* and *lufu*
we often find Middle English *sone, comen,* and *loue,* from which
derive the modern spellings *son, come,* and *love.* But this was a
change in spelling, not in pronunciation: the word *sun* (Old
English *sunne*) has always had the same vowel sound as the
word *son* (Old English *sunu*), and the modern difference in
spelling is a matter of chance.

CHANGES IN PRONUNCIATION

We have already noticed some of the changes in pronunciation that took place in the transition from Old to Middle English: the development of Old English *y* and *ȳ* in different areas,
and the change of Old English *ā* to *oa* south of the Humber.
This *oa* sound (resembling the vowel of our word *law*) was kept
distinct from the long *o* sound descended from Old English *ō*,
which remained a close sound, rather like the vowel of Modern
French *beau*; and the two sounds have been kept distinct to the
present day, for Old English *bāt* has become *boat,* while Old
English (*bōt* 'remedy, compensation') has become *boot.* However, in Middle English the two sounds were not always distinguished in the spelling, and it was not until early Modern
English times that one came to be spelt *oa* and the other *oo*.
Another similar awkward pair in Middle English are the open
and close long *e* sounds. From Old English *ǣ* descended a long
open sound, with a quality somewhat like that of the first
element in our word *air,* while from Old English *ē* descended a
long close sound, more like the vowel of German *zehn.* Once
again, however, the two sounds were often not distinguished in
Middle English spelling, and it was not until early Modern
English times that it became common to spell the first as *ea* and
the second as *ee.* These two sounds were still kept distinct in
the English of Shakespeare's day, but have fallen together in

present-day English, so that we use the same vowel in *sea* (from Old English *sǣ*) as in *see* (from Old English *sēon*); there are still dialects, however, for example in Ireland, where the two sounds are kept distinct. For convenience, I shall refer to these four sounds as the *oa*, *oo*, *ea*, and *ee* sounds of Middle English.

The change from Old to Middle English saw a number of important dependent or combinative changes, i.e. changes in pronunciation that took place only in certain phonetic contexts. One of the most important of these, which has had far-reaching effects both on pronunciation and on spelling, was the lengthening of short vowels in open syllables in two-syllabled words. An open syllable is one that ends with a vowel. Where a single consonant occurs between vowels in English, the consonant normally belongs to the second syllable, and the first syllable is therefore an open one. Thus in the Old English verb *bacan* ('to bake') the syllable division is *ba-can*, and the first syllable is an open one. This word became early Middle English *baken* (still with a short *a*), and then the vowel in the open syllable was lengthened to *ā* (like the *a* in our word *father*), which in Modern English has regularly developed into the sound heard in our word *bake*. When, however, there are two consonants between the vowels, the first consonant normally belongs to the first syllable, which is therefore a closed one. Thus in Middle English *thanken* ('to thank'), from Old English *þancian*, the syllable division was *than-ken*, and no lengthening of the vowel took place.

The short vowels which were regularly subject to this kind of lengthening were *a*, *o*, and *e*. When *o* was lengthened it became a long open sound, and in the standard language it became identical with the *oa* sound; so today we have the same vowels in *boat* and *home* (from Old English *bāt* and *hām*) as in *hope* and *throat* (from Old English *hopa* and *þrote*). When *e* was lengthened it too became a long open sound, and in the standard language it fell together with the *ea* sound, so that today we have the same vowels in *sea* and *to lead* (from Old English *sǣ* and *lǣdan*) as in *meat* and *steal* (from Old English *mete* and *stelan*).

In some dialects, especially in the north, the vowels *i* and *u* were also lengthened under the same conditions, and then became the long close sounds *ee* and *oo*. A few of these lengthened forms have found their way into the modern standard language, for example *week* (Old English *wicu*) and *evil* (early Middle English *ivel* from Old English *yfel*).

Because of the inflexional system of English, the conditions for lengthening were sometimes fulfilled in one form of a word, but not in another. For example, Old English *cradol* ('a cradle') became Middle English *cradel*, and here lengthening of the *a* would occur; but the plural 'cradles' was Old English *cradelas* (early Middle English *cradeles*), and 'in a cradle' was Old English *on cradole* (early Middle English *on cradele*), and no lengthening would take place in these, because they were three-syllabled forms. Similarly, the Old English word *cran* ('a crane') would not have its vowel lengthened in Middle English, but the inflected forms, like *cranas* ('cranes') would do. In such cases Modern English has usually generalized one form or the other for each word; in the two examples given, it is the lengthened vowel that has been generalized, and we use a long vowel in both *cradle* and *cradles*, both *crane* and *cranes*. In some cases, however, it is the short vowel that has been generalized: we use a short vowel in *vat*, *vats*, from the Old English nominative singular *fæt*, not the long vowel that would have arisen from Old English inflected forms like *fatu* ('vats'). Just occasionally it happens that both long and short forms have been retained, so that Modern English has two words where Old English had only one. Thus Old English *stæf* ('a staff') became Middle English *staf*, while the plural *stafas* became Middle English *staves*. From *staves* we have formed a new singular *stave*, while from *staff* we have formed a new plural *staffs*. In present-day southeastern English (though not in Northern and Midland dialects) the word *staff* in fact has a long vowel, but this is a more recent development (as can be seen from the fact that it is a *different* long vowel from that of *stave*).

This Middle English lengthening of vowels in open syllables has affected our spelling conventions. In early Middle English, words like *bake* had two syllables; after the first vowel had been lengthened, the final -*e* was lost, and such words became monosyllables. But the -*e* was often retained in the spelling, and so we tend in Modern English to regard a final -*e* as a mark of a preceding long vowel, provided there is only one consonant between. Thus we use spellings like *home* and *stone*, where the final -*e* has no etymological justification, but is simply inserted to show that the *o* is long. The Old English forms of course were *hām* and *stān*, and the modern words might well be spelt *hoam* and *stoan* (like *oak* and *road* and other words that had *ā* in Old English). Moreover, because of the lengthening in open syllables, we often insert two consonants in the spelling if we have a *short* vowel, so that we write *backer* as distinct from *baker*.

Another set of combinative changes was the lengthening of vowels before certain groups of consonants. This happened earlier than the lengthening in open syllables, and had already begun in late Old English. In many cases the vowels were shortened again later, but long vowels remained in some dialects, especially before the groups *ld*, *mb*, and *nd*. Lengthening before these groups accounts for the modern forms of words like *old*, *bold*, *cold*, *told*; in Old English (Anglian) these had short *a* (*ald*, *bald*, etc.); this was lengthened to *ā* before the twelfth century, and then of course underwent the change of *ā* to *oa* south of the Humber. Other examples of lengthening before these three groups are *field*, *child*, *comb*, *climb*, *blind*, and *ground* (Old English *feld*, *cild*, *camb*, *climban*, *blind*, and *grund*). Neither in Old nor in Middle English, however, did this lengthening take place if the consonant group in question was immediately followed by a third consonant. This accounts for the difference in vowel between *child* and *children*. In most cases, however, either the long or the short vowel has been generalized in Modern English: thus our *lamb* is from the plural (Old English *lambru*, Middle English *lambre*), not from the singular (Old English *lamb*), which had its vowel lengthened. Similarly, the word *wind* ('moving air') probably has its short vowel by analogy with words like *windmill*, where the third consonant prevented the lengthening from taking place; in early Modern English, *wind* had a long vowel, as can be seen from rhymes ('Blow, blow thou winter wind, Thou art not so unkind . . .').

MIDDLE ENGLISH GRAMMAR

In grammar, the Middle English period is marked by a great reduction in the inflexional system inherited from Old English; and Middle English is often referred to as the period of weakened inflexions. There were a number of causes for this. One was the mixing of English with Old Norse; frequently, the English and Scandinavian words were sufficiently similar to be recognizable, but had decidedly different sets of inflexions. In these circumstances, doubt and confusion must undoubtedly arise about the correct form of inflexion to use, and speakers in bilingual situations will have tended to rely on other grammatical devices where these lay to hand. The existence and growth of such other devices must itself have contributed to the decay of the inflexional system, even though it was in part stimulated by this decay; here it is difficult to say which was cause and which was effect, since the two processes undoubtedly fed each other.

Another important cause was the loss and weakening of unstressed syllables at the ends of words, which destroyed many of the distinctive inflexions of Old English. As a result of these changes, Old English *-a*, *-u*, and *-e* all became Middle English *-e*. The endings *-an*, *-on*, *-un*, and *-um* all became *-en*, which in late Middle English was further reduced to *-e*. The endings *-as* and *-es* both became *-es*, while *-aþ* and *-eþ* both became *-eþ*. Moreover the final *-e*, which was all that was left of many of these endings, itself disappeared during the Middle English period; in the North, where the changes took place earliest, it was no longer pronounced as early as the mid-thirteenth century, and in the South it had disappeared by about 1400.

These changes had disastrous effects on the inflexional system of Old English, since many inflexions now became identical.

For example, the Old English noun *sunu* would become Middle English *sone* in all cases except the dative plural, which would become *sonen*; the same would be true of the differently declined nouns *giefu* ('gift') and *wine* ('friend'). As a result of this, the whole inflexional system became simplified. Among nouns, for example, the two declensions with the most distinctive of the remaining inflexions tended to attract all the other nouns to themselves. At the same time, the number of different cases became reduced during the Middle English period, especially in the declension of the adjective and the definite article.

Among the nouns, two main declensions became generalized in the course of the Middle English period. One was the declension that in Old English had its nominative plural in *-as* (*stānas*, 'stones') and its genitive singular in *-es* (*stānes*, 'of a stone'). In Middle English, both these endings became *-es*, so that both the nominative plural and the genitive singular were *stones*. The other declension was the one that in Old English formed both its nominative plural and its genitive singular in *-an*, which in Middle English became *-en*. Thus *ēage* was 'eye', and *ēagan* 'eyes' or 'of an eye'; in Middle English these became *eye* and *eyen*. Of these two declensions, the first became dominant in the northern dialects, so that there all nouns tended to form the nominative plural and genitive singular in *-es*, and forms like *eyes* are normal by about 1200. In the south, on the other hand, it was the *-en* declension that became dominant by the middle of the period, and many nouns that in Old English belonged to other declensions came to use the *-en* plural (though *-es* was common for the genitive singular). So we find forms like *devlen* ('devils') and *englen* ('angels'), where Old English had *deoflas* and *englas*. But in the course of the Middle English period the *-es* plural spread southwards and displaced *-en*, and by the fifteenth century it was almost universal; and of course our normal plural forms are directly descended from it. In Shakespeare's day we still find a few plurals in *-en* which have since disappeared, like *eyen*, *shoon*, *hosen*, *housen*, and *peasen* (the singular of which was *pease*, as still in *pease pudding*). And today we still have *oxen*, *kine*, *children*, and *brethren*.

The last three are curious, in that they are double plurals, the Middle English *-en* having been added to a form that was already plural. The Old English forms were *cū* ('cow') and *cȳ* ('cows'), *cild* ('child') and *cildru* ('children'), *brōþor* ('brother') and *brēþer* ('brothers'); the plural forms would normally develop into Middle English *ky*, *childre*, and *breether*, and to these an additional plural mark *-en* has been added.

We still have a few relics of other declensions: there are the mutated plurals like *feet*, *geese*, and *men*, where the vowel of the plural has been changed by front mutation and there is no plural ending; and there are uninflected plurals like *deer* and *sheep* which are descended from Old English neuter nouns in which the nominative and accusative plural had no ending (*dēor* 'a wild animal', plural *dēor* 'wild animals'). There are also a few curious relics, like Lady Day and Lady Chapel, where *Lady* represents an old genitive form (compare 'Lady Day' with 'the *Lord's* Day'). We have also complicated things a little in Modern English by introducing a few learned plurals in words borrowed from Latin and Greek, like *phenomena* and *nuclei* and *formulae*, but on the whole we have pretty thoroughly generalized the Old English *-as* ending for the plural in Modern English; we now spell it *-s* or *-es*, and (at any rate in southeastern English) pronounce it *-s*, *-z*, or *-iz* according to the preceding sound (compare *caps*, *cabs*, *matches*). And this process of generalization was very nearly complete by the end of the Middle English period.

In early Middle English we find all four of the Old English cases still preserved in both singular and plural, but in the course of the period there is a tendency to reduce the total number of forms to three: one for the nominative and accusative singular (like *eye*), one for the genitive singular (like *eyes* 'of an eye'), and one for all plural uses (like *eyen* 'eyes'). In the north, the second and third forms were identical, so there were only two forms, *eye* and *eyes*. A dative singular with the ending *-e* lingers on for quite a time, especially in the south, but as final unstressed *-e* is lost in all dialects by the fifteenth century this too disappears. Occasionally, too, there are genitive plural forms in *-e* or *-ene* even in late Middle English: we find expressions like *kyngene kyng* ('king of kings'), and Chaucer has *hevene-king* ('king of the heavens'). But such forms disappear by the end of the Middle English period, and we reach the modern situation, where for most nouns we have only two forms (*boy, boys*); we recognize a further two forms in our spelling, though not in pronunciation (*boy's, boys'*), and in fact a few nouns do show four distinct forms (*man, man's, men, men's*). We still have one or two relics of the old case system preserved as fossils in modern words and expressions; the word *alive* comes from Old English *on life*, where *life* is the dative singular of *lif* ('life'); the final *-e* has been lost, of course, but we have retained the voiced *v*, not the voiceless *f* of the nominative. And the archaic word *whilom* comes from Old English *hwilum*, the dative plural of *hwil* ('time, while'), meaning 'at times'.

The same process of loss of case distinctions took place in adjectives and in the articles. In adjectives, the trend was towards the use of only two forms: the normal form (e.g. *fair*), and a form with the ending *-e* (e.g. *faire*) which was used both for the plural and as the weak form. This stage has been reached in Chaucer, who writes 'the weder is fair' and 'she hadde a fair forheed', but 'faire wyves' (where we have the plural form) and 'this faire Pertelote' (where the weak form is used after *this*). When the final *-e* was lost towards the end of the Middle English period, these two forms became the same, and the adjective became indeclinable, as it is today.

In Old English the definite article showed three genders (*sē* masculine, *sēo* feminine, *þæt* neuter), and was declined through all four cases singular and plural, and in fact in the singular even had a fifth case, the instrumental. The form *the* arose as late Old English *þe*, which took the place of *sē* and *sēo*; it had its *þ* from the influence of the other case forms (which all began with *þ*). In the course of Middle English the other forms gradually disappeared, and *the* became used for all of them; Chaucer nearly always uses *the*, though he also has a plural form *tho* (from Old English *þā*). By the end of the Middle English period we have reached the modern position, in which *the* is the only form of the definite article, and *that* (originally the neuter form of the definite article) has acquired a distinct meaning.

We said that the definite article and the adjective played a large part in Old English in the making of case distinctions; the loss of this function by the end of the Middle English period represented a major change in the structure of the language. It also meant that grammatical gender disappeared, and was replaced by 'natural gender': that is, we now refer to female creatures as *she*, male creatures as *he*, and inanimate objects as *it*. Things are in fact a bit more complicated than that (a ship can be *she*, for example, and a dog can be *it*). But still we are a long way from the system of early Old English, where the word *wīfmann* ('woman') was masculine, *ciefes* ('concubine') was feminine, and *wif* ('wife, woman') was neuter, and the forms of the pronoun, the adjective, and the definite article had to be chosen accordingly. Though even in late Old English there is a trend for women to be referred to as 'she' and men as 'he', whatever the gender of the noun that has been used.

As the inflexional system decayed, other devices were increasingly used to replace it. For one thing, word order became more important, and more rigid. In Old English we can say *sē cyning hæfde micel geþeaht* ('the king held a great council'), and as a stylistic variant of this we can say *micel geþeaht hæfde sē cyning*, which is quite unambiguous because of the nominative article, *sē*, but which throws the emphasis on 'a great council'. But in Modern English we can hardly use this second word-order, because 'A great council held the king' would mean something quite different. Not that Old English lacked preferences, and for that matter rules, about word order. Three typical Old English ways of arranging words can be illustrated from a sentence of King Alfred's which begins thus: *þā ic þā þis eall gemunde, þā gemunde ic ēac hū ic geseah* . . . This has three clauses: (1) 'When I then this all remembered', (2) 'then remembered I also', (3) 'how I saw . . .'. Only the third of these has word order in conformity with modern usage. The adoption of the third type as normal, and the disappearance of the other two types, took place in the Middle English period, and we have already looked at a passage of Wycliffe (late fourteenth century) in which the word order is essentially modern.

Another device was the increased use of separate words to perform the functions formerly carried out by inflexions. For example, prepositions like *in*, *with*, and *by* came to be used more frequently than in Old English. A few Old English phrases with their modern equivalents will illustrate this: *hungre ācwelan*, 'to die of hunger'; *meahtum spēdig*, 'abundant in might'; *dæges and nihtes*, 'by day and by night'; *hwilum*, 'at times'; *mildheortnysse Drihtnes full is eorþe*, 'the earth is filled with the mercy of God'.

A parallel development is seen in the verbs. Old English had many inflexions, but only two tenses, a present and a past. In Middle and Modern English the system of inflexions becomes much reduced, but a complicated system of tenses is built up with the help of auxiliary verbs like *be*, *have*, and *shall*. The future tense with *shall* and *will* is established in Middle English. In Old English, as we have seen, *ic sceal* meant 'I am obliged to', and *ic wille* meant 'I wish to'. *Shall* and *will* have never entirely lost the meanings of obligation and desire respectively, but today their main use is to indicate futurity, and this function (already hinted at in occasional Old English usages) developed in the Middle English period, though the distinctions between *shall* and *will* were not exactly what they are today. Thus a character in one of Chaucer's poems says:

> *I shal myself to herbes techen yow*
> *That shul been for youre heele and for youre prow.*

'I shall myself direct you to plants that will be for your health and for your benefit.'

The perfect tenses (forms like *We have eaten*, *He had broken*) became established in the Old English period itself, but were not used as frequently or consistently as they were later.

Originally, sentences like 'He had broken a leg' meant something like 'He possessed a broken leg'; and in fact in the Old English equivalent of this sentence the word *broken* would often have been given an inflexion to make it agree with *leg*. Thus in the Anglo-Saxon Chronicle we read *Hie hine ofslægenne hæfdon*, literally 'They him slain had', where the *-ne* of *ofslægenne* is the inflexion for the accusative singular masculine, making it agree with *hine* ('him'). But even in Old English this habit of inflecting the past participle was dying out, and in Middle English the construction developed into the various perfect tenses of the verb.

The continuous tenses, like *He is coming* and *We were eating*, are a later development, and do not become at all common until the Modern English period. There is indeed an Old English construction that somewhat resembles them. Thus in the Chronicle we read *Ond hie þā ymb þā gatu feohtende wǣron*, which it is tempting to translate 'And then they were fighting around the gates'. Literally, however, it means something more like 'And then they were men fighting around the gates'; and it is probably best translated 'And then they went on fighting around the gates'. The modern continuous tenses did not develop out of such Old English usages. Probably they arose from Middle English sentences like *he was areading*, where *areading* has developed out of *on reading*, and the sentence means 'he was engaged in the act of reading'. Later, *areading* dropped its first syllable, and we arrived at the modern sentence *he was reading*. Originally, this *reading* was a noun, Old English *rǣding*, meaning 'the act of reading'; many nouns of this kind originally ended in *-ung*, like Old English *leornung* ('learning'), but this changed to *-ing* in Middle English.

Specimens of Middle English

We can end this chapter by looking at a couple more examples of Middle English writing, one early and one late. First an extract from the Peterborough Chronicle, which was a continuation of the Anglo-Saxon Chronicle, kept going at the monastery at Peterborough until 1154. Under the year 1137 there is a long annal describing the anarchy and miseries of King Stephen's reign, and I have taken an extract from this. The chronicler has been describing how all the great magnates disregarded Stephen, and used forced labour to build themselves castles:

þa þe castles uuaren maked, þa fylden hi mid deoules and yuele men. þa namen hi þa men þe hi wenden that ani god hefden, bathe be nihtes and be dæies, carlmen and wimmen, and diden heom in prisun efter gold and syluer, and pined heom untellendlice pining, for ne uuæren næure nan martyrs swa pined alse hi wæron. Me henged up bi the fet and smoked heom mid ful smoke. Me henged bi the þumbes other bi the hefed, and hengen bryniges on her fet. Me dide cnotted strenges abuton here hæued and uurythen to that it gæde to þe hærnes. He diden heom in quarterne þar nadres and snakes and pades wæron inne, and drapen heom swa. Sume hi diden in crucethus, that is in an ceste þat was scort and nareu and undep, and dide scærpe stanes þerinne, and þrengde þe man þærinne, that him bræcon alle þe limes. . . . Warsæ me tilede, þe erthe ne bar nan corn, for þe land was al fordon mid suilce dædes, and hi sæden openlice that Christ slep, and his halechen. Suilc and mare þanne we cunnen sæin we þoleden xix wintre for ure sinnes.

This is very early Middle English, and not very easy for the modern reader. A fairly close translation is as follows:

When the castles were made, then they filled (them) with devils and evil men. Then they seized the men that they believed had any property, both by day and by night, men and women, and put them in prison to get gold and silver, and tortured them (with) indescribable torments, for never were martyrs so tortured as they were. They ('One') hanged (them) up by the feet and smoked them with foul smoke. They ('One') hanged (them) by the thumbs or by the head, and hung corslets on their feet. They ('One') put knotted cords about their heads and tightened so that it entered the brains. They put them in a cell in which were adders and snakes and toads, and killed them so. Some they put in a torture house, that is in a chest that was short and narrow and shallow, and put sharp stones in it, and pressed the man in it, so that (they) broke all his limbs. . . . Wherever people tilled, the earth bore no corn, for the land was completely ruined with such deeds, and they said openly that Christ slept, and his saints. Such and more than we are able to tell we suffered nineteen years for our sins.

A text of this early date still reminds us in many ways of Old English. Spellings like *þær* and *bræcon* show that the Old English scribal tradition was not yet quite dead. And the word order often reminds us of Old rather than of Modern English, as in phrases like 'Then seized they the men' and 'for ne were never no martyrs so tortured as they were'. The pronouns also remind us of Old English, *hi*, *heom*, and *her(e)* being used for 'they', 'them', and 'their'. We also notice a verb that is strong (as in Old English), which in Modern English is weak: *slep* (from Old English *slēp*) where we say *slept*. This is one of the verbs that changed from strong to weak during the Middle English period, and Chaucer uses both *he slepte* and *he sleep*.

However, despite these resemblances to Old English, there are also very decided differences, and the text is quite clearly a Middle English one. This is seen especially in the inflexions, which are very much reduced compared with Old English. The adjectives have lost almost all their endings; there is a plural *-e* on some of them (*yuele*, *untellendlice*), but otherwise nothing. Notice for example *mid ful smoke*, which in Old English would have been *mid fūlum smocan*. The definite article, similarly, is almost invariably *þe* or *the* (as in *þe castles*, *bi the fet*), though there is one example of the plural *þa* (in *þa men*). For the nouns, the normal plural ending is *-es* or *-s* (*castles*, *bryniges*), and in several words this ending is used where in Old English there was a different one: for example *thumbes* and *snakes*, which in Old English had the plural forms *þūman* and *snacan*.

There is however one plural ending -*en* in the passage, in the word *halechen* ('hallows, saints'), from Old English *hālgan*. Apart from these plural endings, the nouns have practically no inflexions, though there is a dative singular ending, the -*e* of *quarterne*. An interesting case is the phrase *be nihtes and be dæies*, in which the nouns are not plural but genitive singular. The phrase is in fact a halfway house between the Old English *nihtes and dæges*, in which the genitive inflexion has an adverbial force, and the Modern English *by night and day*; the Middle English writer has introduced the preposition *by*, but has also retained the Old English -*es* genitive ending.

In vocabulary, the passage shows very little French influence, having only *castles* and *prisun*. In several places where Modern English would use a French word, it has an English word that is no longer used, like *halechen* ('saints') and *pining* ('torments'). At this early date, few French words had established themselves in English, especially up in the Northeast Midlands where this was written. Nor are there many Greek or Latin words in the passage; the two words from Greek (*martyrs* and *devils*) are not new loans, but had been borrowed in Old English, and the only new classical word in the passage is *crucethus*, probably from the Latin *cruciatus*.

However, as we might expect from a text from the Danelaw, there are more Scandinavian words, though fewer than in some later texts: *bathe* ('both'), *bryniges* ('corslets'), *carlmen* ('men'), *drapen* ('killed'), and *hærnes* ('brains'). Only one of these has survived in modern literary English, namely the word *both*, from Old Norse *báðir*; the spelling in the Peterborough Chronicle, *bathe*, shows that the change of *ā* to *oa* had not yet taken place in that area.

In reading the passage you may have been struck by the word *nadres* ('adders'). The Old English word is *nædre*, and there are similar words in the other Germanic languages. Why has the initial *n*- been lost in Modern English *adder*? We have already seen that final -*n* in unstressed syllables was lost in Middle English, early in the North and later in the South; there is an example of this in the passage, which constantly uses the form *me* as the unstressed form of *man*, meaning 'one, people' (like French *on* or German *man*). However, this final *-n* was not lost under all circumstances: it was retained when it occurred immediately before a vowel, but was lost when it occurred immediately before a consonant or a pause. Because of this, double forms arose for many words, one form with final *-n* and one without. For example, from the unstressed form of Old English *ān* ('one') we have the two forms of the indefinite article, *a* and *an*, as in *a father* and *an uncle*. Similarly, Old English *mīn* became Middle English *my* and *mine* (*my father* but *mine uncle*). But when there are pairs in the language like *my nephew* and *mine uncle*, mistakes sometimes occur about the point of division between the two words, and there appear forms like *my nuncle*. The word *nuncle* did in fact exist, and is found in Shakespeare (King Lear I. iv. 117, etc.). The word *adder* is of this type, the phrase *a nadder* having been apprehended as *an adder*. Other words that owe their modern forms to this kind of change are *apron* (Old French *naperon*), *umpire* (Old French *nompere*), *nickname* (formerly *ekename* 'additional name'), and *newt* (Old English *efete*). Similarly, the pet names *Nan*, *Ned*, and *Nell* are derived from 'mine Anne', 'mine Edward', and 'mine Ellen'.

It is also clear that in many words a final *-n* would be retained in the inflected forms, while being lost (except before vowels) in the uninflected form. So the Old English *mægden* ('a girl') would become Middle English *maide*, while *mægdenes* ('of a girl') would become Middle English *maidenes*. In such cases, analogy has usually operated to generalize one or other form; thus the forms with final *-n* have been generalized in *heaven* and *weapon*, and those without final *-n* in *holly* (Old English *holen*) and *haughty* (Old French *hautein*). In a few cases, both forms have been preserved, so that in Modern English we have doublets like *maid*, *maiden*; *eve*, *even(ing)*; *no*, *none*; *ope*, *open*; *broke*, *broken*; *morrow*, *morn*. Moreover, because of the example of such pairs, we have even added final *-n* to words that did not originally have it, like *often*, which in Old English is *oft*, and in Middle English either *ofte* or *often*.

For our final passage we can take a few lines from Chaucer's *Canterbury Tales*, dating from the late fourteenth century. Chaucer turned his back on the traditional English alliterative style of verse, and instead used French and Italian models. He uses rhyme, in stanzas or in couplets, and verse lines with a fixed number of syllables, both of which are characteristics alien to the alliterative tradition. In reading his verse, you have to pronounce many of the final -*e* sounds of words, but not all. In speech, this final -*e* was dead or dying in Chaucer's time, but it continued to be used in verse, just as happened later in French poetry. In Chaucer's verse, a final -*e* is not pronounced if it occurs before a vowel or an *h*; otherwise it is usually pronounced, except that there are some words in which it appears to be merely orthographical. In the following passage, which is in ten-syllabled rhymed couplets, I have put a dot over *e* in cases where I think it should be pronounced. The passage is an excerpt from the delightful animal fable, *The Nun's Priest's Tale*. Chauntecleer, the cock, has disturbed his favourite wife, Pertelote, by groaning in his sleep, and he explains to her that he has had a nightmare:

> '*Me mette how that I roméd up and doun*
> *Withinne oure yeerd, wheer as I saugh a beest*
> *Was lyk an hound, and wolde han maad areest*
> *Upon my body and han had me deed.*
> *His colour was bitwixé yelow and reed,*
> *And tippéd was his tayl and bothe hise eeris*
> *With blak, unlyk the remenant of hise heeris,*
> *His snowté smal, with glowynge eyén tweyé;*
> *Yet of his look for feere almost I deyé.*
> *This causéd me my gronyng, doutélees.*'
> '*Avoy,*' *quod she,* '*Fy on yow, hertélees.*
> *Allas,*' *quod she,* '*for, by that God abové,*
> *Now han ye lost myn herte and all my lové.*
> *I kan nat love a coward, by my feith.*
> *For certés, whatso any woman seith,*
> *We alle desiren, if it mighté bee,*

To han housbondès hardy, wise and free,
And secree, and no nygard, ne no fool,
Ne hym that is agast of every tool,
Ne noon avantour. By that God abovè,
How dorste ye seyn, for shame, unto youre lovè
That any thyng mighte makè yow aferd?
Have ye no mannès herte, and han a berd?'

This, plainly, is much nearer to Modern English, and is quite easy to understand. However, there are things in it which may mislead a modern reader, so I had better give a modern version of it:

'I dreamed that I was strolling up and down in our yard, where I saw an animal which was like a dog, and which wished to seize my body and kill me. His colour was between yellow and red, and his tail and both his ears were tipped with black, unlike the rest of his hairs; his muzzle was slender, with two glowing eyes; I still almost die of fear at his look. This caused my groaning, undoubtedly.' 'Why,' she said, 'Fie on you, coward. Alas,' she said, 'for, by God above, now you have lost my heart and all my love. I cannot love a coward, by my faith. For assuredly, whatever any woman may say, we all wish, if possible, to have husbands that are brave, wise, and generous, and secret, and no miser and no fool, not one that is frightened of every weapon, nor a boaster. By God above, how did you dare, for shame, to say to your love that anything could make you frightened? Do you lack the courage of a man, and have a beard?'

The things here that cause most difficulty to the modern reader are words which have changed slightly in meaning since Chaucer's day, like *smal* ('narrow, slender') and *tool* ('weapon'). But it is not difficult by practice to acquire a reasonable facility in reading Chaucer.

Unlike the Peterborough scribe, Chaucer often uses double letters to indicate a long vowel, as in *maad* and *eeris*. In some such words the vowel has since been shortened, e.g. in *deed* ('dead') and *look* ('look'), but in Chaucer we must pronounce it long.

Chauntecleer and Pertelote are a courtly pair of birds, and address one another by the polite pronouns *ye* and *you*, not by the familiar *thou* and *thee*. You will notice that Chaucer consistently maintains the distinction between nominative *ye* and accusative *you* ('Fy on *yow*' but 'Now han *ye* lost myn herte'). A personal pronoun that we have not met in any earlier passage, but which is normal in Chaucer, is *she*. The origin of this word is a bit of a puzzle. The Old English word was *hēo*, and forms like *she* are not found until the twelfth century, the first recorded example being *scæ* in the Peterborough Chronicle under the year 1140. It seems that the form arose in the East Midlands and spread from there, becoming the normal form in literary English by the middle of the fourteenth century. It is possible that both *she* and its Northern variant *sho* in fact developed directly out of Old English *hēo*, since in some dialects there seem to have been sound changes that could have produced these results. Or there may have been influence from *sēo*, the feminine form of the definite article. Whatever its origin, the form probably spread so successfully because it provided a clear distinction between 'he' and 'she'.

Notice the southern plural form *eyen* ('eyes'), but also the non-southern plural *eeris* ('ears') (where Old English had *ēaran*), an example of the gradual displacement of the *-en* plural ending by *-es* spreading from the north. The form *tweye* is from the Old English masculine *twēgen* (from which is also derived our *twain*); the form *two* (which is also found in Chaucer) is from the Old English feminine *twā*.

In the verbs, Chaucer has a singular ending *-eth* or *-th* ('any womman *seith*') and a plural ending *-en* or *-n* ('we alle *desiren*'). The *-eth* type of singular inflexion was normal in the South all through the Middle English period, and we regularly find forms like *he saith* or *he sayeth*, *he walketh*, and so on. The forms with *-s* (*he says*, *he walks*) spread from the North, and were not predominant in the standard literary language until the sixteenth or seventeenth century.

Notice the absence of continuous tenses: Chauntecleer says 'I *romed* up and doun', where it is more natural today to say 'I *was strolling* up and down'. Perfect tenses, on the other hand, are common in Chaucer, as in 'Now han ye lost myn herte'. The opening words of the passage, *Me mette*, have been translated 'I dreamed'; literally, however, they mean something like 'it dreamed to me' (*me* being a dative). Such impersonal constructions are fairly common in Old and Middle English; a survival of one in Modern English is the word *methinks*, from Old English *mē þyncþ*, 'it seems to me'.

The striking thing about the vocabulary of the passage, compared with the Peterborough one, is the large number of words borrowed from French, like *beest*, *areest*, *colour*, *remenant*, *caused*, *coward*, *feith*, and so on. Quite a number of them are names for moral qualities, especially the kind that would be discussed in courtly circles (*hardy*, *avantour*, *coward*, *secree*). It is partly the vocabulary that makes Chaucer seem so much more modern than the Peterborough passage, but partly too it is the word order; in fact there is little in the word order of the Chaucer passage which would not be possible in Modern English, and not much in the syntax. In Chaucer, we feel that Modern English is not so very far away.

CHAPTER XI

EARLY MODERN ENGLISH

THE LATE Middle Ages had seen the triumph of the English language in England, and the establishment once more of a standard form of literary English. This did not mean, however, that English was now entirely without a rival: Latin still had great prestige as the language of international learning, and it was a long time before English replaced it in all fields. Even the natural scientists, the proponents of the New Philosophy, often wrote in Latin. The philosopher of the new science, Francis Bacon, wrote his *Advancement of Learning* in English, but the book that he intended as his major contribution to scientific method, the *Novum Organum*, was in Latin. And the three greatest scientific works published by Englishmen between 1600 and 1700 were all in Latin – Gilbert's book on magnetism (1600), Harvey's on the circulation of the blood (1628), and Newton's *Principia* (1689), which propounded the theory of gravitation and the laws of motion. However, by about 1700 Latin had fallen into disuse as the language of learning in England, and Newton's *Opticks*, published in 1704, was in English.

ENGLISH VERSUS LATIN

In the defeat of Latin and the final establishment of English as the sole literary medium in England, quite an important part was played by the religious disputes that raged from the fifteenth to the seventeenth century. At the time of the Reformation, controversialists wanted to be read by as large a public as possible. Since many of the people who were attracted by Protestantism were of humble origins, and lacked a classical education, this meant that controversial books and pamphlets tended to be written in English. When Sir Thomas More wrote for the entertainment of the learned men of Europe, as in the *Utopia*, he wrote in Latin, but when he was drawn into the domestic religious controversy against the Reformers he wrote books and pamphlets in English. Milton, similarly, more than a century later, wrote defences of the English people and the English republic which were intended for the learned men of Europe, and these were in Latin; but the bulk of his controversial prose (on episcopacy, divorce, the freedom of the press, and so on) was intended to have an immediate impact on English politics, and was written in English.

Another factor that worked in favour of English was the rise of social and occupational groups which had little or no Latin, but which nevertheless had something to say – which of course they said in English. Such were many of the practical men of sixteenth- and seventeenth-century England – skilled craftsmen, instrument makers, explorers, navigators. A gentleman-scientist like Gilbert wrote in Latin, but there were plenty of Elizabethan treatises on practical subjects like navigational instruments, warfare, and so on, which were written in English for the plain man, and sometimes by him. Here, obviously, an important part was played by the invention of printing, and the spread of literacy which followed it.

A third factor in favour of English was the increase in national feeling which accompanied the rise of the modern nation-state in the fifteenth and sixteenth centuries. The medieval feeling that a man was a part of Christendom was replaced by the modern feeling that a man is an Englishman or a Frenchman or an Italian. This change in feeling seems to be the result of changes in economic and political organization. The medieval system of holding land from a lord by personal service, in which a man could be lord and vassal of different fiefs in several countries, and in which power was decentralized, was replaced by a system in which a powerful and centralized state apparatus attended to the interests of a national merchant class, in direct competition with the governments and merchants of other countries. This increase in national feeling led to a greater interest and pride in the national language, while the language of international Christendom, Latin, slowly fell into the background. The new nationalism led to conscious attempts to create a vernacular literature to vie with that of Greece or Rome, and both Spenser's *Faery Queen* (1590) and Milton's *Paradise Lost* (1667) were attempts to do for English what Homer and Virgil had done for Greek and Latin.

But, while English was thus establishing its supremacy over Latin, it was at the same time more under the influence of Latin than at any other time in its history. The Renaissance was the period of the rediscovery of the classics in Europe. In England there was quite a revival of Greek scholarship, symbolic of which was the foundation of St Paul's School by Dean Colet in 1509. But always it was Latin that was of major importance, and we see the constant influence of Latin literature, Latin rhetorical theories, the Latin language.

LOAN WORDS FROM LATIN

One result of this Latin influence on English during the Renaissance was the introduction of a large number of Latin words into the language. We have already seen that the influx of French words in the Middle English period had predisposed English speakers to borrow words from abroad. In the Renaissance, this predisposition was given full scope, and there was a flood of Latin words. The peak period was between about 1550 and 1650.

These were not, of course, the first Latin words to be borrowed by English. We have already seen how words like *street*, *mint*, and *wine* were borrowed while the English were still on the continent, and words like *bishop* and *minster* during the Old English period. Quite a few Latin words were borrowed, too, during the Middle English period: they include religious terms, like *requiem* and *gloria*; words from the law courts, like *client*, *executor*, *conviction*, and *memorandum*; medical and scientific words like *recipe*, *dissolve*, *distillation*, *concrete*, *comet*, and *equator*; and numbers of abstract words, like *adoption*, *conflict*, *dissent*, *imaginary*, *implication*.

In early Modern English, however, the trickle of Latin loans becomes a river, and by 1600 it is a deluge. Some of the words were taken over bodily in their Latin form, with their Latin spelling, like *genius* (1513), *species* (1551), *cerebellum* (1565), *militia* (1590), *radius* (1597), *torpor* (1607), *specimen* (1610), *squalor* (1621), *apparatus* (1628), *focus* (1644), *tedium* (1662), *lens* (1693), and *antenna* (1698). Not, of course, that they were always taken over with their original meaning: *lens*, for example, is the Latin for 'lentil', and was applied to pieces of optical glass because a double-convex lens is shaped like a lentil seed. Other words, however, were adapted, and given an English form. For example, the Latin ending *-atus* is sometimes replaced by *-ate*, as in *desperate* and *associate*. In other cases the Latin inflexion is left out, as in *complex* and *dividend* (Latin *complexus*, *dividendum*). This reshaping is often influenced by the forms of French words derived from Latin; for example, the Latin ending *-tas* sometimes becomes English *-ty*, as in *celerity* (Latin *celeritas*), on the analogy of similar words borrowed via French. And in fact it is often difficult to be sure whether a word has come into English direct from Latin or via French.

These Latin loans tend to be learned words. Many of them are scientific terms, like *pollen*, *vacuum*, *equilibrium*, *momentum*. Some are mathematical, like *area*, *radius*, *series*, and *calculus*. A number are legal terms, like *alias*, *caveat*, and *affidavit*. There are everyday words too, like *album*, *miser*, *circus*. But in general they are the kind of words that are introduced into a language through the medium of writing rather than in speech.

They did not enter the language without opposition, and there are numerous attacks in the sixteenth century on the 'inkhorn terms', as they were called. For example, in Thomas Wilson's influential book *The Art of Rhetoric* (1553) there is a well-known attack on them, of which the following is a part:

Among all other lessons this should first be learned, that wee never affect any straunge ynkehorne termes, but to speake as is commonly receiued: neither seeking to be ouer fine, nor yet liuing ouer-carelesse; vsing our speeche as most men doe, and ordering our wittes as the fewest haue done. Some seeke so far for outlandish English, that they forget altogether their mothers language. . . . The vnlearned or foolish phantasticall . . . wil so Latin their tongues, that the simple can not but wonder at their talke, and thinke surely they speake by some reuelation. I know them that thinke *Rhetorique* to stande wholie vpon darke wordes, and hee that can catche an ynke horne terme by the taile, him they coumpt to be a fine Englisheman, and a good *Rhetorician*.

No doubt such attacks were to some extent provoked by the absurdities of a lunatic fringe, who were also ridiculed in the theatre. Such ridiculous affecters of Latinisms are for example Holofernes in Shakespeare's *Love's Labour's Lost* and Crispinus in Ben Jonson's *Poetaster*. But attacks and ridicule could not stop the tide of Latin loans, and the words held up to ridicule are often ones that have since become fully accepted and now seem quite unexceptionable. For example, the ridiculous words used by Crispinus in *Poetaster* include nice specimens like *lubrical*, *turgidous*, *oblatrant*, and *furibund*; but they also include *retrograde*, *reciprocal*, *defunct*, *spurious*, and *strenuous*. Besides, there were plenty of people to defend Latinisms, and even Wilson admits that some of them are all right. And Shakespeare may make fun of Holofernes and his pedantry, but he himself is no purist, and is a great user of new words.

THE REMODELLING OF WORDS

Not only did Latin influence bring in new words; it also caused existing words to be reshaped in accordance with their real or supposed Latin etymology. An example of this can be seen near the end of the passage from Wilson's *Art of Rhetoric* quoted above: the word *coumpt*. This is simply a respelling of *count*, which was a Middle English loan from Anglo-Norman *counter*, descended from the Latin verb *computare*. Wilson's spelling of the word has been influenced by the Latin, which he no doubt felt was the more 'correct' form. Similarly, we owe the *b* in our modern spelling of *debt* and *doubt* to Renaissance etymologizing, for the earlier spellings of these were *dette* and *doute*, which were their forms in Old French; the *b* was inserted through the influence of Latin *debitum* and *dubitare*. In the case of *debt* and *doubt* the change was merely one of spelling, for the *b* has never been pronounced in English; and the same is true of the *p* inserted in *receipt* and the *c* in *indict*. But there are cases where the actual pronunciation of a word was altered under Latin influence. Thus in Middle English we find the words *descrive, parfit, assaut, verdit,* and *aventure*, which in the Renaissance were remodelled under Latin influence to *describe, perfect, assault, verdict,* and *adventure*. An odd survival of Middle English *aventure* is seen in the phrase 'to draw a bow at a venture' (from *I Kings* xxii. 34), where *at a venture* is a misdivision of *at aventure*, meaning 'at random'.

Some of the Renaissance remodellings are based on false etymologies, so that they have the awkward disadvantage of combining pedantry with bad scholarship. Such is the case with *advance* and *advantage*, remodelled from Middle English *avance* and *avantage*. The modern forms obviously arose from the belief that the initial *a-* represented the Latin prefix *ad-*, but in fact both words derive from French *avant*, which comes from Latin *ab ante*. A similar case is the word *admiral*, a reformation of earlier *amiral*. This word came into English from French, but the French had it from Arabic, where it occurred as the first two words of titles like *amir al bahr*, 'commander of the sea'. In this case, however, we cannot blame Renaissance pedantry alone for the *ad-*, for the form *admiral* is found in Middle English, and conversely *ammiral* is found in Milton. The change in this instance may have been encouraged by the resemblance to *admirable*.

LOAN WORDS FROM OTHER LANGUAGES

Although Latin was the main source of new words in the Renaissance, a number were borrowed from other languages too. Quite a few were from classical Greek, though in many cases these came via Latin or French. They tended to be learned words, and many of them are technical terms of literary criticism, rhetoric, or the natural sciences. Literary and rhetorical terms direct from Greek include *pathos*, *phrase*, and *rhapsody*; via Latin came many more, including *irony*, *drama*, *rhythm*, *trochee*, and *climax*; and there were a few via French, like *ode*, *elegy*, and *scene*. Scientific terms direct from Greek include *larynx* and *cosmos*, while via French came *cube* and *acoustic*, but the majority came via Latin, like *anemone*, *caustic*, *cylinder*, *stigma*, *python*, *electric*, and *energy*.

Quite a number of words were borrowed from Italian and Spanish. Part of a young gentleman's education was the grand tour of the continent, and France, Italy, and Spain were especially favoured. In the sixteenth century there are frequent sarcastic references to the gallant who comes back from the continent affecting foreign clothes, customs, and morals, and larding his speech with foreign words. Italy was particularly influential, and Italian has left its mark on our vocabulary. When we think of Italian words in English, we no doubt think first of words connected with the arts, and especially with music; most of these words are in fact later importations, mainly from the eighteenth century, but a few were borrowed in the Renaissance period: for example, *madrigal* and *opera* in music, *sonnet* in literature, *fresco*, *cameo*, and *relief* in the visual arts, *cornice* and *cupola* in architecture. But in this early period there were other fields of activity where the Italians made an even greater impression. One was warfare, in which we have such Italian words as *squadron*, *parapet*, *salvo*, and *bandit*. Another was commerce, and here belong such Italian loans as *traffic*, *contraband*, *argosy*, and *frigate*.

Fewer words were borrowed from Spanish, but here again commerce and warfare are prominent: *cask*, *cargo*, *anchovy*, *sherry*, *armada*, *galleon*, *parade*. The Spaniards were famous for the formality of their manners, and there is a loan word that puts this in a nutshell: *punctilio*. Their lighter moments are reflected in *guitar* and *spades* (the suit in cards, meaning 'swords'). Since the early exploration of America was to a great extent carried out by the Spaniards and the Portuguese, many early words for specifically American things came into English via Spanish or Portuguese. Thus from Spanish came *mosquito*, *potato*, and *cannibal*, which is a variant of *caribal*, meaning 'Carib, inhabitant of the Caribbean'. And from Portuguese we have *flamingo*, *molasses*, and *coconut*.

The other fair-sized source of loan words in the Renaissance was Low German, in which we can lump together Dutch, Flemish, and the dialects of northern Germany. These regions had had close commercial contacts with England ever since the Norman Conquest, and many of the words borrowed by English have to do with seafaring and trade. From the Middle English period, for example, date *luff*, *skipper*, *firkin*, and *deck*. Sixteenth-century loans include *cambric*, *dock*, *splice*, and *yacht*, while in the seventeenth century we find *keelhaul*, *cruise*, *yawl*, and *smack*. The Dutch were also famous for painting (seventeenth-century *easel*, *sketch*, *stipple*) and for drinking (Middle English *booze*, seventeenth-century *brandy*).

CHANGES IN PRONUNCIATION

In pronunciation, great changes had taken place during the fifteenth century, so that Shakespeare's pronunciation differed considerably from Chaucer's, but differed only in small ways from that of today. The biggest series of changes between Middle and Modern English is often called the Great Vowel Shift. This was a change in the quality of all the long vowels, which went on over a considerable period, and was not fully completed until about 1700, but which was especially rapid in the fifteenth century. The essentials of the Great Vowel Shift are shown in the following table:

| Front vowels | $\bar{a}$ → ea → ee → $\bar{\imath}$ → diphthong |
| Back vowels | oa → oo → $\bar{u}$ → diphthong |

In this table, the symbols stand for the long vowels of Middle English, with the values that we have already assigned them.

That is, $\bar{a}$ is the vowel heard in Modern English *father*, or perhaps better in German *Vater*; *ea* is an open vowel, with a quality like the first element of *air*; *ee* is a close vowel, like that of German *Weh* or French *été*; and *i* is like the *i* of *machine*. Similarly with the back vowels: *oa* is an open sound like the *aw* of *law*; *oo* is a close sound like the vowel of German *wo* or French *beau*; and $\bar{u}$ is the sound heard in Modern English *lunar* or *food*.

The arrows show the direction of the change. It will be seen that similar changes took place among the back and the front vowels, and that all vowels became closer in quality, except for the two which were already as close as they could be, and these became diphthongized. Thus the back open vowel *oa*, used in words like *goat* and *hope*, became the close *oo* sound; in the late eighteenth century this developed in southeastern England into the diphthong which is heard today. At the same time, the close *oo* sound, which was used in words like *tool* and *food*, became even closer, and by 1500 had become the $\bar{u}$ sound heard in those words today. Simultaneously, the $\bar{u}$ sound, often spelt *ou* or *ow* (*house*, *how*), became a diphthong; in Shakespeare's time this probably started from a rather central position, somewhat like the vowel of *go* in southeastern speech today, but during the seventeenth century it reached its present-day quality.

The changes among the long front vowels were somewhat similar. In the fifteenth century, the $\bar{a}$ sound (used in *bake* and *dame*) became closer, and in some dialects it had by the sixteenth century reached the position of *ea*. It did not stop at that point, however, but continued to get closer, and in the second half of the seventeenth century reached the position of *ee*; the diphthongization heard in present-day southeastern speech did not take place until about 1800. Meantime, Middle English *ee* (used in *meet*, *see*, *field*) had been made closer, and by about 1500 had become the $\bar{i}$ sound heard in those words today. At the same time, Middle English *i* (used in *mice*, *five*) became diphthongized; in Shakespeare's time this diphthong probably began from rather a central position, but the modern pronunciation was reached during the seventeenth century.

The development of Middle English *ea* is more problemati-cal, but it is clear that in the sixteenth century it was still kept distinct from *ee* in standard speech: we can be sure that Shakespeare distinguished in pronunciation between *meat* and *meet*, *sea* and *see*. It seems likely that, while *ee* developed into *ī*, *ea* moved up to the position of *ee*, so that round about 1600 the word *see* was pronounced as it is today, while *sea* had a vowel like German *Weh*. When Middle English *ā* also reached this position, in the second half of the seventeenth century, the two sounds fell together, and there is evidence to show that, in the standard language, the same vowel was then used in *sea*, *meat*, *dame*, and *make*. This is no longer the case today, of course, for the *sea* and *meat* vowel has fallen together with the *see* and *meet* vowel in the modern standard language, not with the *dame* and *make* vowel. This can only be explained if we suppose that there were two different styles of speech, perhaps belonging to two different social groups, and that one of them supplanted the other as the standard form of speech. It seems likely, in fact, that there was a variant pronunciation going right back to Middle English, in which the *ea* sound had changed into, or been replaced by, the *ee* sound; and that in the eighteenth century this variant pronunciation replaced the other in educated speech. There are just a few relics of the older style of pronunciation: *great*, *steak*, *break*, and *yea*, as their spelling suggests, all had Middle English *ea*, and they must have been retained from the style of speech in which *ea* became identical with *ā*.

By contrast, there was relatively little change in the short vowels, which continued in early Modern English to be pro-nounced in much the same way as in Middle English. In the seventeenth century, a change took place in the short *u*. In Middle English, this had the sound that it has in present-day *put*, not the sound that it has in *cut*; and words like *cut* then had the *put* vowel. In the seventeenth century it developed into our *cut* vowel, except in certain words where the influence of neighbouring labial consonants or of *l* preserved the old vowel (as in *bull*, *full*, *pull*, *wolf*, *bush*, *pudding*). At this stage the two sounds were merely contextual variants, members of the same phoneme. Since then, however, the two sounds have appeared in other words, and are now sometimes contrasted with each other, and so they constitute two separate phonemes. For example, the word *luck* had the short *u* vowel which regularly underwent the change in the seventeenth century. The word *look*, on the other hand, originally had a long *ō*, as its spelling suggests; this became *ū* in the Great Vowel Change, and this was later shortened. But the shortening took place *after* the operation of the change in the seventeenth century, and so was not affected by this change. In consequence, we now have the two words *luck* and *look* which are distinguished from one another solely by the two different short *u* sounds, which must therefore belong to different phonemes.

The changes in the consonants in the transition from Middle to Modern English were also relatively unimportant. For example, the *w* was lost in words like *sword* and *two*; the final *b* was lost in words like *climb*, *comb*, and *lamb*; words like Middle English *fader* and *hider* became Modern English *father* and *hither*; and the *gh* sound (pronounced rather like the *ch* in German *Licht*) was lost in words like *light*, *eight*, *height*, and *high*. There were also a number of small changes in the course of the early Modern English period: in the seventeenth century, for example, the initial *k* was lost in words like *knee* and *knight*, and the *t* was lost in words like *castle*, *bristle*, *Christmas*, and *soften*.

A Specimen of Early Modern English

As an example of early Modern English I have chosen an extract from a sixteenth-century sermon in praise of thieves and thievery, said to have been delivered by one Parson Haben, standing on a molehill at Hartley Row near Bagshot, at the commandment of seven thieves, who, after they had robbed him, commanded him to preach to them. The parson gave them a splendid extempore sermon in praise of their profession, but it had a sting in its tail:

As for stealinge, that is a thinge vsuall: who stealeth not? For not only you that haue besett me, but many other in many places. . . . And if you liste to looke in the whole course of the Bible, you shall find that theves have bin belovid of God. For Iacobe, when he came oute of Mesopotamia, did steale his vncles lambes; the same Iacobe stale his brother Esawes blessinge; and that God saide, 'I haue chosen Iacob and refused Esawe'. The Children of Israell, when they came oute of Egippe, didd steale the Egippsians Iewells and ringes, and God comaunded them soe to doe. David, in the dayes of Ahemelech the preiste, came into the temple and stole awaye the shewe bread; and yet God saide, 'This is a man accordinge to myne owne harte'. Alsoe Christ himsellfe, when he was here vppon earth, did take an asse, a colte, which was none of his owne. And you knowe that God saide, 'This is my nowne sone, in whome I delighte'.

Thus maye you see that most of all God delighteth in theves. I marvell, therefore, that men can despise your lives, when that you are in all poynts almost like vnto Christe; for Christ hade noe dwellinge place – no more haue you. Christe, therefore, at the laste, was laide waite for in all places – and soe are you. Christe alsoe at the laste was called for – and soe shall you be. He was condemned – soe shall you be. Christe was hanged – soe shall you be. He descended into hell – so shall you. But in one pointe you differ. He assendid into heauen – soe shall you never, without Gods mercye, which God graunte for his mercyes sake. Toe whom, with the Sonne and the Holye Goste, be all honour and glory for euer and euer. Amen.

After this good sermon ended, which edefied them soe much, they hadd soe muche compassion on him, that they gave him all his mony agayne, and vij s. more for his sermon.

And seven shillings was quite a lot of money in those days, when a labourer's wage was sixpence a week.

If the passage has a quaintly archaic look to the modern eye, that is surely due mainly to the spelling: if you put it into modern spelling it is really very close to present-day usage. There are of course small differences. The author says 'many other' where we should say 'many others'. He has an obsolete form *stale*, though in fact a little later he also uses the modern form *stole*, which is a sixteenth-century formation on analogy with the past participle *stolen*. He has the archaic phrase *if you liste* ('if you like'). He writes *myne* before a vowel, where we write *my*, and makes an incorrect word division in *my nowne*, which is exactly like *my nuncle* and similar cases that we discussed earlier. He writes *when that*, instead of *when*. He says that the thieves gave the parson his money *again*, where we should say that they gave it *back*. And there are small ways in which the word order differs from our own usage, for example in *a thinge vsuall* and *Thus maye you see*.

These differences are small, however, compared with the ways in which the passage differs from Middle English usage. The adjective and the definite article have lost all their inflexions, and so are indeclinable. The noun inflexions are as today, with the plural in *-s* (*theves, ringes, poynts*) and the genitive singular also in *-s* (*his vncles lambes, Esawes blessinge*). In the latter case we should nowadays put an apostrophe before the *s* (*uncle's, Esau's*), but this is merely a spelling convention, and does not affect the pronunciation. The verbs have lost the *-n* inflexion which in the Chaucer passage we saw used for the plural and the infinitive: where Chaucer wrote *desiren* and *han*, Parson Haben says *differ* and *have*. He has indeed one verb inflexion that we no longer use, the third person singular *-eth* in *stealeth*, where we say *steals*. As we have already seen, this was the southern form in Middle English, and in the sixteenth century was being driven out by the northern *-s*. Shakespeare uses both forms, writing *he loveth* as well as *he loves*, but uses *-s* a good deal more frequently than *-eth*. The 1611 Bible, which regularly uses *-eth*, is consciously archaic. The final *-e* on words like *stealinge, steale, Iacobe*, and so on, is not an inflexion, since it was not pronounced.

Among the personal pronouns, you will notice that Haben uses the Scandinavian *them*, where Chaucer still used the English form *hem*. And he regularly uses *you* as the nominative, whereas Chaucer had distinguished between nominative *ye* and accusative *you*. The disappearance of the distinction between *you* and *ye* also affects the phrase *if you liste*. Originally, *list* (Old English *lystan*) was an impersonal verb, meaning 'it pleases': so *him lyste* meant 'it was pleasing to him', and *ēow lyst* meant 'it is pleasing to you', the pronouns being dative. Similarly in Middle English we find forms like *me list* and *you list*. In Middle English and early Modern English there is a tendency for such impersonal constructions to disappear, and this process is encouraged by the acceptance of *you* as a nominative, for then phrases like *you list* can be read as if *you* were the subject of an ordinary personal verb, parallel to *you wish*, *you desire*, and so on. In fact in our passage it is impossible to tell whether the author thought of the construction as personal or impersonal, for there are clear examples to show that both types existed in the language when he wrote: the personal construction (e.g. *he list*) had existed since Middle English times, but there are examples of the impersonal construction (e.g. *me list*) well on into the seventeenth century.

The Dummy Auxiliary

There is however one way in which the passage differs from modern usage, and which is more important than it appears at first sight. The parson asks 'Who stealeth not?', where today we should use the auxiliary verb *do* and say 'Who doesn't steal?'. On the other hand, Haben sometimes uses auxiliary *do* in places where we should not: he says for example that Jacob *did steal* his uncle's lambs, where we should say *stole*; in this case, Haben's *did steal* is not emphatic, but is merely a stylistic variant of *stole*, and he uses the two forms indifferently. The same is true of other sixteenth-century writers: Shakespeare can say 'I know him' or 'I do know him' indifferently, and 'Know you him?' or 'Do you know him?' equally indifferently.

So auxiliary *do* was used in early Modern English, but its use was not regulated as it is today.

In present-day English, auxiliary *do* is used in much the same way as the other English auxiliary verbs (*be, have, can, could, will,* etc.). As a class, they have four key uses: (1) They are used immediately before *not* (or its weak variants *n't* and *'t*) when a sentence is made negative: 'He may not come', 'I can't remember', 'They wouldn't know', 'He isn't coming'. (2) They are used before the subject of the sentence to form questions: 'May John come?', 'Can you remember?', 'Would they know?', 'Is he coming?'. The use of this construction serves to keep the subject of the sentence in front of the verb, thus preserving an important feature of Modern English word order. (3) They are used in echo repetitions: 'John will come, won't he?', 'You can't remember, can you?', 'He isn't coming, is he?'. (4) When stressed, they are used to assert emphatically the truth of the sentence as a whole: 'John *will* come', 'They *wouldn't* know', 'He *is* coming'. This gives a different effect from stressing any other word in the sentence, which produces only a partial contrast. Thus if I say '*John* will come' I mean 'John and not somebody else'; if I say 'John will *come*' I mean 'come but not do something else'; but if I say 'John *will* come' I am underlining my belief in the truth of the whole sentence.

These four ways of using auxiliaries are a central feature of the syntax of present-day English. If you look back to the Robert of Gloucester passage in Chapter IX, you will see a negative sentence of the form 'I ween there ne beeth in all the world countries none that ne holdeth to their own speech'. In the passage from the Peterborough Chronicle in Chapter X there is a negative sentence of the form 'Ne were never no martyrs so tortured'. These typical Middle English methods of negating sentences are no longer possible – we have to use an auxiliary followed by *not*.

Now the importance of auxiliary *do* in our present-day scheme is that it is the *dummy* auxiliary: it performs the four key functions of an auxiliary verb, but is empty of meaning. So we use it when we want to ask a question, or negate a sentence, or have an echo repetition, or underline the truth of a sentence, but when none of the other auxiliaries has an appropriate meaning: 'Do you know him?', 'We didn't go', 'She wants to come, doesn't she?', 'But John *does* live there'. Foreigners learning English are often puzzled by these uses of *do*, which they find queer; but it is important to see that, in terms of the structure of Modern English, they are not queer at all, but absolutely normal and central. What on the contrary *is* abnormal in present-day English is the survival of sentences like 'Have you a match?', which seem natural to most foreigners but which in fact are not in line with normal English usage for other verbs. It is notable, in fact, that such sentences are commonly replaced by ones like 'Have you got a match?' (British) or 'Do you have a match?' (American).

The establishment of *do* as a dummy auxiliary took place in early Modern English, but the present-day regulation of its use had not been reached in Shakespeare's day. The use of *do* as an auxiliary of some kind goes back to Old English (though there it is found mainly in close translations from the Latin), and is not uncommon in Middle English. Originally, however, it was not a dummy auxiliary, but had a *causative* sense. Thus we find Middle English sentence with the structure *He did them build a church*, which meant 'He caused them to build a church'. In some dialects we also find sentences with the structure *He did build a church*, which originally meant 'He caused a church to be built'. The non-causative use of *do* arose from sentences of this second type. It is not difficult to see how this happened: a sentence like *He built a church* can itself have a causative meaning, since we do not necessarily take it to mean that the person referred to built the church with his own hands; consequently, *He built a church* and *He did build a church* can mean exactly the same thing; and it is only a small step from this to use *did build* as equivalent to *built* in non-causative sentences.

The development of this non-causative use of *do* took place in the southwestern dialects in the late thirteenth century, and spread from there. At first it was mainly used in poetry, because it was a convenient device for putting a verb into rhyme position at the end of a line. For example, the late medieval poet John Lydgate, in his poem *London Lyckpeny*, writes the line

Then I hyed me into Est-Chepe

which he rhymes with 'heape'; but elsewhere in the same poem he has the line

Then vnto London I did me hye

which he rhymes with 'crye'. Here the choice of *hyed* or *did hye* is clearly a matter of metrical and rhyming convenience and nothing more. From verse the usage spread to prose, where it is first found about 1400. It spread slowly in the fifteenth century, and rapidly in the sixteenth, and at the same time the old causative use of *do* died out, its place being taken by *make* and *cause*. In Shakespeare's time, *do* is commonly used as an auxiliary empty of meaning, but its use is not yet regulated as it is today. This regulation takes place during the seventeenth century: *do* gradually drops out of affirmative sentences (except for the emphatic use), and comes to be used more and more regularly in negative and interrogative ones. The present-day situation was reached by about 1700.

CHAPTER XII

ENGLISH IN THE SCIENTIFIC AGE

BY ABOUT 1700, the main changes in pronunciation that made up the Great Vowel Shift were all completed. Forms like *loveth* had disappeared in ordinary educated speech, and been replaced by ones like *loves*. The pronouns *thou* and *thee*, and the corresponding verb forms like *lovest*, had disappeared from everyday educated use. Auxiliary *do* had come to be used as we use it today. And, all in all, the language had reached a stage at which its differences from present-day English were very small. This can be seen if we look at a piece of writing from the early eighteenth century. The following is an extract from one of the numbers of the *Spectator* for the year 1711; it was written by Joseph Addison, who was fond of ridiculing the Italian opera, which was then in vogue in London:

The next Step to our Refinement, was the introducing of Italian Actors into our Opera; who sung their Parts in their own Language, at the same Time that our Countrymen perform'd theirs in our native Tongue. The King or Hero of the Play generally spoke in Italian, and his Slaves answered him in English: The Lover frequently made his Court, and gained the Heart of his Princess in a Language which she did not understand. One would have thought it very difficult to have carry'd on Dialogues after this Manner, without an Interpreter between the Persons that convers'd together; but this was the State of the English Stage for about three Years.

At length the Audience grew tir'd of understanding Half the Opera, and therefore to ease themselves Entirely of the Fatigue of Thinking, have so order'd it at Present that the whole Opera is perform'd in an unknown Tongue. We no longer understand the Language of our own Stage; insomuch that I have often been afraid, when I have seen our Italian Performers chattering in the Vehemence of Action, that they have been calling us Names, and abusing us among themselves; but I hope, since we do put such an entire Confidence in them, they will not talk against us before our Faces, though they may do it with the same Safety as if it were behind our Backs. In the mean Time I cannot forbear thinking how naturally an Historian, who writes Two or Three hundred Years hence, and does not know the Taste of his wise Fore-fathers, will make the following Reflection, *In the Beginning of the Eighteenth Century, the Italian Tongue was so well understood in* England, *that Operas were acted on the publick Stage in that Language*.

If we feel that that piece of writing is very typical of its age, this is largely a matter of tone and style and outlook; there is very little in grammar, syntax, or vocabulary that would not be acceptable in present-day English. Addison writes *sung* where we use *sang* (though *sung* is common in substandard speech, and may yet come back into the literary language). We should perhaps write *At* instead of *In* at one point ('In the Beginning of the Eighteenth Century'). And there is one example of *do* used in an older way ('since we do put'), though this may possibly be an example of the emphatic use.

THE STANDARDIZATION OF SPELLING

Addison's spelling, too, is almost identical with ours. There are minor differences, like *carry'd* and *publick*, and there are small differences in punctuation and in the use of capital letters; but essentially the system of orthography is the one we use now. In Middle and early Modern English there had been no standard spelling: it varied from writer to writer, and even within the work of one writer. Even proper names were not fixed, and Shakespeare, in the three signatures on his will, uses two different spellings of his own surname (*Shakspere* and *Shakspeare*). A powerful force for standardization was the introduction of printing, and by the middle of the sixteenth century, although there was still no standard system, there were quite a number of widely accepted conventions. There was considerable discussion of the problem by grammarians and spelling reformers in both the sixteenth and the seventeenth century, partly because of the increased interest in the vernacular, and partly because people with a classical education wanted English to be 'fixed' in the way that classical Latin was fixed. This classical desire for a stable language was even stronger in the eighteenth century, a great age for grammarians and lexicographers, among whom the most famous is Dr Johnson; but in fact the standardization of English spelling had effectively taken place before that century opened, in the second half of the seventeenth century; and it has changed only in minor ways since that time.

However, the standardized spelling which became established in the late seventeenth century was already an archaic one, and broadly speaking it represented the pronunciation of English as it had been in late medieval times. This explains many of the oddities of present-day English spelling. We still preserve letters in our spelling which represent sounds that long ago ceased to be pronounced, like the *k* and *gh* of *knight*, the *t* in *castle*, the *w* in *wrong*. In some cases a sound change has taken place, but the spelling represents the older pronunciation, as in *clerk* and *Derby* (which would more reasonably be spelt *clark* and *Darby*). Distinctions are made in spelling where there is no longer any distinction in pronunciation, as in *meat* and *sea* beside *meet* and *see*. Conversely, new distinctions have arisen without being recognized in the spelling, so that we use the same letter to represent the vowels of *put* and *putt*. Diphthongs, like the vowel of *mice*, are often represented by a single letter, because the sound was a pure vowel in Middle English; and, conversely, modern monophthongs are sometimes represented by digraphs, like the *au* of *author* or the *ou* of *cough*, because in Middle English the sound was a diphthong. And superimposed on all this are the effects of Renaissance etymologizing, which accounts for such things as the *b* in *subtle* and the *p* in *receipt*. Such things have introduced inconsistencies into our spelling, and these are what is bad about it; within quite wide limits, the spelling conventions that a language adopts are a matter of indifference, but it is important that it should use them consistently.

One result of the inconsistencies of our spelling is the prevalence of *spelling pronunciations*. These arise when a word is given a new pronunciation through the influence of its spelling. This is especially likely to happen when universal education and the wide dissemination of books and newspapers introduce people to words in printed form which they have never heard pronounced in their home environment. But even ordinary everyday words may be given spelling pronunciations: thus the influence of the spelling leads many people to pronounce the *t* in *often* and *waistcoat*, the *th* in *clothes*, the *h* in *forehead*, the *l* in *Ralph*, and the *w* in *towards*; these had been lost in the traditional pronunciation, which would be better represented by the spellings *offen*, *weskit*, *cloze*, *forrid*, *Rafe*, and *tords*; in all six of these words, with the sole exception of *forehead*, the spelling pronunciation is now fully accepted in educated speech.

CHANGES IN PRONUNCIATION

In pronunciation no major changes have taken place since Addison's time, but there have been a number of minor ones. Perhaps the most important has been the disappearance of *r* before consonants and before a pause. Formerly, the *r* was always pronounced in words like *barn* and *person* and *father*; but today, in southeastern English and also in many kinds of American speech, the *r* is never pronounced in words like *barn* and *person*, and is pronounced in words like *father* only if they occur immediately before a vowel (as in the phrase 'father and mother'). The weakening of *r* before consonants and before a pause had begun in the sixteenth century or even earlier, but the final disappearance of the *r* in educated speech did not take place until the middle of the eighteenth century.

However, although *r* has disappeared from such positions, it has left its mark on the words where it was formerly pronounced, for, before disappearing, it caused changes in the vowel that preceded it. In Middle English, *arm* had the same vowel as *cat*, *birch* the same vowel as *chin*, *here* the same vowel as *see*. The *r* caused three kinds of change: lengthening, change of quality, and diphthongization. The changes mostly occur in early Modern English, but one of them goes back to Middle English times, and some were not completed until the eighteenth century.

Examples of the lengthening process are *arm*, *bark*, *card*, and *corn*, *horse*, *storm*. These originally had short *a* and *o*, which were lengthened in the seventeenth century.

An example of change of quality is the development of *er* (with a short vowel as in *bed*) to *ar* (with a short *a*). This took place in late Middle English, and affected many words, though not all. So Middle English *sterre*, *ferre*, and *ferme* became early Modern English *star*, *far*, and *farm*; then the *a* was lengthened in the seventeenth century, and the *r* lost in the eighteenth, giving our present-day pronunciation. In words in which *er* failed to develop into *ar*, like *certain* and *verse*, the *e* developed in the seventeenth century into a central vowel (like the *er* of *father*); in the eighteenth century, this vowel was lengthened and the *r* was lost, giving the present-day pronunciation. In a few words, double forms were preserved, one with *er* and one with *ar*; such doublets include *person* and *parson*, *university* and *varsity*, *errant* and *arrant*, *perilous* and *parlous*.

The process of diphthongization before *r* took place in the long vowels. In Middle English, *care* had the same vowel as *bake* (a long *ā* sound), and *deer* the same vowel as *deep* (the *ee* sound of Middle English); but before *r* these vowels became diphthongs round about 1600. Similar changes have produced the diphthongs in *poor*, *flour*, *scarce*, and *pear*.

Various other dependent changes have taken place in Modern English, though none as far-reaching in their effects as those caused by *r*. For example, after *w* there has been a change of *a* to *o*, so that *swan* and *watch* no longer have the same vowel as *ran* and *match*; this change began in the seventeenth century and was completed in the eighteenth; it did not take place, however, when the *a* was followed by a velar consonant, as in *wax*, *wagon*, and *twang*. Another change has been the lengthening of short *a* and *o* before the voiceless fricatives *f*, *s*, and *th*, as in *after*, *castle*, *bath*, *often*, *cross*, *cloth*. These lengthenings took place in the seventeenth century, and became fashionable in the eighteenth, but forms with short vowels have continued to exist beside them in some styles of speech. The short *a* is normal in the north of England, for example; and in the present century the forms with lengthened *o* (now pronounced like the vowel of *law*) have been dropping out of use in the standard language, the forms with short *o* being used instead: so that it now sounds rather old-fashioned to use a long vowel in words like *often* and *cross*.

Shortening of vowels has taken place in the modern period in numerous words, especially words of one syllable. You can often recognize such shortenings from the spelling, which shows that the word had a long vowel in Middle English, for example *book*, *foot*, *dead*, *sweat*, *sieve*, *Greenwich*. In the proverbial phrase 'to lose (or spoil) the ship for a ha'porth of tar', the word *ship* is a shortening of *sheep*.

THE INFLUENCE OF SCIENTIFIC WRITING

The seventeenth century saw the triumph of the scientific outlook in England, and science has had a pervasive influence on the language and the way it has been used during the past three hundred years. We have already seen how Latin gave way to English as the language of science and scholarship. The rise of scientific writing in English helped to establish a simple referential kind of prose as the central kind in modern English. Other kinds of prose continued to exist, of course, but a rhetorical style ceased to be the norm, and what we may call *the plain style* became central, the background against which other kinds of prose were examined. The plain style is not of course confined to science; it is found in all kinds of expositional writing – history, philosophy, literary criticism, and so on. Nor, unfortunately, do all scientists write in a plain style. But scientific writing, and the scientific attitude in general, undoubtedly played a part in the establishment of this style.

In the second half of the seventeenth century, the influence of science on the way language was used was quite conscious. In 1667 Thomas Sprat wrote a history of the Royal Society, the first scientific society in England, and still the most famous. In this book, he made an attack on rhetorical and figurative language, which he said the members of the Royal Society had rejected:

> They have therefore been most rigorous in putting in execution, the only Remedy that can be found for this *extravagance*: and that has been, a constant Resolution, to reject all the amplifications, digressions, and swellings of style: to return back to the primitive purity, and shortness, when men delivered so many *things*, almost in an equal number of *words*. They have exacted from all their members, a close, naked, natural way of speaking; positive expressions; clear senses; a native easiness; bringing all things as near the Mathematical plainness, as they can: and preferring the language of Artizans, Countrymen, and Merchants, before that of Wits, or Scholars.

Sprat's primitive purity and shortness is of course a myth: the kind of style he is describing is a highly sophisticated achievement, and not at all primitive. But the passage shows clearly that the seventeenth-century scientists had their own ideas about the way language should be used.

THE SCIENTIFIC VOCABULARY

However, the more obvious influence of science on the language has been in the expansion of the scientific vocabulary. Scientists have needed technical terms for an enormous number of things: for example, for the names of the branches and sub-branches of science (*zoology*, *chemistry*, *histology*, *genetics*);

for newly discovered or invented substances (*oxygen, uranium, benzene, nucleic acid, nylon*); for the various parts of an organism (*femur, flagellum, pericarp*); for the various kinds of plant and animal (*Angelica sylvestris, Calidris ferruginea, Homo sapiens*); for various kinds of scientific instrument (*barometer, electroscope, vernier, cyclotron*); for units of measurement (*metre, micron, dyne, erg, ohm*); for states and processes and relationships (*anaesthesia, photosynthesis, symbiosis*); for the description of shapes and qualities (*ovate, glabrous*); for postulated entities (*phlogiston, ether, gene, neutrino*); and in general for an enormous number of objects and concepts of all kinds. One authority has estimated that the technical vocabulary of the natural sciences now runs into several *millions* of items. Nobody, obviously, can know more than a fraction of this vocabulary: the greater part of it must belong to the narrowly specialist field. However, there is a considerable scientific vocabulary which is more widely known, and some of the very common words are familiar to the man in the street (like *cell, atom, nucleus, volt, molecule*).

In forming this enormous vocabulary, the scientists have drawn on various sources. One device is to take a word already in everyday use and give it a special scientific meaning; this is what the chemists have done with *salt*, the botanists with *pollen* and *fruit*, the biologists with *parasite*, the metallurgists with *fatigue*, and the physicists with *work, force, power, current*, and *resistance*. Another way is to take over words bodily from another language; thus from Latin have been taken such words as *bacillus, corolla, cortex, focus, genus, quantum, saliva*, and *stamen*; fewer words have been lifted from Greek, but there are some, like *cotyledon, iris, larynx, pyrites*, and *thorax*. But by far the commonest way of providing new scientific words is to invent them, using Greek and Latin material. Thus there is no Greek word *chlorophyll*, but the English word is made up of Greek elements – *chloros* ('light green') and *phyllon* ('leaf'); the whole word does not of course mean 'light green leaf', but is the name for the substance in plants that gives them their green colour. Similarly, there is no Latin word *vitamin*, but this word has been coined from Latin elements, of which the main one is *vita* ('life'). Some words are mixed Latin and Greek, for example *haemoglobin*; this is the name of a protein substance in the blood, and is built up from a Greek word for 'blood', a Latin word for 'ball', and a suffix *-in* which could be equally well Greek or Latin.

The number of such words formed from classical elements, and especially Greek ones, is now enormous. It is sometimes objected to them that they are opaque, i.e. that their meaning is not self-evident to an Englishman in the way that a word formed from English elements might be. And there were some folksy reformers in the nineteenth century who wanted to re-place such classical coinages by English ones: electricity, for example, could be called *fireghost*, and the horizon would be called the *sky-sill*. Such arguments have had no effect, how-ever; and the classical words have the advantage of being in-telligible *internationally*. Moreover, in any specialist field, the research worker presumably gets to know the meanings of the classical elements commonly used there, so that the words are not opaque to him. Indeed, there are Greek elements that are so commonly used in forming English words that their mean-ing is understood by most educated Englishmen, even if they know no Greek. Such, for example, are elements like *mono* ('single'), *pyro* ('fire'), *bio* ('life'), *graph* ('write, draw'), *photo* ('light'), *phono* ('speech, sound'), *morph* ('shape, form'), *hydro* ('water'), *thermo* ('heat'), *micro* ('small'), and many more.

The great expansion of the scientific vocabulary during the last three hundred years has gone on at an ever-increasing pace. The sixteenth century had introduced especially words to do with the human body, like *skeleton*, *tibia*, *abdomen*, and *tendon*, and also a number of names of diseases, like *catarrh*, *epilepsy*, *mumps*, and *smallpox*. In the seventeenth century, too, the new scientific words were predominantly medical and biological (*vertebra*, *tonsil*, *pneumonia*, *lumbago*); but there were also quite a few new words in chemistry (including *acid*), in physics (including *atmosphere*, *equilibrium*, and *gravity*), and in mathematics (including *formula*, *logarithm*, and *series*). In the eighteenth century came an enormous expansion in the vocabulary of the biological sciences, for this was the great age of biological description and classification, as seen for example in the work of Linnaeus; from this period, therefore, come many of the descriptive terms of zoology and botany, like *albino*, *coleoptera*, *anther*, *fauna*, *dicotyledon*, *habitat*, *pistil*, and so on. The great changes in chemical theory in the late eighteenth century also produced many new words, including *hydrogen*, *oxygen*, *nitrogen*, and *molecule*. In the nineteenth century, the expansion became explosive; many specialized scientific fields were developing rapidly, and the majority of the new words have never had any circulation outside their own narrow sphere; a few, however, have got into common use, like *accumulator*, *dynamo*, *cereal*, *hibernate*, *pasteurize*, *conifer*, *ozone*, *metabolism*, and *aspidistra*.

In our own century, the flow has continued, especially in the newer fields like genetics and nuclear physics. Once again, a certain number of the new words have got into the language of the non-specialist. Nuclear physics, for example, has had a profound effect on us all, both in changing our conceptions of the universe and in confronting us with new and terrifying problems of war and human survival, and we all know words like *proton*, *neutron*, *electron*, *reactor*, *radioactive*, and *isotope*. This last word is especially connected in the popular mind with the medical applications of radioactive isotopes; and other new words that bear closely on our health have also obtained a wide circulation: *vitamin*, *penicillin*, *antibiotic*. Other words have obtained general currency because they are connected with new and widely used products of technology: *stratosphere* and *supersonic* are linked in our minds with airliners, and we all know about *nylon*, *television*, and *transistors*, because they are popular consumer goods. Some scientific words get taken into popular speech and used with a quite different meaning; this has recently happened, for example, with *atomic* (often used popularly to mean 'powerful, shattering') and with *allergic* (a word now commonly used to indicate disinclination or dislike).

The Expansion of the General Vocabulary

The expansion of the English vocabulary in the modern period has by no means been confined to scientific words. As a community changes, there is a constant demand for new words – to express new concepts or new attitudes, to denote new objects or institutions, and so on. During the past few centuries the change has been particularly great and society has become increasingly complex. And the growth of our vocabulary has been correspondingly great. New methods develop in commerce, and bring new words with them: *capital, discount, insurance, finance, budget*. New ideas and new institutions demand a new political vocabulary: *legislator, cabinet, prime minister, democrat, socialism*. New configurations of human experience emerge in the arts, and new words crystallize round them: *sentimental, romantic, aesthete, expressionist*. Even new recreations and pastimes produce new words, like *jazz* and *aqualung*, and so do new fashions, whether it be *doublet, crinoline, jeans*, or *bikini*. And so on.

The flood of new words in Modern English has had various sources. We have seen that most of the new scientific words are learned formations using classical elements, but this has not been the main way of acquiring new words in other spheres.

Loan Words.

We have continued to borrow words from other languages. Because of the growth of world trade, and Britain's large part in it, we have borrowed words from distant and exotic countries: *pyjamas* from India, *bamboo* from Malaya, *maize* from the West Indies, *budgerigar* from Australia, *tomato* from Mexico, *coffee* from Turkey, and *tea* from China. And many more. Nearer home, we have continued to borrow words from French – words connected with the arts (*critique, connoisseur, pointillism*), with clothes and fashion (*rouge, corduroy, suede*), with social life (*etiquette, parvenu, elite*), and more recently with motoring and aviation (*garage, hangar, chauffeur, fuselage, nacelle*). From the Dutch we have taken more nautical terms (*taffrail*, *schooner*), and from the Italians more words from the arts (*studio*, *replica*, *scenario*, *fiasco*). From German have come quite a few scientific words, especially in chemistry and mineralogy, like *paraffin*, *cobalt*, and *quartz*; the Germans have also given us a few words in wartime, like *strafe*, *blitz*, and *ersatz*. From other languages we borrow words occasionally when there is some special reason – like Afrikaans *apartheid* and Russian *sputnik* and *lunik*.

Altogether, loan words have continued to make a very respectable contribution to our vocabulary throughout the late Modern English period. But they cannot compare in number with the flood of French words in Middle English or of Latin words in the Renaissance. And in fact there have been other sources of new words which have been more important.

Affixation

An important method has been the use of prefixes and suffixes, which are added to existing English words or stems to form new words. Thus the prefix *un-* can be added to enormous numbers of words to give words like *unlucky*, *unconditional*, *untie*, *unfunny*, and so on. The prefix *de-* can be added to verbs to give forms like *denationalize*, *decontrol*, and *deration*, or can replace another prefix, as when *demote* is coined as the opposite of *promote*. And similarly with many other prefixes, like *dis-*, *pre-*, *anti-*, *pro-*, *mis-*. An example of a suffix is *-ize*, which can be added to adjectives (*national*, *miniature*, *tender*) or to nouns (*carbon*, *vitamin*, *vapour*) to form new verbs (*nationalize*, *carbonize*, etc.). From these in turn can be formed a new abstract noun ending in *-ization* (like *nationalization*, *carbonization*). Other active suffixes in Modern English include *-er* (*walker*, *bumper*), *-ee* (*detainee*, *employee*, *evacuee*), *-ist* (*anarchist capitalist*, *stockist*), and *-y* or *-ie* (*civvy*, *goalie*, *nappy*, *undies*). Most of these prefixes and suffixes are not of native origin, i.e. they have not come down to us from Old English but have been taken over from Greek, Latin, or French; this of course is of no importance – they have now become part of the English language and their origins are irrelevant. Many of them are in fact so familiar to us that we can use them for making spontaneous coinages in speech or writing ('anti-Common-Market', 'pre-Stalin', 're-transcribe', and such like).

Compounding

Another method of word formation that has been very prolific in the modern period is compounding, that is, the making of a new word by joining together two existing ones. In this way we have obtained such words as *airscrew*, *bandmaster*, *childlike*, *graveyard*, *nosedive*, *oatcake*, *offside*, *oilcloth*, *outcry*, *pigtail*, and so on. Some words are particularly prolific in forming new compounds: there are large numbers ending in *man* (like *postman*, *frogman*, *business-man*), and in present-day American there are large numbers of new adverbs ending in *-wise* (like *examinationwise*, *discussionwise*, and so on). We tend to treat such compounds as single words (*a*) if their meaning cannot be deduced from the sum of their parts, as in the case of *air-umbrella* and *bubble-car*, or (*b*) if they have the stress pattern of a single word, as in the case of *paperback* and *redbrick*. The importance of stress, and of the accompanying intonation pattern, can be seen if you compare *a blackbird* with *a black bird*, or *the greenhouse* with *the green house*.

When a compound word has become established, it may then in the course of time undergo phonetic changes which make it quite different from the words that originally made it up. The unstressed element is especially likely to change: for example, *nobleman* is an old compound word (going back to Middle English), and its second syllable no longer has the same vowel as the independent word *man*, but has been weakened down to an *er* sound (at any rate in the southeast of England). Sometimes the pronunciation of both elements diverges from that of their originals: *breakfast* is derived from *break* and *fast*, but no longer has the vowel of either. Other similar examples (all going back to the Middle English period or earlier) are *sheriff* ('shire reeve'), *holiday* ('holy day'), *woman* ('wife man'), *twopence*, and *garlic* ('gore leek', where the first element originally meant 'spear', and survives in dressmaking in the sense of 'gusset'). There are also cases where only the stressed element has diverged in pronunciation from its original, like *tadpole* ('toad poll', i.e. 'toad head'). Many of these vowel changes represent a shortening of the vowel at some period, either because it was unstressed (as in the *-lic* of *garlic*), or because it occurred before a group of consonants (*tadpole*), or because it occurred in the first syllable of a three-syllable word (*holiday*).

When such changes of pronunciation have taken place, a word-element with the new pronunciation may itself be used for making new compounds. Thus in southeastern English the ending *-man* (from words like *nobleman*) has been used to form new words like *postman* and *frogman*, in which the ending has never had the same pronunciation as the independent word *man*. In some cases, the pronunciation of such an element can change so much that it is no longer recognized as identical with the original word. An example is the ending *-ly*, in adjectives like *lovely*, *kingly*, *bodily*. This goes back to an Old English ending *-lic*, which originally was identical with the Old English independent word *lic*, meaning 'form, shape, body'. This survives in the word *lychgate*, so called because it was the roofed gate leading into the churchyard under which the body was placed while the funeral procession awaited the arrival of the clergyman. Moreover, our preposition *like* ('similar to') goes back to the Old English adjective *gelic* ('similar, equal'), which was derived from *lic* and basically meant something like 'having the same form as'. But phonetic change has obscured for us the relationship between *-ly*, *lych*, and *like*, which originally were all the same word. And now we think of *-ly* as a suffix, not as the second half of a compound word. It is in fact an example of the way in which a suffix can develop out of a full word. Now that we no longer feel any relationship between *-ly* and *like*, we can use the latter for forming a new series of compound words; so beside the word *lively*, which goes back to Old English *liflic*, we have the more recent formation *life-like*, which consists of what are, historically speaking, exactly the same two elements.

Conversion

A process which has led to quite a considerable expansion of the vocabulary, in both Middle and Modern English, is the one called 'conversion'. This is the transfer of a word from one grammatical category to another, for example from noun to verb, or from adjective to noun. The word *market*, borrowed from Norman French in the eleventh century, was originally used only as a noun, as when we say 'a market is held here every Saturday'; but since the seventeenth century we have also been able to use the word *market* as a verb, as when we say 'this detergent is marketed by I.C.I.'. This kind of change is very easy in Modern English, because of the loss of so many of our inflexions. There is nothing in the word *market*, taken in isolation, to show what part of speech it is, whereas the Latin *mercatus* (from which it is ultimately derived) shows immediately by its ending that it is not a verb.

In Old English, similarly, the ending of a word often proclaims what part of speech it is, and related words are formed by suffixes rather than by conversion. Thus there is an Old English noun *dōm* and a related verb *dēman*; these became Modern English *doom* and *deem*, but now we also have a verb *to doom*, formed by conversion from the noun, and recorded from the fifteenth century.

An example of a noun being formed from a verb is *ambush*; this was borrowed from the French in Middle English times, in the form *to enbush* or *to embush*, and is not found used as a noun until the late fifteenth century. The word *black*, on the other hand, was originally only an adjective (as in *a black hat*); later it came to be used also as a noun (*to wear black*) and as a verb (*to black boots*).

The process of conversion is especially popular in the present century. There are new verbs like *to feature*, *to film*, *to pinpoint*, *to headline*, *to process*, *to service*, *to audition*, *to garage*. New nouns include *a highup* and *a must*. And perhaps we could say that there are new adjectives like *key* ('a key man'), *teenage*, *backroom*, *off-the-record*, and *round-the-clock*; but it is in fact debatable whether these should be called adjectives, because they cannot be used in all positions which adjectives can normally occupy in the sentence: we can say that a man is *very important*, but not that he is *very key*. One particularly common type in recent years has been the compound noun formed by conversion from a corresponding verb: from the verb *to hand out* is formed the new noun *a handout*, and similarly with *buildup*, *walkout*, *setup*, *blackout*, *hairdo*, and *knowhow*. In these cases the verb usually has double stress (*to hánd óut*) and the noun single stress (*a hándout*).

Shortening, Blending, Proper Names

We have now covered the major sources of the great expansion of the vocabulary in the modern period, but there are also a number of minor ways in which new words have been acquired, and we can look at a few of these. One is the process of *shortening*. Most often, this is done by cutting off the end of the word, as when *cabriolet* becomes *cab*, or *photograph* becomes *photo*. Sometimes it is the end of a whole phrase that is cut off, as when *public house* becomes *pub* or *permanent wave* becomes *perm*. And occasionally it is the *beginning* of the word that is lopped off, as when *acute* becomes *cute*, or *periwig* just *wig*. Other examples of shortening are *bus* (*omnibus*), *van* (*caravan*, *vanguard*), *telly* (*television*), *nylons* (*nylon stockings*), *prefab* (*prefabricated house*), *plane* (*aeroplane*), and *bra* (*brassière*).

A few new words are made by *blending*, that is by combining part of one word with part of another: *brunch* (breakfast and lunch), *motel* (motorists' hotel), *subtopia* (suburban utopia), *smog* (smoke and fog).

Another minor source of words is illustrated by *ohm* and *bikini*: the first is taken from the name of the German scientist G. S. Ohm, and the second from the name of a Pacific atoll which was used for atomic bomb tests. Sometimes such proper names are combined with a suffix, as in the verb *to pasteurize*; sometimes a pet name is taken, as in *bobby* ('policeman'), from Sir Robert Peel. But often the name of a person or place is taken unchanged and used as the name for something: *mackintosh*, *cardigan*, *derrick* (from the name of an eighteenth-century hangman), *doily*, *diesel*, *sandwich* (from the fourth Earl of Sandwich, who was unwilling to leave the gambling table even to eat). Similarly, a few proprietary trade names have been made into common nouns, like *thermos* (flask) and *primus* (stove).

Internal Loans

Another means by which words come into the standard language is by borrowing from regional dialects or from the language of specialized groups within the speech community. Such borrowings are called *internal loans*. An internal loan is not a new word, of course, but it is a new acquisition as far as the *general* vocabulary of the language is concerned. The Industrial Revolution, centred on the North and the Midlands, brought a certain number of words from regional dialects into wider circulation: the word *bogie* (on railway rolling stock) is from a northern dialect; *flange* (although originally borrowed from French) has also come into the standard language via regional dialect; and *trolley* was originally a Suffolk word.

The flow of northerners, and especially Scots, to London in the last few centuries has no doubt also played a part in the borrowing of words from the north, and helps to explain the presence in the standard language of such words as *glen*, *tarn*, *bracken*, *rowan*, *cairn*, *bard*, *kipper*, *scone*, *eerie*, *canny*, and *bonny*. Some of these are not native English words, but are loans from Scandinavian (like *rowan* and *tarn*) or from Gaelic (like *glen* and *bard*), but they have entered the standard language via regional dialect, and so are internal loans as far as their immediate provenance is concerned. The adoption of Scots words has been facilitated by our knowledge of Scots literature, especially no doubt by the former popularity of Sir Walter Scott.

Words also creep into the standard language from lower-class speech and from the argot of occupational groups: *gadget* is first heard of as sailors' slang in the late nineteenth century, *wangle* began as printers' slang, *scrounge* has regional dialect origins but was popularized as army slang, *spiv* has come from the language of race gangs, and recently the word *square* has come in from jazzmen's slang. These particular words, indeed, are still hardly respectable; but there are many words which were once considered 'low' or 'vulgar', but which are now fully accepted: they include such perfectly respectable words as *banter*, *coax*, *flimsy*, *flippant*, *fun*, *sham*, and *snob*, all of which were frowned on in the eighteenth century.

As a result of the growth of vocabulary by all these methods, we now have an enormous number of words in English. The great *Oxford English Dictionary* (originally called the *New English Dictionary*) runs to twelve large volumes and a supplement. It excludes all narrowly technical words, but nevertheless records about a quarter of a million words, plus their derivatives. We are fortunate in having this magnificent historical dictionary for Modern English, and this is the first work you should turn to when you want to know anything about the origins and history of an English word.

The Loss of Words

Besides acquiring new words, we have lost some of the old ones. In the passages of Old English that we have looked at, there are words that have not survived into the modern language, like *swēg* ('noise') and *wered* ('crowd'). There are many reasons for the loss of words. There is the obvious one that the word is no longer needed; we no longer need the words for the various parts of a suit of armour or for outdated concepts like *phlogiston* or *fee simple*. Another reason is the danger of confusion when phonetic change has caused the pronunciation of two different words to become identical. For example, the words *queen* and *quean* ('woman, shameless woman') originally had different pronunciations: in Old English the first was *cwēn* and the second *cwene*, and they were still distinct in Shakespeare's time, *queen* having its present-day pronunciation while *quean* had a vowel like that of German *Weh*. But when their pronunciations became identical (in the eighteenth century) there was obviously danger of ambiguity, and it is not surprising that one of them has fallen out of use.

Another possible reason is that phonetic change makes a word too short to be distinctive, and speakers replace it by a longer word, which gives a bigger safety margin. This may explain the loss of the Old English word for 'river'. This word, related to Latin *aqua* and Gothic *ahwa*, was prehistoric Old English **ahu*, which by normal phonetic change became **eahu* and then Old English *ēa*. This would give a Modern English word **ea*, but it has not survived, having been replaced in Middle English by *river*, borrowed from the French.

But it is not always possible to say exactly what has caused one word to die out and another to survive. In Middle English, French loan words had cultural prestige compared with native words, but this was not always enough to ensure the replacement of the native word by the loan: the French loan words *orgel* and *cete* are found in Middle English, but they did not succeed in displacing the earlier words *pride* and *whale*. We can be sure that *noise* had advantages which enabled it to oust *swēg*, but it is difficult to pinpoint them. And in general the causes of the death of a word are complex, and often obscure.

CHAPTER XIII

ENGLISH AS A WORLD LANGUAGE

TODAY, WHEN English is one of the major languages of the world, it requires an effort of the imagination to realize that this is a relatively recent thing – that Shakespeare, for example, wrote for a speech community of only a few millions, whose language was not thought to be of much account by the other nations of Europe, and was unknown to the rest of the world. Shakespeare's language was confined to England and southern Scotland, not having yet penetrated very much into Ireland or even into Wales, let alone into the world beyond. In the first place, the great expansion in the number of English speakers was due to the growth of population in England itself. At the Norman Conquest, the population of England was perhaps a million and a half. During the Middle Ages it grew to perhaps four or five million, but then was held down by recurrent plagues, and was still under five million in 1600. It was approaching six million in 1700, and nine million in 1800, and then expanded rapidly to seventeen million in 1850 and over thirty million in 1900. At the same time, English penetrated more and more into the rest of the British Isles at the expense of the Celtic languages. But the populations of other European countries were expanding too, and even in the eighteenth century, when England was beginning to be powerful and influential in the world, the English language still lacked the prestige in Europe of French and Italian; and it was not until the nineteenth century that it became widely respected as a language of culture, commerce, and international communication.

However, English has become a world language because of its establishment as a mother tongue *outside* England, in all the continents of the world. This carrying of English to other parts of the world began in the seventeenth century, with the first settlements in North America, and continued with increasing impetus through the eighteenth and nineteenth centuries. Above all, it is the great growth of population in the United States, assisted by massive immigration in the nineteenth and twentieth centuries, that has given the English language its present standing in the world. In 1790, when the Federal Constitution was finally ratified, there were about four million people in the United States, most of them of British origin. By 1830, the population was nearly thirteen million; by 1850 it was twenty-three million, and had overtaken that of England; and then it shot ahead – to fifty million by 1880, seventy-six million by 1900, and a hundred and fifty million by 1950. At the same time there was a less grandiose but nevertheless important expansion of native speakers of English elsewhere in the world, so that today there are some twelve million in Canada, ten million in Australia, two and a half million in New Zealand, and over a million in South Africa.

There are very few native speakers of English in South America or in Asia, but English is an important medium of communication in many parts of the world where it is not a native language. In India, with its three hundred and fifty million people and its two hundred and twenty-five different languages, English is still the main medium of communication between educated speakers from different parts of the country, and is widely used as a language of administration and commerce. As could be expected, the Indian schools have changed over to teaching in the regional languages since Independence, but English is still used as the medium of instruction in most Indian universities, and university students rely to a very large extent on textbooks written in English. A similar situation is found in other countries, especially former British colonies: in Nigeria, for example, where there are three main regions with different languages, English is still an essential language for internal communication, and the universities carry out their teaching in English. This situation cannot continue for ever: such countries will ultimately change over to teaching and adminstering and publishing textbooks in one or more of their own languages, and nobody will want to quarrel with them for that. But it is clear that for a long time ahead English will be an important language for them, playing a role somewhat like that of Latin in medieval Europe.

Moreover, the use of English as a medium of international communication is not confined to such countries. In the past few hundred years the English-speaking peoples have played a large part in seafaring and international trade, and English has become one of the essential commercial languages of the world. So that if a Norwegian or Dutch business firm wants to write to a firm in Japan or Brazil or Ceylon, it will probably do so in English, and will expect to receive a reply in English. In science, too, the English-speaking peoples have played a large part, and in recent years there has been an increasing tendency for scientists in other countries to publish in English, which in this field has gained at the expense of German. Of course, English is not the only important international language. Arabic, French, German, Malay, and Spanish all play an important part in certain areas. Russian has become of greater international importance than ever before, and will undoubtedly continue to go up; and we can confidently expect that Chinese will soon follow. But at the moment it does seem that English is the most important of the international languages.

DIVERGENT DEVELOPMENT IN MODERN ENGLISH

As new English-speaking communities have been set up in different parts of the world – North America, Australia, South Africa, and so on – a certain amount of divergent development has inevitably taken place in their languages. Fortunately, a standard form of English had already established itself pretty firmly in England before the expansion over the world began, otherwise the divergence might have been greater, and English might not have survived as a single language. Even so, it is clear that some of the groups that emigrated had social or regional peculiarities in their language which made it different right from the start from the standard form of the language in

England. This was probably the case, for example, with some of the groups that settled in North America in the seventeenth century: these tended to be drawn from the puritan middle classes, not from the landowning gentry whose language had the greatest prestige in England. Moreover, once the group was settled in its new home, far from the influence of the original speech community, its language took its own course: changes in pronunciation took place; new words were coined to cope with the new environment; there was influence from other languages spoken in the region; and in general the community put the stamp of its own personality on the language.

AUSTRALIAN ENGLISH

So today there is, for example, a distinctively Australian form of English. It has its own pronunciation: for example, the long vowel in words like *park* is made further forward than in Britain (somewhere near the vowel of our *cut*), and is often slightly nasalized; many vowels are diphthongized; and the unstressed endings -*es* and -*ed* (in words like *boxes* and *waited*) are not pronounced -*iz* and -*id*, as in Britain, but with the short *er* vowel. There is also a specifically Australian vocabulary: words have been borrowed from the local aboriginal language, like *dingo*, *billabong*, *gunyah*, and *joey* ('young kangaroo'); new words have been invented, like *outback*, *tuckerbag*, *stockman*, and *cuppa* (which has now spread to England); old words have been given new meanings, like *wattle* ('acacia') and *paddock* (used for any piece of fenced land, whatever its size); and old dialect words which have been lost in England have been retained, like *larrikin* ('hooligan'), *fossick* ('to seek'), and perhaps *wowser* ('puritanical fanatic'). Characteristic Australian idioms and phrases have grown up, and Australian slang in particular has been enriched to the stage where it is incomprehensible to the outsider.

When local developments take place like this, they may then react back on the English spoken in Britain. The influence of the Commonwealth countries on British English has on the whole been limited to vocabulary, like Australian *boomerang*, *kangaroo*, *bush telegraph*, *cuppa*. But American influence has been more pervasive, and has increased considerably in recent years, because the Americans now form the largest, richest, and most powerful group within the English-speaking community.

AMERICAN ENGLISH

That British and American English have diverged in the three hundred odd years since the first settlements is obvious enough, and many of the differences are apparent to speakers on both sides of the Atlantic. There are differences in pronunciation, especially of the vowels, so that British and American speakers use different vowel sounds in words like *home, hot,* and *aunt*. There are differences of grammar, so that an American can say *Do you have the time?* while an Englishman says *Have you got the time?* And there are differences of vocabulary, so that every after-dinner speaker knows that British *braces* are American *suspenders*, while British *suspenders* are American *garters*. Some of the divergences are due to the fact that British English has changed, while American has not: thus American *dove* is more archaic than British *dived*, which shows the normal tendency of Modern English to change strong verbs into weak ones. On the other hand, the American use of the word *creek* to mean 'tributary' is an innovation, and the British meaning 'inlet' is the original one. In other cases, both Englishmen and Americans have made innovations, but different ones, for example in the naming of new objects, so that we find American *railroad, auto, antenna, sidewalk,* and *subway* beside British *railway, car, aerial, pavement,* and *underground*. People on both sides of the Atlantic have at different times tried to make a virtue either of archaism or of innovation, usually claiming of course that the virtue belonged particularly to their own form of the language. Some, indeed, have managed to claim a monopoly of both virtues simultaneously. Such disputes are pointless: neither archaism nor innovation is a virtue in itself.

American Dialects

The American language is not monolithic, any more than the British, but consists of an agglomeration of dialects, both regional and social. The regional dialect areas are larger than those of Britain, a relatively uniform style of speech often stretching over hundreds of miles of country, where in Britain it would be tens of miles. There are three major dialect regions in the United States, the Northern, the Midland, and the Southern, the Midland being divided into North Midland and South Midland. Each of these main regions can in turn be subdivided into subdialect areas, the exact number of which is uncertain, as the American dialect survey is not yet finished. These dialect areas show differences in pronunciation, grammar, and vocabulary. For example, in the Midlands, the *r* sound has been retained before consonants and pauses (as in *barn, father*), but in the South it has been lost; in the North it is generally retained, but is lost in eastern New England and in New York City. Britain and the United States are similar in this respect: it is not true, as is sometimes popularly thought, that all Americans pronounce the *r* in these positions, and that no Englishmen do. In fact, in both countries the *r* is pronounced in some regions but not in others (in England, for example, it is pronounced in the West Country); but this fact has been obscured by the great prestige enjoyed in Britain by 'public school English', which is one of the styles where the *r* is lost. In vocabulary, an example is the pair of words *pail* (which is Northern) and *bucket* (which is Midland and Southern); here again the situation resembles that in England (where, however, *bucket* is northern and *pail* southern). In grammar, the form *dove*, which we have already noticed, is characteristic of the North, the other areas using *dived*.

The American dialect areas have no direct correspondence to those of Britain. The early settlers were a mixed lot, as indeed can be seen from the place names they took with them, like Portsmouth, Norwich, Bangor, Boston, Worcester, York, Belfast, Exeter, and Ipswich. Each community must have had its own particular mixture, which was gradually levelled out into a local dialect. As the frontier was pushed westwards, the original dialect groups on the east coast expanded along fairly well marked lines, and of course underwent modifications in the process.

American Pronunciation

The differences in pronunciation between British and American English are not as simple as they seem to the casual listener. It is not possible to take an English and an American speaker and simply say that where the Englishman produces sound A the American produces sound B. There is not usually any such one to one correspondence, for the *distribution* of the phonemes often differs in the two forms of the language. For example, the lengthening of short *a* before voiceless fricatives, which took place in England in the seventeenth and eighteenth centuries, did not occur in most American dialects, so that in words like *fast*, *bath*, and *half* an American uses the same vowel as in *cat*, whereas a southern Englishman uses the same vowel as in *father*. Sometimes the distribution of a phoneme varies considerably in different American dialects. This can be illustrated with an example given by the American dialectologist Professor W. Nelson Francis: the words *cot*, *bomb*, *caught*, and *balm*. Some American speakers make the same distinctions as British speakers in their treatment of these four words, i.e. they recognize three different vowels, those in *cot* and *bomb* being the same. There are other speakers, however, who recognize only two different vowels. Some of these have one vowel for *cot* and *bomb* (a short *ah* sound) and a second vowel for *caught* and *balm* (a long *ah* sound). Others, however, have one vowel for *cot* and *balm* (a short *ah* sound) and a second one for *caught* and *bomb* (a short *o* sound). And there is yet another group of speakers which uses only one vowel for all four words, namely a short *o* sound.

There are also differences between British and American English in stress and intonation. In general, southeastern English uses more violent stress contrasts and a wider range of pitch than American does. Where the Englishman gives a word one heavy stress and several very weak ones, the American often gives it a secondary stress on one of the weak syllables. This is the case, for example, with words ending in *-ary*, like *military* and *temporary*, where the American has a secondary stress on the third syllable. As a result, southeastern English on the whole moves faster than American English, since there are fewer stresses: and the whole rhythm of English, as we have seen, tends to an equal spacing of stresses. And it tends to have more reduced vowels than American English (as in the third syllable of *military*). Northern English speech, however, is closer to American in movement than southeastern English is.

American Grammar

In grammar and syntax, the differences between British and American usage are not great, at any rate if we confine ourselves to educated speech and writing. We have already noticed two minor differences: the form *dove* for *dived*, and the American use of *do have* where an Englishman says *have got*; of course, we also use *do have* in Britain ('Do you have dances in your village?'), but the distribution of the two forms is different. Again, American has the two forms *I have got* (meaning 'I have') and *I have gotten* (meaning 'I have acquired' or 'I have become'), where British English uses only the first form. An American can use impersonal *one*, and then continue with *his* and *he*; for example *If one loses his temper, he should apologize*. This sounds odd to an Englishman, who replaces *his* and *he* by *one's* and *one*. The American in his turn is likely to be surprised by the British use of a plural verb and plural reflexive pronoun in sentences like *The government are considering the matter themselves*. Prepositions, too, are sometimes used differently: an Englishman lives *in* Oxford Street, whereas an American will usually live *on* it; and an Englishman caters *for* somebody, while an American caters *to* him. But, while examples of this kind could be multiplied, they are all minor things: in all essentials, British and American syntax are identical.

American Vocabulary

The largest divergences are perhaps in vocabulary. Expanding across a new continent, with new flora and fauna and different natural features from those of Europe, building up a new society, with its own political institutions, its own social customs, its various ways of earning its living, the Americans were impelled to adapt old words or invent new ones to meet their many needs. The very names for topographical features evoke a specifically American atmosphere, and words like *gulch*, *bluff*, *creek*, *rapids*, and *swamp* seem as much out of place east of the Atlantic as *moor*, *heath*, *fen*, and *coomb* do west of it.

A large part of the specifically American vocabulary was borrowed from other languages. The first contacts of the settlers were with the American Indians, and quite a number of words were borrowed from them, especially in the seventeenth century. Many of the Indian words were rather long, and they were often shortened and simplified by the borrowers: thus *seganku* became *skunk*, and *pawcohiccora* was borrowed as *hickory*. Occasionally the form of the word was altered to give it English elements with a meaning of their own, as when *wejak* was borrowed as *woodchuck*; this is the process known as popular etymology. Many of the words borrowed were the names of the American flora and fauna, like *chipmunk*, *hickory*, *sequoia*, *skunk*, and *terrapin*. Others were words connected with American Indian culture, like *wigwam*, *totem*, *wampum*, and *powwow*; this last word originally meant 'medicine man', and passed through a whole series of changes of meaning before reaching its present one of 'informal conference, discussion'. Among the other words borrowed are some in the sphere of politics, like *caucus* and *Tammany*. And some American place and river names are also Indian: *Mississipi* means 'big river', and *Chicago* perhaps means 'place of wild onions'.

Even more words, several hundred in all, were borrowed from Spanish, for the Spaniards had established solid and permanent settlements in the New World, and the American pioneers encountered them at many points during their expansion. Borrowings are especially common in the southwest of the United States. Many of the loans go back to the seventeenth century, though there are also a large number from the nineteenth. A number of them, again, are topographical, like *sierra* and *canyon*, or words for flora and fauna, like *alfalfa*, *armadillo*, and *cockroach*. A large number come from ranch life, like *ranch*, *corral*, *lasso*, *stampede*, *mustang*, and *bronco*; perhaps with these we can group words for clothing, like *poncho* and *sombrero*. One other interest of the Spanish settlers, mining, is seen in such loans as *bonanza* and *placer*, and there are also words connected with the administration of justice, like *calaboose*, *desperado*, and *vigilantes*. Miscellaneous loans include *filibuster*, *hombre*, *pronto*, *stevedore*, *tornado*, and *vamoose*. There are also many Spanish place names, especially saints' names like *Santa Barbara* and *San Francisco*.

In the north, there was contact right from the beginning with the French, and a number of words were borrowed from them, especially in the eighteenth century. They again include topographical words, like *prairie* and *rapids*, and flora and fauna, like *pumpkin* and *gopher*. This last word is from French *gaufre*, which means 'honeycomb', but has been borrowed as the name of a small rat-like animal, because of its honeycomb of burrows. From French, too, come names of coins, *cent* and *dime*; the latter word in fact already existed in England, having been borrowed in Middle English times, and it is found in Shakespeare, but as an American monetary term it is a reborrowing.

There were also a few borrowings from the Dutch settlers in North America, who were centred on New Amsterdam (which in 1644 was taken by the British and became New York). The loans include food names like *cookie* and *waffle*, and miscellaneous words like *boss*, *boodle*, *dope*, *snoop*, and perhaps *Yankee*, which may be derived from the Dutch *Jankin* ('little John') or *Jan Kees* ('John Cheese'), in which case it will have been a patronizing name given by the Dutch to the English settlers of New England.

Later, in the nineteenth and twentieth centuries, large numbers of immigrants of many nationalities entered the United States. But their contribution to the American vocabulary is remarkably small, because the language of the immigrant has low prestige in the United States, and he is usually anxious to Americanize himself as thoroughly as possible. The largest number of loans are from German, for the German influx in the nineteenth century was particularly massive, and there is still a considerable German-speaking population in the United States. These borrowings include food names like *delicatessen* and *hamburger*, educational terms like *semester* and *seminar*, and a number of miscellaneous words like *loafer* and *nix*.

These contacts with other languages are not the only sources of the specifically American vocabulary. The same processes of word formation have been going on in Britain and America – affixation, compounding, conversion, and so on – and sometimes, inevitably, different words have been coined for the same thing: petrol and gasoline, tram and street car, lift and elevator, and so on. Nor are all the names for specifically American phenomena borrowed from other languages. Native material has been used for coining new words, like *groundhog* and *bullfrog*, or existing English words have been given a new application, like *robin* (used for a bird of the thrush family) and *corn* (specialized to mean what an Englishman calls *maize*). Indeed, in the coining of new words and phrases, the Americans in modern times have been more exuberant and uninhibited than the British. After the American Revolution, the Americans broke away even more fully than before from English traditions, linguistic as well as social and political, and were much less restrained by upper class ideals of decorum in their treatment of the language. The exuberance and the love of novelty were encouraged by the existence of the ever-moving frontier, which for over two hundred years kept bringing new American communities into existence, and encouraged the pioneer spirit. The frontier spirit is no doubt partly responsible for the American gift for coining lively and telling new phrases, like *flying off the handle* or *barking up the wrong tree*. It may also be responsible for the love of the grandiloquent that turns an undertaker into a *mortician* and a spittoon into a *cuspidor*.

STANDARD ENGLISH

The divergent development that has taken place in the English language as it has spread over the world during the last three hundred years raises the question of Standard English. Does it exist? If so, what is it?

Inside England, as we have seen, one form of the language, basically an East Midland dialect, became accepted as a literary standard in the late Middle Ages. This does not mean, of course, that dialect differences disappeared within England, or even that all educated Englishmen spoke in the same way: in the plays and the novels of the seventeenth and eighteenth centuries we often meet country gentlemen who are represented as speaking a local dialect. But in the last century or two there has been a strong tendency for the English upper and upper middle classes to adopt a uniform style of speech. One of the causes of this has been the influence of the great public schools, which have dominated the education of the English gentry at least since the time of Arnold of Rugby in the early Victorian age. This 'public school' English is obviously a variant of southeastern English, but it has in fact ceased to be a regional dialect and has become a class dialect, spoken by members of the English gentry whatever part of the country they come from. It has great prestige, and by many English people is considered the only really 'correct' form of speech. But of course it is not spoken by all educated English people, unless we equate 'educated' with 'educated at a public school': and that is really rather too flattering to the public schools. Today, in fact, the majority of English people educated to university level are *not* from public schools, and there is an increasing tendency for educated people to speak the educated form of their regional dialect. On the other hand, the more 'educated' a regional dialect is, the more nearly it approximates to public school English.

However, while educated southeastern English, and the class dialect of the public schools derived from it, have established themselves as prestige languages in England, their claims to be the only standard form of English speech do not meet with much sympathy in other parts of the English-speaking world. Even in the British Isles there are rivals, for Irishmen and Scots have their own forms of educated speech, and see no reason why they should be considered inferior to the speech of Eton or Harrow. Nor have the inhabitants of New Zealand, Australia, Canada, or the United States any reason to mimic the language of the English upper classes, since they fail to see any way in which it is superior to their own language. The American attitude to regional dialects is more tolerant than the English one: an educated man is expected to speak the educated form of his regional dialect, and no region has special prestige in this respect; still less is there a non-regional class dialect with super-prestige. This attitude would be a sensible one for us to adopt towards the varieties of English as a whole. The English language is not the monopoly of the inhabitants of Britain: we have no sole proprietary rights in it, which would entitle us to dictate usage to the rest of the English-speaking world. Nor is it the monopoly of the Americans, or the Australians, or any other group: it belongs to us all. It would be reasonable to give parity of esteem to all educated forms of English speech, whatever country they are found in, and in whatever region of that country.

Fortunately, there is a solid core of common usage in all English-speaking countries which makes it possible to talk of 'standard world English'. The regional variations that we have been discussing are especially marked in the *spoken* language (many of them are differences in pronunciation), and are greatest in informal, slangy, and uneducated speech. But if we examine the more formal uses of language, and especially if we confine ourselves to a formal style of *written* language, the differences become small. In formal writing, the essential structure of the language is practically the same throughout the English-speaking world; the differences in vocabulary are perceptible but not enormous; and the differences in spelling negligible. There is, therefore, a standard *literary* language which is very much the same throughout the English-speaking community, and it is this, if anything, which deserves to be called Standard English.

The reality of this literary standard can be seen from the fact that it is often difficult to say what part of the world a piece of writing comes from. Of course, a good deal depends on the kind of writing – how familiar it is in style, how nearly it models itself on everyday speech: if you are presented with a page from Mr Brendan Behan's autobiography or from Mr J. D. Salinger's *Catcher in the Rye*, you do not need to be much of a detective to guess that the authors are from Ireland and the United States respectively. But suppose you open a novel and find that it starts like this:

> Love conquers all – *omnia vincit amor*, said the gold scroll in a curve beneath the dial of the old French gilt clock. To the dial's right, a nymph, her head on her arm, drowsed, largely undraped, at the mouth of a gold grotto where perhaps she lived. To the dial's left, a youth, by his crook and and the pair of lambs with him, a shepherd, had taken cover. Parting fronds of gold vegetation, he peeped at the sleeping beauty. On top of the dial, and all unnoticed by the youth, a smiling cupid perched, bow bent, about to loose an arrow at the peeper's heart. While Arthur Winner viewed with faint familiar amusement this romantic grouping, so graceful and so absurd, the clock struck three.

Is the nationality of its author really so evident? Perhaps an Englishman would have written *To the right of the dial* rather than *To the dial's right*, but this is by no means certain. And there is hardly any clue beyond this. In fact it is the work of an American, the opening of *By Love Possessed*, by James Gould Cozzens, published in 1957; but it is difficult to see anything in it that could not have been written by an

Englishman or an Irishman or an Australian: it is Standard World English.

Of course, the existence of a standard literary language does not in itself prove that spoken English is a single language. But experience shows that educated English-speaking people from any part of the world have no serious difficulties in understanding each others' speech. Things are a little more difficult when the speakers are uneducated, especially if they are old and have spent their whole lives in small isolated communities. An aged agricultural labourer from a village in Norfolk or in Cornwall who had never lived outside his birthplace would no doubt have some difficulty in conversing with a backwoodsman from the Rocky Mountains or with a bushwhacker from the Australian outback. But even in this case there is a *chain* of mutual comprehension which could easily be established. The old Norfolk labourer can converse easily with the younger men of his own village, they can converse easily with the townsfolk in Norwich, the latter can converse easily with educated people from New York, and so on along the chain. For all their rich variety and regional diversification, the dialects spoken in the British Isles, in the Commonwealth countries, and in the United States still form one single entity, the English language.

CHAPTER XIV

CHANGES IN MEANING

IN THE course of this book we have come across a number of words that have changed their meaning: the Old English word *æcer* meant 'field', not 'acre'; and similarly *whole* once meant 'well, safe', *lore* 'learning', and *knave* 'boy'.

TWO KINDS OF MEANING

When we use the word *meaning* here, we are talking about the relationship between language and the real world, between the signalling system and the things that the signals refer to or stand for. We can call this *referential meaning*. We can only detect referential meaning by observing how language is used in actual situations, and this is how a child discovers the meaning of words and sentences when it learns its mother tongue. Often, of course, the verbal context by itself can show us what a word means, and if we are trying to discover the meaning of a word in, say, sixteenth-century English, we simply examine a large number of passages of sixteenth-century English in which the word occurs. But we can only discover meaning in this way because (1) we have already learnt the meanings of the other words in the passages by meeting them in actual situations, and (2) the passages are therefore able to present us, by what they say, with fairly clear situations. If, on the other hand, we are given extensive tape recordings of people talking in a completely unfamiliar language, with no indication of the situations in which the utterances were made, we can never hope to discover the meaning of a single word or utterance in that language. We cannot even get very far in analysing the structure of the language, because, in the absence of situation, we can never be quite sure what things in the language operate as signals, what features are contrastive and what are not.

There is however another sense of the word *meaning* which is often used by linguists. This is what we can call *formal meaning*, and refers to the place of the word (or other linguistic item) in the language system. Formal meaning is the *ability* of the item to carry information, and depends on the other items that it can be contrasted with in the system. Consider the signalling system of an ordinary set of British traffic lights. These have four possible positions: green alone, amber alone, red alone, and red and amber together. The amount of information that can be carried by each of these signals depends entirely on the fact that it is one of this set of four. If we add a fifth signal (for example, a purple light alone) we increase the amount of information carried, and alter the 'meaning' of each signal. And this formal meaning is quite independent of the referential meaning which we decide, quite arbitrarily, to assign to each of them. In a language, similarly, we have sets of items that contrast with each other, and so have formal meaning. In English, for example, we have a set of personal pronouns, *I*, *he*, *she*, *it*, *we*, *you*, *they*; if we were to lose one of these, or to add a new one, we should change the formal meaning of each member of the set.

There has been a tendency for modern linguists to confine their attention to formal meaning, and to argue that referential meaning is not their concern; indeed, in some circles *meaning* itself has become a dirty word. There have been good historical reasons for this, because in the present century the science of language has had to free itself from definitions and criteria drawn from other disciplines (e.g. logic, psychology), and to assert the necessity for purely formal and linguistic criteria in establishing its categories and making its analyses; and this has been extremely fruitful. Nevertheless, it seems to me that the escape from referential meaning into a world of pure linguistic form is an illusion. My example of the tape recording of an unknown language suggests that we cannot even discover what the structure of a language is (and thereby discover the formal meanings carried by its elements) without paying attention (however covertly) to referential meaning.

Change of Meaning and Polysemy

This chapter is about changes in referential meaning, which henceforth I shall simply refer to as meaning. In discussing the development of the English language from its earliest known forms up to the present day, I have given no systematic account of changes of meaning. This is for a good reason: changes in meaning do not lend themselves to such treatment, because there are no regular laws or large-scale trends such as we find in phonology or in grammar. However, we can still see some kind of order in these changes of meaning: changes of various kinds can be distinguished, and similar causes can often be seen at work to bring them about. In this chapter I shall look at a few examples of change of meaning in English, and illustrate some of the common types of change.

When a word develops a new meaning, it sometimes loses the old one. Thus the word *wan* (Old English *wann*) at first meant 'dark', or even 'black', being applied for example to a raven and to night. In late Middle English it developed its modern sense of 'pale'. This remarkable change of meaning seems to have taken place partly through the application of the word to human faces discoloured by disease, and partly through its use to describe the colour of lead. From meaning 'darkened by disease' it came to mean 'livid', 'the colour a person's face is when they are ill', and hence 'pale'. When one word has two such contradictory meanings as 'dark' and 'pale' there are grave dangers of confusion, and it is not surprising that one of them died out; the meaning 'dark' is last recorded in the sixteenth century.

Often, however, there is no such sharp contradiction between the old and the new meaning; or each meaning is found in one characteristic kind of context so that there is no danger of confusion; and in such cases the two meanings may continue to exist side by side, and even branch out again and give more meanings. Thus the original meaning of *horn* was 'one of a pair of pointed projections on the heads of oxen, sheep, goats, etc.'; but already in the Old English period it was extended to mean 'one of these used as a musical instrument'. Later, similar musical instruments were made of other materials, such as brass, but they were still called horns; and later the word became used for other kinds of noise-producing instruments, like those used on motor-cars. There is really no danger of confusion from the coexistence of these different meanings, because they all occur in characteristic contexts: 'He plays the horn in the Hallé'; 'Jack jammed on his brakes and sounded his horn'; 'Let's take the bull by the horns.' And the word has more meanings yet. Besides meaning 'a wind instrument', it can mean 'a person who plays such an instrument' ('for five years he was first horn in the Hallé'). Besides referring to the projections on the heads of animals like cows, it can be used for projections on the heads of insects and snails, and for tufts of feathers on the heads of birds; it is the snail usage that has given us the phrase 'to draw in your horns'. It can also be used as the name of the material that animals' horns are made of ('a handle made of horn'). And we still have meanings like 'drinking vessel', and the horns of a bow, or of the moon, or of a dilemma. And all in all you will agree that the word *horn* now has a positive welter of meanings, which have all developed out of the original one referring to the things on an animal's head.

The coexistence of several meanings in one word, which is extremely common, is called *polysemy*. Some words develop a whole family of meanings, each new meaning often forming yet another starting point for more; if in a good dictionary you look up such words as *natural*, *good*, *loose*, *free*, and *real*, you will be surprised at the number of meanings listed. If you look them up in the big *Oxford English Dictionary*, available in any big public library, you will find brief dated quotations illustrating each meaning, including the first recorded example of each in English; from these you can get some idea of the way in which the various meanings have evolved.

It sometimes happens that a word develops meanings very remote from one another, and the reader of a dictionary will be puzzled or intrigued to find a word operating in such different fields. Such is the word *collation*, which in present-day English has two main meanings: 'the act of bringing together and comparing (different manuscripts or editions)' and 'a light meal'. How does it come to have such oddly assorted meanings? The first of the two meanings is very close to the meaning of the Latin word *collatio* to which the English word ultimately goes back, and which meant 'a bringing together'. In Late Latin, *collatio* also had the meaning 'a conference, discourse', and this too was one of the early meanings of English *collation*, though it has not survived into our time. In Benedictine monasteries, it was the custom before Compline for the monks to hear a reading from a Latin work on the lives of the fathers, the *Collationes* ('Conferences, Discourses') of Cassian; and the name *collation* was then applied to these readings. Next, it seems, it became applied to the light meal which the monks took after the readings. This can easily have happened simply from the constant closeness of the two events in time: a reference to something happening before or after the collation, for example, might often equally well refer to the readings or to the meal. Having become the name of this particular meal, the word was later extended to refer to any light meal.

When a word develops very different meanings like this, and has no intermediate ones to link them together, the native speaker may feel that there are two different words, not one word with two meanings. Thus historically the word *mess* meaning 'group of people who take their meals together' is identical with *mess* meaning 'state of disorder'; but most people probably feel these as two separate words, because they occur in such different contexts. In such cases, it sometimes happens that two different spellings develop for the word, one for each meaning. This is so with *mettle*, which historically is the same word as *metal*. The specialized meaning 'temperament, spirited temperament, ardour' arose from the figurative application of *metal* (referring to the temper of a sword blade) to the qualities of human beings or animals. But this meaning is so remote from the other meanings of metal that the word has split in two, and this is reflected in the spelling. The same is true of *flower* and *flour*, which are simply spelling variants of what was originally the same word. One meaning that developed for *flower* was 'the best part' (as in 'the flower of chivalry'), and *flour* is simply 'the best (or finest) part of the wheat'.

The existence of polysemy has obvious dangers: it makes language rather slippery, so that in the course of a piece of reasoning we may be led astray because a key word in our argument is used with different meanings in different places. This often happens in political or moral disputes, where words like *freedom* and *natural* get thrown around in ill-defined and shifting senses. On the other hand, the kind of 'play' that polysemy gives to language makes it easier to use: communication would really be too difficult if, in every utterance, we had to practise the strictness of definition demanded by mathematics or by symbolic logic. And of course reasoned demonstration is only one of the many functions of language; in some uses, polysemy plays an essential part, enabling us to achieve a complexity and a compression otherwise impossible. The kind of impact Shakespeare produces in his major works would be impossible without the richness given to the language by polysemy – the fact that every word is clustered around with associations, derived from the different types of context in which it can be used.

CHANGES IN THE REFERENT

One reason why a word changes its meaning is that the thing it refers to changes. The word *ship* has been used in English for over a thousand years to denote a vessel for travelling on the sea, but the kind of machine actually used for this purpose has changed enormously: the word used of the long boats of the Vikings is now also used of a modern liner or aircraft carrier, and it seems reasonable to say that its meaning has changed. The same applies to other products of our material culture, like *house*, *lamp*, *weapon*, *hat*. It also applies to the names of institutions, like *parliament*, *king*, and *law*, for they too have changed. And it applies to words that involve moral or aesthetic judgements: the words *good*, *virtuous*, *modest*, and *beautiful* do not mean the same today as they did in 1600, because our moral and aesthetic standards have changed: our idea of what constitutes virtuous conduct, or a modest woman, or a beautiful painting does not tally with the ideas of Shakespeare and his contemporaries.

SHIFT IN THE FOCUS OF INTEREST

At first sight it might seem that the change in meaning of the word *horn* (from 'animal weapon' to 'musical instrument') was also of this kind: just as ships changed from sail to steam, but kept the same name, so musical instruments were made of a new material, but were still called horns. But the change in *horn* is not as simple as this: even before horns came to be made of brass, it is clear that a new meaning had appeared, namely 'musical instrument'. This meaning had arisen by a shift in the speaker's and hearer's centre of interest when the word was used – from animals and their weapons to the fact that a noise could be produced from the thing; and the shift arose because the implement came to be used regularly in a different kind of situation. Consequently, when the word *horn* was used in certain types of context, it had a musical meaning.

Many changes of meaning are of the kind where a shift takes place in the focus of interest, in the aspect which is given prominence, though the mechanism of change is not always identical with that for *horn*. The adjective *fair* (Old English *fæger*) originally meant 'fit, suitable' (which is the meaning of the Gothic *fagrs*), but in Old English it had come to mean 'pleasant, joyous, agreeable, beautiful'. When used of conduct, it must have been used frequently in situations in which 'pleasant conduct' meant 'conduct free from bias, fraud, or injustice', so that *fair* came to mean 'equitable, just'; this meaning is recorded from the fourteenth century, and remains one of its chief ones. In the sense of 'beautiful', *fair* is often used of human beings, and especially women, from Old English times onwards; but for various historical reasons, which were touched on in Chapter V, the ideal of beauty in medieval and early modern England was a blonde one: hair and complexion had to be light in colour. Consequently, a beautiful woman was also a blonde one, and *fair* came to mean 'light in colour', a meaning first recorded in the mid-sixteenth century. The existence side by side of the meanings 'beautiful' and 'blonde' is demonstrated by a famous Shakespeare sonnet, in which he asserts that his love is fair although she is dark. But the existence of these two different meanings, which would obviously occur in similar contexts, offers too many possibilities of ambiguity, and the meaning 'beautiful' has dropped out of use, except in a few consciously archaic (and often jocular) phrases like 'a fair lady' and 'the fair sex'. On the other hand, there is little danger of conflict between the meanings 'equitable' and 'blonde', because the context usually shows clearly whether we are talking about conduct or appearance.

Somewhat similar is the way in which words denoting occupation or social rank often develop meanings referring to the moral or intellectual qualities (real or supposed) of people in that station. When the word *gentle* was borrowed from French in the Middle English period, it was used mainly to refer to social rank, and meant 'well-bred, of good family'. The meanings 'docile, courteous, merciful', and so on, arose because these were the qualities conventionally attributed to people of that class. Of course, we know that not all gentlemen were gentle, but the idealized picture that a ruling class has of itself may be more influential than the actual facts. The influence of the *dominant* social class in these matters is shown by the rather different history of the word *villain*: this originally meant 'peasant', but then came to mean 'scoundrel, criminal'. In this case, plainly, it is the gentleman's view of the peasant that has determined the change of meaning, not the peasant's view of himself. The word *lady*, similarly, from meaning 'woman of the upper classes', has come to mean also 'woman of delicacy and refinement'. And *noble*, from meaning 'pertaining to the aristocracy', has come to mean 'lofty, magnanimous, imposing, holding high ideals', because these qualities, as we know, are especially characteristic of members of the House of Peers. Other examples are *churl* (originally 'man of low rank'), *boor* (originally 'peasant, countryman'), and *bourgeois*.

A particularly striking example of a change of meaning arising from a movement of the focus of interest within a situation is given by the word *bead*, discussed in detail by Gustaf Stern in his book on change of meaning in English. The word originally meant 'prayer'. The meaning 'small pierced ball for threading on a string' arose from the medieval habit of counting one's prayers on a rosary: *to tell your beads* meant 'to count your prayers', but what anyone would actually *see* when a man was 'telling his beads' was the movement of the small balls on the rosary; hence the word *beads* came to be apprehended as referring to these balls, and the modern meaning arose.

THE INFLUENCE OF FORM

Sometimes a change of meaning is caused by the *form* of a word: one word is confused with another that resembles it in some way, or its meaning is affected by the meanings (or supposed meanings) of its constituent parts. For example, in early Modern English, *obnoxious* often had the meaning of its Latin original, 'liable to harm or punishment, exposed to injury'; its modern meaning, 'offensive, objectionable', is due to the influence of the word *noxious*.

This kind of change is encouraged in English by the large number of words of Greek or Latin origin, which are often 'opaque', that is, their meanings cannot be deduced from their constituent parts by an unlearned speaker. Our literature is full of comic characters who use long words incorrectly, like Sheridan's Mrs Malaprop, who says 'illegible' when she means 'eligible', and remarks that she has very little affluence over her niece. Indeed, Mrs Malaprop has given a new word to the language, *malapropism*, and it is perhaps significant that English speakers feel a need for such a word. Of course, one malapropism doesn't make a change of meaning; but if there is some factor that causes a large number of people to make the same mistake, then a new meaning will indeed arise. Malapropism, for example, may have played a part in the development of a new meaning for *aggravate* ('annoy' instead of 'make worse'), *decimate* ('destroy' instead of 'kill one man in ten'), *peroration* ('speech' instead of 'final section of a speech'), *disinterested* ('not taking an interest' instead of 'impartial'), and *protagonist* ('supporter' instead of 'main character'). The new meaning of *peroration* is probably due quite simply to confusion with *oration*, of which it is considered a more mouth-filling variant, and the new meaning of *disinterested* to confusion with *uninterested*. The change in *protagonist* is probably due to the influence of *antagonist*: speakers feel half-consciously that these two words contain the prefixes *pro-* ('for') and *anti-* ('against'), and are therefore the opposites of one another. It is quite true that the first syllable of *antagonist* represents *anti-*, but the first syllable of *protagonist* is from the Greek *protos* ('first'), and the word originally meant 'first competitor' or 'first actor'. These particular changes of meaning are still not accepted by all speakers, but the new usages are extremely common, and look like obtaining ultimate acceptance.

A rather different kind of influence of one word on another is illustrated by the adjective *fast* (Old English *fæst*). Today this has two main meanings: (1) 'firmly fixed' (*make a boat fast with a painter*); and (2) 'swift, rapid' (*a fast train*). The first meaning was the original one, and in Old English we find it in such phrases as *fæst hūs* ('a firm house, a strong house'), *mid fæstum gelēafan* ('with firm faith'), and *fæst innoþ* ('constipated bowels'). Then, in the second half of the fourteenth century, we suddenly find alongside this meaning the new one of 'swift, rapid' (in phrases like *a fast fleeing*), with no intermediate ones to form a bridge. The explanation is that the adjective *fast* was influenced by the related adverb *fast* (Middle English *faste*, Old English *fæste*), in which we can trace a continuous chain of meanings from 'firmly' to 'rapidly'. Like the adjective, the adverb at first had a passive kind of meaning, 'firmly, securely', and is found in Old English in phrases like *fæste tosomne gelīmed* ('firmly cemented together'); this meaning, of course, it still possesses. However, when it was used with verbs like *to hold*, it could easily acquire a more active sense, 'strongly, energetically, vigorously', because in order to hold a thing securely you often have to exert effort. Next it was used with verbs like 'strike, beat, fight', in which it could only have an active meaning, 'strongly, vigorously, violently'. Among other verbs of vigorous action, it was used with verbs of motion, like 'run' and 'ride'. But to run vigorously or strongly usually means to run *quickly*, and in the second half of the thirteenth century the word acquired this meaning; this becomes clear round about 1300, when *faste* begins to be used in the sense 'rapidly' with verbs not denoting motion, like *sell*, *eat*, and *fail*. Once the adverb *faste* had acquired the meaning 'rapidly', it was not long before the adjective *fast* acquired the parallel meaning 'rapid'; this is an example of analogy, for related pairs of adjectives and adverbs usually have related meanings.

NARROWING AND WIDENING OF MEANING

One common change is a narrowing or widening of reference. An example of narrowing is the verb *to starve* (Old English *steorfan*), which originally meant simply 'to die'. In Middle English it was sometimes specialized to mean 'die of cold' (and in some northern English dialects it still means 'to be cold'), but a sixteenth-century specialization, 'die of hunger', is the meaning that has survived in the modern standard language. This is a grim reflexion on the hardships of our ancestors, since it implies that a verb meaning 'to die' was very often used in contexts where the death had in fact occurred from lack of food. Similarly, *accident* once meant 'happening, chance event'; *science* meant 'knowledge' (while what we call science was called *natural philosophy*); a *desert* was 'any uninhabited place'; and an *undertaker* was 'anybody who undertakes something'. Other examples are *deer*, which originally meant 'animal' (like German *Tier* and Swedish *djur*), and *meat*, which originally meant 'food', a meaning which survives vestigially in stereotyped phrases ('meat and drink', 'one man's meat is another man's poison'). More recent examples are *photogenic*, which used to mean 'suitable for being photographed' but which has now been narrowed to 'good-looking, glamorous', and the verb *to discipline*, which used to mean 'to provide discipline, to train', but which is now commonly used in the sense 'to punish'.

An example of widening is the word *rubbish*, which in early Modern English meant 'rubble', but which soon developed the wider meaning of 'waste matter, anything worthless'. Words often take on a wider meaning when they move out of the language of some special group and get adopted by the speech community as a whole. For example (since we are talking of rubbish) the word *junk* was originally sailors' slang, and meant 'old rope', but now that it has moved out of that restricted sphere it has the wider meaning of 'useless stuff, rubbish'. Similarly, *gambit* is a technical term in chess, meaning 'an opening in which White offers a pawn sacrifice', but when it is used outside chess it means simply 'opening move'. Similar widenings of meaning can be seen in the popular use of words from other fields: *allergic* from medicine, *complex* from psychology, *alibi* from the law courts, and so on.

AMELIORATION AND DETERIORATION

A special kind of narrowing of meaning is the acquisition by a word of favourable implications (called 'amelioration') or of unfavourable ones (called 'deterioration'). Amelioration is seen, for example, when *success* changes its meaning from 'result' to 'favourable result', and when *knight* changes from 'servant' to (among other things) 'loyal and chivalrous servant'. Amelioration is often the result of a general change in social or cultural attitudes. Thus in the late seventeenth century the words *enthusiasm* and *zeal* were pejorative, implying violence and fanaticism, at any rate in the mouths of polite society, because of their association with revolutionary puritanism, but as English society changed and the civil wars were forgotten these associations were lost. At the same period, *Gothic* and *romantic* were also pejorative words, to describe a style or quality that was felt to be rude, inelegant, barbarous; but as taste changed in the course of the eighteenth century, the same style or quality came to be admired, and they became words of praise. Among political words, we may note *politician*, which in Shakespeare's day was a sinister word (implying scheming and machiavellian trickery), and *democratic*, which is now usually a term of praise, but which not so very long ago was more often a term of reproach (like *red* today).

Human nature being what it is, deterioration is commoner than amelioration: we are only too prone to believe the worst of anybody, and this is reflected in the way our words change. An example is *lust*, which in Old English meant 'desire, pleasure', but which today means 'illicit or intemperate sexual desire'. We have already noticed the deterioration of *villain*, which from 'peasant' came to mean 'scoundrel'; a similar example is *knave*, which at one time meant 'boy, servant', but which now means 'rogue'. Another such case is *lewd*, which in Old English meant 'lay' (as opposed to 'clerical'), and so also 'ignorant'; hence it came to mean 'common, vulgar', and in early Modern English this progressed to the present meaning of 'unchaste, lascivious'. Other adjectives which are now pejorative, but which formerly were not, include *coy* ('quiet, modest'), *cunning* ('skilful'), *gaudy* ('brilliant, gay'), *notorious* ('well known'), *obsequious* ('compliant'), *officious* ('obliging'), and *uncouth* ('unknown'); the meanings given in brackets are ones found in Middle English or early Modern English.

EUPHEMISM

Euphemism is the habit of avoiding an unpleasant or taboo reference by substituting some indirect word or expression for the blunt direct one, as when we say that somebody 'passed away' when we mean that he died. But of course, when such a euphemism has been used for some time, it ceases to work as a

euphemism any longer, because it is now simply one of the possible expressions for the thing in question. In effect, therefore,
a change of meaning has taken place. Very often, of course, a
new euphemism will now be coined, only to suffer the same
fate in turn.

Euphemism is often caused by things that are painful and
distressing to contemplate. Death is one of these, and the language is full of expressions like 'she lost her husband', 'if anything should happen to me', 'the departed', and 'they must
be liquidated', not to mention the kinds of slang expression
that were current in the armed forces during the war, like 'to
go for a Burton', 'to buy it', 'to hand in your chips', and so
on. War is another subject for euphemism, and official publica-
tions tend to refer delicately to small wars as 'local operations'
and to a possible nuclear war as 'an emergency'. Economic
crises are also unpleasant to think about, and the prewar word
slump was soon replaced by *depression*, which in turn had to be
replaced by *recession*, which is now showing signs of being displaced by *downturn*. And nowadays, of course, nobody becomes
unemployed – merely redundant. Another delicate subject is
imbecility, which has led to such euphemisms as *silly* (which
originally meant 'blessed, innocent'), *natural* (a common word
for 'imbecile' in Shakespeare's day), *innocent*, *crazy*, *simple*,
batty, *potty*, *mental*, *nutty*, and so on. In our own times, people
seem more reluctant than formerly to speak bluntly about
social class, which is often referred to indirectly in terms of
'niceness', 'roughness', 'refinement', and 'education': nowadays, an *uneducated man* often means one who is not quite our
class, dear; riches have been converted into a *higher income
bracket*; and the poor have become *the underprivileged*.

The other main cause of euphemism is social taboo. There is
nothing intrinsically unpleasant in sex, but the subject is so
hedged around with taboos that many people refer to it only
indirectly: there are, for example, innumerable slang words for
the sexual organs and for the sexual act. Because of sexual
euphemism, there is a constant tendency for words meaning
'woman' to acquire pejorative overtones; this has happened

with *mistress*, which has developed as one of its meanings 'paramour'; it happened earlier with *quean*, which meant simply 'woman', and then came to mean 'flaunting, shameless woman'; and it happened with the word *hussy*, which is simply a variant form of *housewife*. The word *harlot* at one time meant 'vagabond', and in Middle English was used about men as well as about women, but its use as a euphemism for *whore* has led to its modern meaning. The other major sphere of taboos is defecation, and this has led to innumerable euphemisms for 'lavatory'; indeed, the word *lavatory* is itself one of these, for originally it meant 'a place for washing oneself', but through being used as a euphemism for a jakes or privy (the Elizabethan words) it has come to mean this. Words for this place lose their 'niceness' so rapidly that new ones have continually to be invented, and what with toilet, ladies' room (or ladies'), washroom, bathroom, cloakroom, gents, convenience, closet, and the rest, choosing the right one is a major proof that one is socially *au fait*.

LOSS OF INTENSITY

Another type of change going on all the time is loss of intensity. When you want to emphasize the strength of your feelings about something, or to impress your hearer suitably, you tend to exaggerate. But of course the meaning of a word is determined by the situations that it is normally used in. So if, for example, the word *hellish* becomes commonly used to describe, not the agonies of the damned or sufferings resembling them, but the kind of discomfort experienced in the rush hour in the London tube, then it comes to *mean* a discomfort of this degree of intensity. The word fades, or loses its intensity. The word *awful*, which once meant 'causing reverence and fear', has been weakened to a kind of omnibus term of deprecation ('The weather was awful') or omnibus intensifier ('It's an awful nuisance'). Similar weakening has occurred in the words *dismal*, *dreadful*, *fearful*, *frightful*, *horrible*, *horrid*, *monstrous*, and so on. The very fact of loss of intensity leads to rather a rapid turnover in words of this kind, since they wear out so quickly, and new words have to be found in their place. But it is not only words of this type that suffer loss of intensity. In Shakespeare's English, the word *naughty* meant 'wicked, evil', and *to annoy* meant 'to harm, to injure'. In the nineteenth century the adjective *fair*, some of whose meanings we have already examined, lost its intensity in some types of context and came to mean 'moderately good' (as in 'He has a fair chance of success'). The adverb *quite* still retains in some contexts the meaning 'entirely' ('I think she is quite superb'), but in others has been weakened to mean 'fairly, in a moderate degree' ('I think she is quite good'). Fading often occurs in words to do with punctuality, since we have an incurable tendency to exaggerate our own promptitude: thus Old English *sōna* meant 'immediately', but has become Modern English *soon*; and in early Modern English, *presently* meant 'immediately, at once', but has now been weakened to 'soon, after a short time'.

FIGURATIVE LANGUAGE

Many of the changes of meaning that we have examined have been slow and insensible affairs; even when not slow, they have mostly been unintentional, as with malapropisms. However, some changes of meaning are conscious affairs. This is the case, for example, when we use a word in a figurative sense, which in due course becomes one of its meanings. The first man to speak of the *foot* of a hill or of the *mouth* of a river was consciously coining a metaphor; but, by constant use, these innovations have ceased to be figurative: they are simply two common meanings of the words *foot* and *mouth*. Language is full of dead metaphors of this kind. They are especially common in words for mental phenomena, and indeed for abstract things in general, since originally these often took their names from some physical or concrete analogy. Thus we talk about *grasping* an idea, on the analogy of the action of the hand; the verb *to comprehend*, similarly, comes from a Latin word which originally meant 'to grasp, to seize', and then came to be used of mental acts as well; we say that we *see* when we mean that we understand; and *lucid* comes from a Latin word that means 'bright, shining'. Metaphors of this kind are old and deeply embedded in the language, but new figurative uses constantly arise: consider in our own times such words as *target* (of production), *ceiling* (of prices, wages, aircraft, mental attainments), *freeze* (of wages, prices), *bottleneck* (in a transport system, on a production line), *blanket* (meaning 'comprehensive, all-embracing'), *package* ('group of proposals which must be accepted or rejected as a whole'), and *headache* ('problem'). These usages are still felt as figurative, but they are well on the way to becoming simply new meanings, dead metaphors.

THE ARGUMENT FROM ETYMOLOGY

It is perhaps change of meaning that produces the most violent reactions among those who are conservative about language, and there are frequent letters to the papers condemning the misuse of this or that word. Every speaker has the right to refuse to adopt an innovation in the language, and we all draw the line somewhere. But, if we refuse to adopt a new meaning, we should often be prepared to recognize that we are fighting a lost cause, and that, after a certain stage has been reached, it is mere pedantry to insist that the earlier meaning is the 'right' one. Above all, we should be wary of resorting to the argument that the 'real meaning' of a word is so and so. There is no intrinsic meaning to any word. A word means what the speech community makes it mean, and if people use the word *aggravate* in the sense 'annoy', then it *means* 'annoy'.

Sometimes the opponent of the new meaning triumphantly produces the etymology of the word, to prove that his meaning is the right one: the word *climax* is from the Greek *klimax*, he says, and so the English word does not mean 'culmination' but 'rising series of events leading to a culmination'. But the meaning of a word in English is the meaning that speakers of English give to it, not the meaning of some earlier word from which it

is descended. Besides, if we are to play this game of etymological meanings, where are we to stop? After all, the *original*
Greek meaning of *klimax* is not 'rising series of events', but
'ladder, staircase'; so why should we not argue that this is the
'real' meaning of English *climax* ('He climbed up the climax
to clean the window')? And if we are going to claim that meanings must be etymological, we shall have to say that *wan* means
'dark', *idea* means 'look, form', *idle* means 'empty', *idiot*
means 'a private person', *deer* means 'animal', *try* means 'rub
down, pulverize', *beam* means 'tree', and so on.

I am not arguing that we should accept all innovations automatically and uncritically: but that we should accept the fact
that change exists, and come to terms with it.

CHAPTER XV

ENGLISH TODAY AND TOMORROW

In the present century, the English language seems to have entered on a period of quite considerable change. One encouraging feature is that the divergent tendencies that have been apparent over the past few centuries now seem to have been slowed down, and perhaps even reversed. We have seen how, as English spread over the world from the seventeenth century onwards, local varieties inevitably sprang up – in North America, in Australia, and so on. This is not to be regretted: the rich variety of English is one of the things that make it an exciting language to speak and to hear. But an indefinite continuation of the divergent processes would ultimately break up English into a number of separate languages, as Primitive Germanic was broken; and this would be an unhappy thing for us, and for the world. As it is, we have some reason to feel optimistic about the continuing unity of English, and about its prospects as a major medium of world intercourse.

Dialect Mixing

The slowing down of the divergent trend has been due to the great development of communications (steamships, aircraft, telegraph, telephone) and the rise of the mass media (the popular press, the cinema, broadcasting, television). These things have enabled the different regional varieties of English to influence one another, and so to reduce their differences. Such influences have been mutual, but at present the major influence in the English-speaking world is undoubtedly the language of the United States, and this influence penetrates everywhere that English is spoken as a mother tongue. Not only do Americans form by far the largest single body of speakers of English, but also of course they have a preponderance of economic and political power and prestige. And considerations of this kind play a major part in the influence of a language: Latin became the dominant cultural language of Western Europe, not because it was intrinsically superior to Greek or Arabic, or was the vehicle for a finer literature than they, but simply because of the political and administrative achievements of Imperial Rome. Similarly the wealth and power of the United States make her a creditor nation in linguistic matters, as in others.

American influence shows itself especially in vocabulary. In Chapter XIII, when I was giving examples of new words which had arisen in America, you were probably surprised to learn that some of them *were* of American origin. Words like *cockroach*, *stevedore*, *tornado*, and *loafer* are so familiar to us that we do not think of them as Americanisms; and the same is true of phrases like *having an axe to grind* and *barking up the wrong tree*. More recent importations, like *gimmick* or *package deal* or *blurb* or *cagey* or *rugged* (in the sense of 'robust') are still conscious Americanisms, but will no doubt become naturalized in Britain in due course.

Inside Britain a somewhat similar process is going on: the different dialects are being mixed and levelled. In addition to the influence of the mass media, there has been that of universal and compulsory education, dating from the last quarter of the nineteenth century, which has worked against the broader dialect elements, both regional and social. Moreover, the population has become more mobile: the small self-contained community has practically disappeared, there has been continuing migration to the great cities, and in two world wars there has been mixing of men in enormous conscript armies. As a result, the traditional rural dialects have now virtually vanished, and have been replaced by new mixed dialects. This does not mean, of course, that dialect differences have disappeared: a Manchester man still speaks differently from a London man; and a Manchester millhand still speaks differently from a Manchester company director. But it does mean that the *range* of variation has been reduced, and that the more idiosyncratic usages are disappearing, in vocabulary, in grammar, in pronunciation.

RECEIVED PRONUNCIATION AND THE DIALECTS

In an earlier chapter, I talked about the prestige language of the English gentry, and the influence of the public schools in making it more or less universal among the upper and upper-middle classes in recent times. It is above all in pronunciation that this form of the language differs from other educated forms, since, as we have seen, the grammar and vocabulary of educated English vary relatively little in different parts of the world. The pronunciation of the public-school speaker is often called Received Pronunciation, or just RP. Now the levelling process that is going on among the English dialects, while it tends to produce standard grammar and a common vocabulary, does not necessarily produce speakers of RP. Many English schoolteachers, for example, do not speak RP, but the educated form of their regional dialect; and it is towards this, rather than towards public-school English, that the influence of the schools works.

It also seems likely that RP has itself lost some of its prestige in the present century, with the rise of democracy and the consequent loss of the monopoly in power and education formerly enjoyed by public-school men. This has been especially so since the Education Act of 1944, which threw open a higher education to the children of the lower and lower-middle classes who were talented enough and tough enough to survive the rat race in the schools. Today, the majority of English university students are not speakers of RP, and of course it is from the universities that a large part of the English professional classes are recruited. Consequently, it is becoming increasingly common for professional men to speak the educated form of their regional dialect, as in America. I do not wish to suggest that public-school speech has lost all its magic. It still has great prestige, for example in the City, in many parts of the Civil Service, and among officers of the armed forces. But it surely is true that the public schools are no longer felt to have a *monopoly* of 'correct speech', and that the prestige of educated regional speech has risen enormously in the present century. Indeed, many people would no longer define Standard English or Received Pronunciation as that of the upper classes or of the public schools, but rather as that of educated people in south-eastern England, thus making an educated form of regional dialect into the standard. It is perhaps symptomatic that Daniel Jones, in his celebrated *Pronouncing Dictionary*, gives both criteria, for he claims that his dictionary records the pronunciation of people from the southeast of England who were educated at public schools.

There is, consequently, a tendency in present-day England to draw the boundaries of 'Standard English' and of 'Received Pronunciation' rather wider than formerly, and to take into account the usages of a larger part of the population. Hence some of the changes that seem to be taking place in the language may be more apparent than real: they may be changes in acceptance, rather than actual substantive changes. What formerly existed as a usage in some group, but was considered substandard, may now come to be accepted as standard, because of the changing definition of 'standard'. It does seem, however, that there are also substantive changes going on in the language, in pronunciation, in grammar, in vocabulary.

CHANGES IN VOCABULARY

The expansion of the vocabulary seems to be going on at a great rate in our time. Many new words continue to be coined from Greek and Latin roots for use in science and technology. More popular words also continue to arise in large numbers, especially by affixation, conversion, and compounding. Examples of such new words have already been given in Chapter XII, and there is no need to repeat them here; in any case, you only have to read the newspapers to find more examples of your own. Changes in meaning also continue, as always; here again, contemporary examples have been included in Chapter XIV, and there is no need to enlarge on them here.

CHANGES IN PRONUNCIATION

In the educated speech of southeastern England, there seems to have been a change in the quality of some vowels during the present century: the vowel of words like *cut* and *jump* is now made farther forward than it was, farther away from *ah* and nearer to the vowel of French *chat*; the vowel of words like *law* and *horse*, on the other hand, has become closer, farther away from *ah* and nearer to the vowel of French *beau*. The long pure vowels *ee* (as in *keep* and *see*) and *oo* (as in *hoop* and *too*) are becoming diphthongized: in the speech of many people, *ee* is now a glide, which begins in the position of the vowel of *bit* and then moves up to the *ee* position; *oo*, similarly, begins in the position of the vowel of *put* and then glides to the *oo* position. In substandard speech, these diphthongs often begin at an even opener and more central position, for example from the position of the vowel of *er*.

In unstressed syllables, the short *er* sound is spreading at the expense of other short vowels. For example, it is often heard instead of short *i* in the unstressed syllables of *system*, *waitress*, *remain*, *kitchen*, and *women*; and it sometimes replaces other vowels too, for example in words like *sawdust* and *boycott*. In this respect, British pronunciation is following in the wake of American and Australian.

Among the consonants, the long-term historical process of weakening and loss at the ends of words seems to be continuing. Final consonants which are especially often lost in familiar speech are *t*, *d*, and *n*. For example, the *d* is often lost in phrases like *old man*, the *n* in *fifteen miles*, and the *t* in *half past five*. There are also various minor changes going on: for example, assimilations, such as the pronunciation of *tenpence* as *tempence*, or of *due* as *Jew*; and the continuing spread of 'intrusive *r*', heard in such phrases as *the idear of it*, *Indiar and Ghana, the lawr of the sea*. Intrusive *r* arises by analogy with words like *father* and *beer*, which (for historical reasons discussed in Chapter XII) quite regularly have a final *r* before a vowel, but not before a consonant or a pause.

There are also changes going on in the way words are stressed. In a number of words of two syllables, the stress has been moved within living memory from the second to the first syllable: *garage*, *adult*, *alloy*, *ally*. In some words of more than two syllables, there is an apparent tendency to move the stress from the first to the second syllable: *doctrinal*, *communal*, *formidable*, *aristocrat*, *pejorative*, *hospitable*, *controversy*, and many others. However, the forms with the stress on the second syllable are not new ones, and it seems that here we have a change of acceptance (or the beginnings of it) rather than a substantive change. The pronunciations with first-syllable stress are upper-class ones, and the other forms are permeating up from below, as part of the dialect mixing of our time.

A trend which has been encouraged by the spread of secondary education is the adoption of what can be called 'continental pronunciations'. Words borrowed from abroad soon get assimilated to an English style of pronunciation, either by passing through normal English sound changes or because of the influence of the spelling. Nowadays, however, such words are sometimes given a 'foreign' kind of pronunciation again. Thus in the traditional pronunciation the words *gala*, *Gaza*, *Copenhagen*, and *armada* have their stressed *a* pronounced as in *gale*, but it is now common for the vowel of *father* to be used instead, and in *armada* this pronunciation is universal. Similarly, *valet* and *beret* and *ricochet* are now often pronounced without their final *t*; *proviso* sometimes has its *i* pronounced as in *machine* instead of as in *mine*; Marlowe's *Dr Faustus* is frequently given the vowel of the German *Faust* instead of that of the English *author*; and *chivalry* is almost universally pronounced with a *sh* sound instead of the traditional *ch*. Such changes obviously imply a realization that the word is of foreign origin, and some knowledge of foreign languages; they must be due to some extent to the expansion of education and the increased popularity of foreign travel.

However, there is probably another influence at work too, namely the 'new' pronunciation of Latin, which has continental-style vowels, whereas the 'old' pronunciation had anglicized vowels. The majority of Englishmen under middle age, if they have learnt Latin at all, have learnt the new pronunciation. This no doubt explains why many younger people are reluctant to use the traditional pronunciation of those Latin tags which are commonly used in English, like *a priori*, *quasi*, *sine die*: the traditional pronunciation sounds wrong, and they tend to use an approximation to the new Latin pronunciation. This even affects Latin proper names; of course, there is no danger that a well-known name like *Julius Caesar* will lose its traditional pronunciation; but it is now quite common to pronounce Shakespeare's *Coriolanus* with an *ah* vowel instead of the vowel of *lane*. The same change of vowel is sometimes heard in *status*, *apparatus*, and *stratum*, and even occasionally in *data*. Besides affecting words which are obviously direct from Latin, this 'new Latin' influence also affects a few words which are more remotely derived from Latin, but whose origin is nevertheless plain: thus the words *deity* and *vehicle* traditionally have their *e* pronounced like the vowel of *deed*, but are now often given the vowel of *day*. The 'new Latin' and 'continental' tendencies must obviously reinforce one another.

CHANGES IN GRAMMAR

In grammar we can see the continuation, in small ways, of the long-term historical trend in English from synthetic to analytic, from a system that relies on inflexions to one that relies on word order and on grammatical words (prepositions, auxiliary verbs, etc.). For example, the form *whom* is dropping out of use, at any rate in speech, and *who* tends to be used in all positions. Admittedly, we still have to use *whom* after a preposition, as in 'To whom shall I give it?'; but in fact this is not what we say in ordinary speech – we say 'Who shall I give it to?' Another example of the trend is in the comparison of adjectives, where *more* and *most* are spreading at the expense of the endings *-er* and *-est*. Formerly, *-er* and *-est* were used more widely than today, and in the seventeenth century you meet forms like *famousest* and *notoriousest*. At the beginning of the present century, adjectives of more than two syllables always had *more* and *most* ('more notorious, most notorious'); adjectives of one syllable normally had *-er* and *-est* ('ruder, rudest'); the adjectives of two syllables varied, some normally being compared one way ('more famous, most famous') and some the other ('commoner, commonest'). In this group of two-syllabled adjectives, there has been a tendency in the course of the century for *-er* and *-est* to be replaced by *more* and *most*, and it is now quite normal to say 'more common, most common'; and similarly with *fussy, quiet, cloudy, cruel, simple, pleasant*, and others. Recently, moreover, *more* and *most* have been spreading to words of one syllable, and it is not at all uncommon to hear expressions like 'John is more keen than Robert' and 'It was more crude than I expected'.

Changes are also taking place among the auxiliary verbs. Thus *shall* and *should* are dropping out of use in some positions, and being replaced by *will* and *would*: it is now quite normal to say such things as 'We will all die some day' and 'I would prefer not to'. For giving or asking permission, *can* is now common instead of *may*, so that children say 'Can I leave the table?' And, especially in the United States, *might* seems to be spreading at the expense of other auxiliaries, especially *may*. The verbs *need* and *dare* are ceasing to be auxiliaries, and coming more and more to be used as ordinary verbs: thus it is increasingly normal to say 'Do you need to do it?' and 'I don't dare to do it', and less common to say 'Need you do it?' and 'I dare not do it.' In substandard speech, the same has happened to the auxiliaries *ought to* and *used to*, for you hear expressions like 'He didn't ought to' and 'He didn't used to', and such forms are now spreading into educated speech.

It also seems that changes are taking place in the use of the definite article, which is sometimes omitted where formerly it was obligatory, for example in phrases like '*the* Bank Rate', '*the* United States', '*the* Government', 'on *the* radio', 'the art of *the* theatre', 'to go to *the* university'. It is also becoming common to put titles or descriptive phrases in front of proper names, in cases where this would formerly have been impossible, for example *prime minister Macmillan* (instead of *the prime minister*, *Mr Macmillan* or *Mr Macmillan, the prime minister*); and similarly with *actress Flora Robson, centre-forward John Charles, twenty-seven-year-old pretty London housewife Betty Smith*, and so on. This trick comes from the newspapers, but is no longer confined to them, and is even heard in speech. Another development where the newspapers may have had an influence is the use of expressions like *London's East End* and *a symphony's first movement*, where formerly it was normal to say *the East End of London* and *the first movement of a symphony*; the newspapers no doubt find the new forms shorter and snappier for headlines. This development is contrary to the normal run of grammatical change in English: the replacement of the preposition *of* by the inflexion *'s* is a move from analytic to synthetic.

ENGLISH TOMORROW

It is dangerous to extrapolate or to prophesy, and none of us can even guess what the English language will be like in a hundred years time. The changes of the last few decades suggest what forces are at work in the language today, and the likely shape of things in the next few decades; but the history of the language in the coming century will depend, as it always has done, on the history of the community itself.

One of the striking things at the moment is the remarkable expansion going on in the vocabulary; we cannot tell whether this will continue at its present rate, but if it does the change in a hundred years will be comparable to that of such earlier periods as 1300 to 1400 or 1550 to 1650. Another clear trend at the moment is large-scale dialect mixing, with American influence predominant; if this continues, the divergent tendencies of the language will be held in check, and a unified

English language will continue to be available as a medium of international communication. Inside England, it seems quite on the cards that public-school English will lose its privileged position, and be replaced by local educated standards, or by a new standard (perhaps educated London English); but here, obviously, a great deal depends on the course of English social history. In pronunciation, such trends as the diphthongization of the long close vowels may well continue, and might be expected to lead to further changes in the vowel system. In grammar, nothing revolutionary seems to be happening, but the trends of the past thousand years continue in small ways.

It is clear, at any rate, that the process of change, which we have traced from the earliest records up to modern times, is still going on. As long as a language is being used, it will be in flux; and English is changing today, as it has always changed. It requires an effort of detachment to recognize this change for what it is. We are so thoroughly trained in the use of one particular form of the language, which seems to us so absolutely 'right', that we are likely to dismiss innovations as mistakes, as vulgarisms, as the slipshod barbarism of that shocking younger generation. On the other hand, when our own elders make similar deprecating noises about *our* use of the language, we are likely to dismiss them as old-fashioned, as pedants, as stuffy old fuddy-duddies who haven't yet been dragged into the twentieth century. This conservatism is inevitable, and indeed necessary to the stability of the language. As users of the language, we inevitably feel that there is some unique rightness about our own particular form of it, and we try to teach this form to our children. But, if we are to understand the language, we must learn to step outside this attitude, and view the whole speech community with scientific detachment. As users of the language, we are fully entitled to deplore an innovation, and to refuse to adopt it ourselves. But, as scientific observers, we must recognize that our own behaviour in doing so is simply that of one group at one point in time, and that in the next generation the innovation may well have become completely respectable, and indeed uniquely right for its user.

It is natural to long for stability in a universe of change, to try to pin things down and fix them. But it can't be done. The whole of nature is in flux, and so is the whole of the life of man, and we might as well accept the fact. It's not really much good clinging to the bank: we have to push out into the flux and swim.

GLOSSARY

References to other items in the Glossary are indicated by capital letters. Page-references to the text are given where this seems helpful.

ABLAUT: *see* GRADATION.

ACCENT: a combination of STRESS and INTONATION. See p. 113.

ACCUSATIVE: one of the CASES of nouns, pronouns, and adjectives in Indo-European languages. Used in a variety of situations, especially for the OBJECT, and often after PREPOSITIONS. See pp. 109–10.

ADJECTIVE: a word-class (*see* PARTS OF SPEECH). Examples of English adjectives are italicized in the following sentences: (1) The *new* ship was very *fast*. (2) Who is more *beautiful*, you or your *young* sister? See also WEAK DECLENSION OF THE ADJECTIVE.

ADVERB: a word-class (see PARTS OF SPEECH). Examples of English adverbs: *quickly, often, here, always, backwards*.

AFFIX: a PREFIX or SUFFIX.

AFFIXATION: the formation of a word by means of an AFFIX. See pp. 216–17.

AFFRICATE: a STOP consonant in which the release is relatively slow, e.g. the *ch* of *church*. See p. 16.

AFRIKAANS: form of Dutch, spoken in South Africa.

AKKADIAN: eastern branch of the ancient SEMITIC languages, including classical Babylonian and Assyrian. See pp. 73–4.

ALPHABETIC WRITING: writing in which (at least in principle) the symbols stand for single sounds or PHONEMES.

ALTAIC: family of languages, including Turkish and Mongol. See p. 75.

ANALOGY: the process of inventing a linguistic item in conformity with some existing pattern in the language; e.g. the invention of a plural form *mans* (instead of *men*) on the analogy of the many English plurals in -*s*. See p. 69.

ANGLIAN: a dialect of OLD ENGLISH, consisting of Mercian and Northumbrian. See pp. 126–8 and Figure 11.

ANGLO-NORMAN: the form of the NORMAN FRENCH dialect which developed in England after the Norman Conquest.

ANGLO-SAXON: an older name for the stage of the English language now usually called OLD ENGLISH.

ARABIC: language of the SEMITIC family. See pp. 73–5.

ARTICLES: *see* DEFINITE ARTICLE; INDEFINITE ARTICLE.

ARTICULATE: (*a*) to articulate is to produce a speech sound or speech sounds; (*b*) when we say that a language is articulate, we mean that it has structure; see ARTICULATED.

ARTICULATED: literally 'jointed'; when we say that language is articulated, we refer to the fact that it has structure: phonemes forming words, words forming sentences, and so on. See pp. 17–24.

ARTICULATION: the production of a speech sound, or the method of producing it. See also ARTICULATOR.

ARTICULATOR: the speech organ (or part of a speech organ) that approaches some other part of the vocal apparatus in order to produce a speech sound. E.g. for the English *t* sound the articulator is the tip of the tongue; this is brought up against the teethridge, which is called the PLACE (or point) OF ARTICULATION. See pp. 10–17 and *Figure 1*.

ARYAN: a branch of the INDO-EUROPEAN language-family, consisting of an Indian group (Sanskrit, Hindi, etc.) and an Iranian group (Persian, etc.). See p. 85.

ASH: the Old English symbol æ. See p. 129.

ASPIRATED CONSONANT: one followed by a puff of breath resembling an *h* sound.

ASSIMILATION: the change of a sound under the influence of a neighbouring sound, by which the articulations of the two sounds become more similar. See pp. 63–4.

ASSYRIAN: ancient language belonging to the SEMITIC family.

AUXILIARY: a word-class (*see* PARTS OF SPEECH). In English, a closed class with such members as *shall, can, might, must*. Also called *auxiliary verbs*.

AUXILIARY VERB: *see* AUXILIARY.

AVESTAN: form of ancient PERSIAN, found in the Avesta (the sacred writings of the Zoroastrians).

BABYLONIAN: ancient language of the SEMITIC family.

BALTIC: a branch of INDO-EUROPEAN, including Lithuanian and Lettish. See p. 86.

BILINGUAL: speaking two languages.

BLENDING: the formation of a new word by combining parts of two existing words. See p. 220.

BRITANNIC: a branch of CELTIC, including Welsh and Breton.

BURGUNDIAN: extinct language of the eastern branch of GERMANIC.

CASE: any one of a set of variant forms of a NOUN, PRONOUN, or ADJECTIVE, used according to the different grammatical relationships it enters into. See pp. 108–12.

CELTIC: a group of related languages belonging to the INDO-EUROPEAN family, and including Welsh, Gaelic, and Breton. See p. 86.

CENTRAL FRENCH: dialect of OLD FRENCH, spoken in the Ile-de-France and Paris, from which standard modern French is descended.

CENTRAL VOWEL: one in which the highest part of the tongue is neither far forward in the mouth nor far back, but in an intermediate position, e.g. the vowel of *bird*. See p. 13 and *Figure 2*.

CLAUSE: a linguistic structure consisting of a SUBJECT and a PREDICATE, whether or not it constitutes a SENTENCE.

CLOSED SYLLABLE: one that ends with a consonant.

CLOSE VOWEL: one in which the tongue is high in the mouth, e.g. the vowels of *sea, who*. See p. 13 and *Figure 2*.

COGNATE: (of words) derived from the same word in the parent language.

COMBINATIVE SOUND-CHANGE: a change in pronunciation that takes place only when the phoneme in question occurs in some certain position (e.g. at the end of a word, or when it precedes some other specified phoneme). Also called a *dependent* sound-change. Contrasted with ISOLATIVE SOUND-CHANGE. See also SOUND LAW.

COMPOUND: word formed by joining together two existing words, e.g. *blackbird*. See pp. 136, 217–18.

CONJUGATION: a set of INFLEXIONS for a VERB.

CONSONANT: a speech sound in which at some time the mouth passage is obstructed. See pp. 15–17.

CONVERSION: the production of a new word by the transfer of an existing word to a different word-class. See pp. 219–20.

CORNISH: an extinct language of the Britannic branch of CELTIC. See p. 86.

CUNEIFORM: form of ancient writing, in which the symbols consist of groups of wedge-shaped marks made on a clay tablet with a reed stylus. See pp. 43–5.

DANELAW: the part of England left under Scandinavian rule after the partition of the country between King Alfred and the Danes. See p. 143 and *Figure 12*.

DATIVE: one of the CASES of a noun, pronoun, and adjective in Indo-European languages. See pp. 108–10.

DECLENSION: a set of CASE endings for NOUNS or ADJECTIVES. See pp. 108–11.

DEFINITE ARTICLE: Modern English *the*, and the corresponding forms in earlier stages of English and in some other languages.

DENTAL: having the teeth as PLACE OF ARTICULATION.

DEPENDENT SOUND-CHANGE: *see* ISOLATIVE SOUND-CHANGE.

DIALECT: the particular form of a language used by some sub-group of the speech-community. If the group is a geographical one, it is a *regional dialect* (e.g. Lancashire English); if the group is a social one, it is a *social dialect* or *class dialect* (e.g. public school English). It is not always possible to draw a sharp distinction between a dialect and a language. See pp. 70–3.

DIGRAPH: a combination of two letters used to represent a single phoneme, e.g. *sh* in Modern English spelling.

DIPHTHONG: vowel in which the speech organs change their position in the course of the sound, but constituting only one syllable; e.g. the vowels of English *boy*, *mice*. See pp. 14–15.

DRAVIDIAN: language-family of southern India, including Tamil and Telegu.

DUAL: special form of a word to show that *two* persons or things are referred to; contrasted with SINGULAR and PLURAL. See pp. 110, 112.

DUMMY AUXILIARY. See pp. 201–4.

EGYPTIAN: Ancient Egyptian was a HAMITIC language. The language of modern Egypt is ARABIC, a Semitic language.

ETH: the Icelandic name for the symbol ð. See p. 130.

ETYMOLOGY: the derivation of a word.

FAROESE: language of the Faroe Islands, belonging to the northern branch of GERMANIC.

FINNISH: a language of the FINNO-UGRIAN family.

FINNO-UGRIAN: a group of related languages belonging to the URALIAN family, including Finnish, Estonian, and Hungarian. See p. 75.

FIRST SOUND SHIFTING: change that took place in the consonant system of PROTO-GERMANIC during the first millenium BC, whereby aspirated voiced stops changed to voiced stops, voiced stops to voiceless stops, and voiceless stops to voiceless fricatives. Also known as Grimm's Law. See pp. 114–16.

FLEMISH: a form of Dutch, spoken in Belgium.

FRANKISH: extinct language of the western branch of GERMANIC, spoken by tribes living east of the Rhine in the first millenium of the Christian era.

FRICATIVE: a consonant in which the air passage is narrowed so much that audible friction is produced, e.g. s, z, f, v, th. See pp. 15–16.

FRISIAN: a language of the western branch of GERMANIC, closely related to English. See pp. 106–7.

FRONT MUTATION: a series of sound changes in prehistoric Old English, whereby a number of vowels were changed when there was an *i*, *i*, or *j* in the following syllable. Also called *i-umlaut*. See pp. 133–4.

FRONT VOWEL: one in which the highest part of the tongue is far forward in the mouth, e.g. the vowels of *beat*, *bit*, *bet*, *bat*. See p. 13 and *Figure 2*.

FUNCTIONAL LOAD: the amount of work in a language that some
  item or feature has to do. See p. 66.

FUTHORC: the Old English form of the Runic alphabet, corresponding to the Scandinavian *futhark*. See p. 129.

GENDER: a set of categories (given such names as *masculine, feminine,
  neuter*) into which the NOUNS of some languages are divided.
  The category a noun falls into determines the selection of the
  PERSONAL PRONOUN used to replace it (e.g. in English *he,
  she,* or *it*). In languages with *natural gender*, the categories correspond fairly well with the sex or sexlessness of the person or
  thing referred to by the noun. In languages with *grammatical
  gender* there is no such correspondence, and the allocation of a
  noun to a gender is arbitrary. In some languages, ADJECTIVES
  and ARTICLES are also divided into such categories, and have
  to be selected according to the gender of the noun that they
  accompany. See pp. 110–11.

GENITIVE: one of the CASES of nouns, pronouns, and adjectives in
  Indo-European languages. Used to indicate a variety of relationships, including possession, for which reason it is sometimes
  called the *possessive* case. See p. 109.

GERMAN: a language of the western branch of GERMANIC, made up
  of both HIGH GERMAN and LOW GERMAN dialects.

GERMANIC: group of related languages belonging to the INDO-
  EUROPEAN family, and including English, German, Gothic, and
  the Scandinavian languages. See pp. 79–82, and Chapter VI.

GERMANS: besides being used of the inhabitants of modern Germany,
  this word is used to translate the Latin *Germani*, and so to refer
  to speakers of PROTO-GERMANIC and of ancient GERMANIC
  languages.

GLIDE: sound made while the speech organs are moving from one
  position to another. Glides include DIPHTHONGS and SEMI-
  VOWELS, and also often occur automatically in the transition
  from one phoneme to the next in the chain of utterance.

GLOTTIS: the opening between the VOCAL CORDS.

GOTHIC: extinct language of the eastern branch of GERMANIC.
  See p. 106.

GRADATION: in Proto-Indo-European, the alternation of different
  vowels in related forms (as in English *sing, sang, sung*). Also
  called *ablaut*. See pp. 118–19.

GRADE: any one of a series of vowels used for GRADATION.

GRAMMAR: the structure of a language at the level of closed systems
  (i.e. ones in which all the items can be enumerated, and which
  can be described exhaustively). Contrasted with vocabulary (or
  lexis), at which level no complete description or definitive list of
  items can be given.

GRAMMATICAL GENDER: *see* GENDER.

GREAT VOWEL SHIFT: series of changes in the English long vowels, which took place in late Middle English and early Modern English. See pp. 195–7.

GREEK: language of the INDO-EUROPEAN family. See pp. 85–6.

GRIMM'S LAW: *see* FIRST SOUND SHIFTING.

GUTNISH: language of the Swedish island of Gotland, belonging to the northern branch of GERMANIC.

HAMITIC: a family of languages, including Ancient Egyptian and modern Berber and Somali. Related to SEMITIC. See pp. 74–5.

HAMITO-SEMITIC: a large language-family, consisting of HAMITIC and SEMITIC. See pp. 73–5.

HELLENIC: the GREEK branch of INDO-EUROPEAN.

HIGH GERMAN: group of dialects of southern Germany, belonging to the western branch of GERMANIC, and including modern standard literary German. Distinguished from the other West Germanic languages by the consonant changes known as the *High German Shift* or *Second Sound Shifting*, which produced forms like *Schiff, beissen, machen*, compared with English *ship, bite, make.*

IDEOGRAM: a visual sign which stands directly for an idea or object, and so is not tied to one specific language. See pp. 42–3.

IMPERATIVE: form of the VERB used in giving commands.

IMPERSONAL VERB: one where the grammatical subject is a formal one, and does not refer to any person or thing, as in *it is raining.*

INDEFINITE ARTICLE: Modern English *a, an*, and the corresponding forms in earlier stages of English and in some other languages.

INDICATIVE: *see* SUBJUNCTIVE.

INDO-EUROPEAN: large language-family with many branches, to one of which, Germanic, the English language belongs. See Chapter V.

INDO-GERMANIC: another name for INDO-EUROPEAN.

INDO-IRANIAN: another name for ARYAN.

INFINITIVE: form of the VERB in Indo-European languages, roughly corresponding to Modern English forms like *to walk.*

INFLEXION: variation in the ending of a word for grammatical purposes. See pp. 108–13.

INTERJECTION: one of the traditional PARTS OF SPEECH. An interjection is an exclamation, like *Ah!, Alas!*, etc.; its distinctive feature is that it does not enter into sentence structures.

INTERNAL LOAN: word borrowed from another dialect of the same language.

INTONATION: the patterns of musical pitch in speech; the way the voice rises and falls on the musical scale as you talk. See pp. 21–2.

IRISH or IRISH GAELIC: a language of the Gaelic branch of CELTIC. Sometimes called *Erse*. See p. 86.

ISOLATIVE SOUND-CHANGE: a change in the pronunciation of a phoneme that takes place in *all* positions that it occurs in. Contrasted with COMBINATIVE SOUND-CHANGE.

ISOGLOSS: a line drawn on the map to show the geographical limit of some specified linguistic feature, or the boundary between two alternative features. See p. 93 and *Figure 9*.

ITALIC: a branch of INDO-EUROPEAN, spoken in ancient Italy, including LATIN, Oscan, and Umbrian. See pp. 76–7, 86.

I-UMLAUT: *see* FRONT MUTATION.

KENTISH: a dialect of OLD ENGLISH. See p. 126 and *Figure 11*.

KENTUM LANGUAGES: Indo-European languages in which Proto-Indo-European palatal *k* became velar *k*. See pp. 90–1.

KOINE: form of Greek widely used in the eastern Mediterranean from the time of Alexander the Great. See pp. 77–8.

LANGUAGE: for an attempt at a definition, see pp. 10–26.

LANGUAGE FAMILY: group of related languages, i.e. ones that have all evolved from some single previous language. See Chapter VI.

LATERAL CONSONANT: one in which the centre of the mouth is blocked by the tongue, while the air is allowed to escape down one side or down both. See p. 17.

LATIN: a language of the ITALIC branch of Indo-European, spoken in ancient Rome and thence spread over the Roman Empire. Ancestor of the ROMANCE LANGUAGES. See pp. 71–3, 76–7, 86, 109–12.

LITHUANIAN: language of the BALTIC family.

LOAN WORD: word borrowed by one language from another.

LOW GERMAN: in the widest sense, all forms of the western branch of GERMANIC which are not HIGH GERMAN. Used in a narrower sense to exclude English and Frisian, but to include Dutch and Flemish. In the narrowest sense of all, refers only to the dialects of northern Germany. Distinguished from HIGH GERMAN by the absence of the Second Sound Shifting.

MEANING. See pp. 239–40.

MELODY: same as INTONATION.

MERCIAN: a dialect of OLD ENGLISH. See p. 126 and *Figure 11*.

MIDDLE ENGLISH: the English language from about 1100 to about 1450 or 1500.

MID VOWEL: one in which the tongue is neither very high in the mouth nor very low, but at a medium height, e.g. the vowels of *bed*, *bird*. See p. 13 and *Figure 2*.

MODERN ENGLISH: the English language from about 1450 or 1500 to the present day.

MONOPHTHONG: a PURE VOWEL.

NASAL CAVITY: the air passage behind the nose, linking the nostrils to the back of the mouth cavity; see *Figure 1*, p. 11.

NASAL CONSONANT: one in which the nasal passage is open, but the mouth passage blocked, e.g. *m, n*. See p. 17.

NASAL VOWEL: one in which the nasal passage is open, e.g. the vowel of French *bon*. See p. 12.

NATURAL GENDER: *see* GENDER.

NOMINATIVE: one of the CASES of nouns, pronouns, and adjectives in Indo-European languages, used especially for the SUBJECT of the sentence. See pp. 108–10.

NORMAN FRENCH: northern dialect of OLD FRENCH, spoken by William the Conqueror and his followers.

NORTHUMBRIAN: a dialect of OLD ENGLISH. See p. 126 and *Figure 11*.

NOUN: a word-class (*see* PARTS OF SPEECH). Examples of English nouns are italicized in the following sentence: 'My *brother* got a few *ideas* from the *library*.' The traditional definition of a noun is 'the name of a person, place, or thing'. Modern grammarians prefer to define it by formal characteristics, e.g. in English by its occurrence after determiners (words like *the*, *my*) and its use of a plural inflection.

OBJECT: in Indo-European languages, many sentences have a position in the PREDICATE which is called the *object* or the *direct object*. Examples of the object are italicized in the following sentences: (1) The master beat *the servant*; (2) I dislike *him* heartily; (3) His father gave him *sixpence*; (4) He underwent *an operation*.

OLD ENGLISH: the English language from the time of the first Anglo-Saxon settlements in England to about 1100.

OLD FRENCH: the French language up to about the fourteenth century.

OLD HIGH GERMAN: the HIGH GERMAN language up to about 1100.

OLD ICELANDIC: the Icelandic language up to about 1350.

OLD IRISH: the IRISH GAELIC language up to about 1000.

OLD NORSE: the early form of the northern (Scandinavian) branch of GERMANIC. Sometimes treated as synonymous with OLD ICELANDIC, because this is the early Scandinavian language with the fullest records.

OLD PERSIAN: ancient form of PERSIAN, found in inscriptions from about 500 BC.

OLD SAXON: ancient West GERMANIC language, ancestor of the modern LOW GERMAN dialects of Northern Germany.

OLD SLAVONIC: oldest recorded form of SLAVONIC. See p. 86.

OPEN SYLLABLE: one that ends in a vowel.

OPEN VOWEL: one in which the tongue is low in the mouth, e.g. the vowels of *hot* and *ah*. See p. 13 and *Figure 2*.

PALATAL CONSONANTS: ones in which the PLACE OF ARTICULATION is the PALATE.

PALATE: the front part of the roof of the mouth, behind the teeth-ridge. Also called the *hard palate*. See *Figure 1*, p. 11.

PARTS OF SPEECH: the traditional name for the different categories of words. Traditional grammar recognizes eight: NOUNS, PRONOUNS, ADJECTIVES, VERBS, ADVERBS, PREPOSITIONS, conjunctions, and INTERJECTIONS. It tends to regard these as universal categories, applicable to any language. It defines them in various ways, but with a bias towards definitions in terms of meaning: thus traditional-style school-grammars often define a verb as 'a word which describes an action or a state'. It is not difficult to show the inadequacy of definitions of this kind, and modern grammarians prefer to use *formal* criteria for defining a part of speech: the kind of sentence-patterns it can occur in, the inflexions it can be given, and so on. This means that there is no universal definition for a noun or a verb, but only definitions for a given language at a given time; and there are languages for which the categories of noun and verb have no relevance. Many modern grammarians object to the term *parts of speech*, and prefer to talk about *word classes* or *form classes*. In general, modern grammarians of English use more word-classes than the eight traditional ones, setting up such categories as *determiners* (e.g. *the*, *a*, *my*) and *auxiliaries* (e.g. *could*, *shall*). They also tend to distinguish two main types of word-class: (1) closed classes, where a complete list can be given of the members (e.g. prepositions, determiners); (2) open classes, where no such complete list can be given (e.g. nouns, adjectives).

PASSIVE: special forms of the VERB, to indicate that an action is suffered, not performed; e.g. *he was eaten*, contrasted with the non-passive *he ate*.

PAST PARTICIPLE: part of the VERB in Indo-European languages, like English *given*, *sung*, *seen*.

PERSIAN: a language of the Iranian branch of ARYAN.

PERSONAL PRONOUN: a word-class (*see* PARTS OF SPEECH). In present-day English: *I*, *me*, *you*, *he*, *him*, *she*, *her*, *we*, *us*, *they*, *them*. Also similar sets in other languages, like French *je*, *me*, *moi*, *tu*, etc., German *ich*, *mich*, *mir*, etc.

PHOENICIAN: an ancient West SEMITIC language.

PHONEME: in any one language, a family of similar speech-sounds which do not contrast with each other; e.g. the different varieties of the *p* sound that occur in English according to the neighbouring sounds. See pp. 18–20.

PHONETIC CONTEXT: the sounds which occur before and after the item under consideration, including the conditions of stress and intonation under which it occurs.

PHONOLOGY: the sound-system of a language, e.g. its PHONEMES, the permissible ways of combining them, its patterns of STRESS and INTONATION.

PICTOGRAPH: a picture intended to convey an idea or a message. See pp. 41–3.

PLACE OF ARTICULATION: when a speech-sound is produced, some moving organ (the ARTICULATOR) approaches some other part of the vocal apparatus; the part which is thus approached is called the place (or point) of articulation. E.g. in the English *k* sound, the back of the tongue (the articulator) is brought up against the velum (the place of articulation). And see *Figure 1*, p. 11.

PLOSIVE: a STOP consonant in which the release is very rapid, e.g. *p, d, k*. See p. 16.

PLURAL: special form of a word used to indicate that more than one (or in some cases more than two) persons or things are referred to. Contrasted with SINGULAR. E.g. singular *boy, is*; plural *boys, are. See also* DUAL.

POLYSEMY: multiple meaning. See pp. 241–4.

PREDICATE: *see* SUBJECT.

PREFIX: element which can be placed before a STEM or root to make a word, e.g. *un-* (*unpin, unhappy*), *re-* (*rehouse, receive*), See pp. 216–17.

PREHISTORIC OLD ENGLISH: the OLD ENGLISH language in the period from which no written records have survived, i.e. before about AD 700.

PREPOSITION: a word-class (*see* PARTS OF SPEECH). Examples of English prepositions are italicized in the following sentences: (1) I live *in* London, *near* St Paul's. (2) Why did you give it *to* him? (3) It was you that I gave it *to*. They are normally followed by a NOUN or PRONOUN or something equivalent, which they are said to govern; but in some cases (as in sentence 3) the preposition is separated from the word it governs.

PRONOUN: a word-class (*see* PARTS OF SPEECH). In English, pronouns have functions similar to those of NOUNS, but differ from them in some ways (e.g. they cannot be preceded by *the* or by adjectives). There are various sub-groups, including: (1) PERSONAL PRONOUNS; (2) Relative Pronouns, *who, which*, and *that* (in sentences like 'I know the man *who* did it', 'He bought a book, *which* he took away with him'); (3) Demonstrative Pronouns, *this, that, these, those* (in sentences like '*This* is what I want', 'I don't like *that*'); (4) Interrogative Pronouns, *who, which, what* (in sen-

tences like 'Who knows?', 'Which will you have?'); (5) Indefinite
Pronouns (e.g. *none, any, each*); (6) Reflexive Pronouns (*myself,
himself, ourselves,* etc.).

PROTO-GERMANIC: the postulated ancient language, a dialect of
Indo-European, from which all the GERMANIC languages
have evolved. Also called *Primitive Germanic.* See pp. 103–
20.

PROTO-INDO-EUROPEAN: the postulated ancient language from
which all INDO-EUROPEAN languages have evolved. Also called
Primitive Indo-European. See pp. 83–97.

PURE VOWEL: one in which the position of the speech-organs does
not change appreciably in the course of the sound. Contrasted with
DIPHTHONG.

RECEIVED PRONUNCIATION: the pronunciation of English heard
from speakers educated at the great English public schools. Also
called *RP.* See pp. 259–60.

REFLEXIVE PRONOUN: *see* PRONOUN.

RELATED LANGUAGES: languages which have evolved from some
single earlier language. See Chapter VI.

RELATIVE: see PRONOUN, and p. 139.

RESONANT CONSONANT: one in which use is made of resonant
cavities, while there is some kind of obstruction in the mouth
passage, e.g. *m, n, l.* See pp. 16–17.

ROMANCE LANGUAGES: languages descended from Latin, such as
French, Italian, Spanish. See pp. 71–3.

ROMANSCH: a ROMANCE LANGUAGE, spoken in parts of Switzerland and Italy.

ROUNDED VOWEL: one accompanied by a rounding of the lips, e.g.
those of English *cot, caught,* French *tu, peu.* See pp. 13–14.

RUNES: system of writing used for inscriptions by the early Germanic
peoples. See pp. 128–9.

SANSKRIT: extinct language of northern India, belonging to the
Indian branch of ARYAN.

SATEM LANGUAGES: Indo-European languages in which Proto-
Indo-European palatal *k* became a palatal fricative. See pp.
90–1.

SCANDINAVIAN: general name for languages of the northern branch
of GERMANIC (see p. 105) and their speakers.

SECOND SOUND SHIFTING: *see* HIGH GERMAN.

SEMITIC: large family of languages, including Akkadian, Hebrew, and
Arabic. Related to HAMITIC. See pp. 73–5.

SEMIVOWEL: a GLIDE which is not merely an accidental linking-
sound, but which does not constitute a syllable, e.g. the *y* of *yes,*
the *w* of *water.*

SENTENCE: there have been many definitions. Here is a useful working definition: 'a sentence is a linguistic structure which is not a constituent of some larger one.'

SHIFT: *see* FIRST SOUND SHIFTING; GREAT VOWEL SHIFT.

SHORTENING: loss of part of a word, not as the result of a SOUND LAW. See p. 220.

SINGULAR: form of word used when only one person or thing is referred to. *See* PLURAL and DUAL.

SINO-TIBETAN: family of languages, including Thai, Burmese, Tibetan, and Chinese.

SLAVONIC: branch of INDO-EUROPEAN, including Russian, Czech, and Polish. See p. 86.

SOFT PALATE: see VELUM.

SOUND LAW: a regular change in pronunciation that occurs in a language or dialect during some given period of its history. *See* COMBINATIVE SOUND-CHANGE; ISOLATIVE SOUND-CHANGE.

SOUND SYMBOLISM: the alleged correspondence between sound and meaning in language, whereby words seem to enact what they denote. See pp. 31–2.

SPEECH COMMUNITY: the group of people that uses a given language or dialect.

SPEECH ORGANS: the parts of the body used to produce speech sounds. See pp. 10–17 and *Figure 1*.

SPELLING PRONUNCIATION: a new pronunciation of a word that arises through the influence of its spelling.

STANDARD ENGLISH. See pp. 159–61.

STANDARD LANGUAGE: one particular dialect of a language which is given a special prestige or status. See pp. 77–8.

STEM: the invariable kernel of a word to which INFLEXIONS can be added; e.g. the stem of Latin *dominus* (p. 109) is *domin-*.

STOP: a consonant in which pressure is built up behind a complete blockage of the air-passage, and then suddenly released by removal of the blockage, e.g. *b*, *ch*, *k*. See pp. 15–16.

STRESS: degree of loudness of a syllable. See pp. 20–1.

STRONG VERBS: in GERMANIC languages, VERBS that show change of TENSE by changing the vowel of their STEM, e.g. English *run, ran*. Contrasted with WEAK VERBS. See pp. 112–13.

SUBJECT: many sentences in English, and in other Indo-European languages, can be analysed into two main parts, a subject and a predicate. Roughly speaking, the subject offers something for consideration, and the predicate offers some statement about it. In the following sentences, the subject is italicized, and the remaining words constitute the predicate: (1) *The master* beat the servant; (2) *The servant with red hair* was soundly beaten by his master; (3) *Walking* is good for you; (4) Did *you* go to the pictures?

The subject always contains a NOUN or something equivalent, while the predicate always contains a VERB. In any given language, there will be specific criteria for identifying the subject and the predicate (e.g. word order, inflexions).

SUBJUNCTIVE: particular forms of the VERB, found in some languages (e.g. Latin, German, Old English), and used in circumstances that vary from language to language, but often implying doubt, uncertainty, or unreality. Often contrasted with *indicative*, the forms of the verb that lack these special implications. See p. 112.

SUFFIX: element which can be added after a STEM or root to form a word, e.g. *-ize* (*tenderize*), *-ly* (*quickly*). See pp. 135, 216–17.

SUMERIAN: extinct language of the ancient Sumerians, unrelated to any other known language.

SYLLABIC: forming a SYLLABLE: e.g. the English word *button* contains a syllabic *n*.

SYLLABIC WRITING: script in which the symbols stand for syllables. See pp. 47–9.

SYLLABLE: a peak of loudness in the chain of utterance. See p. 15.

SYMBOL: see pp. 24–5 and *Figure 4*. *See also* SOUND SYMBOLISM.

SYNTAX: permissible ways in which words of a given language can be arranged to form utterances; sentence-patterns.

TAMIL: a DRAVIDIAN language of southern India.

TEETH-RIDGE: the convex part of the roof of the mouth immediately behind the upper teeth. See *Figure 1*, p. 11.

TENSE: variant form of a VERB, used to indicate such things as time, duration, instantaneity, completion, etc. Different tenses are seen in *I sing, I sang, I am singing, I have sung*.

THAI: language of Thailand (Siam), belonging to the Sino-Tibetan family.

THORN: the runic symbol þ, used in Old and Middle English writing. See p. 130.

TOCHARIAN: extinct language of the INDO-EUROPEAN family. See p. 87.

URALIAN: family of languages consisting of Samoyed and FINNO-UGRIAN. See p. 75.

UVULA: the small fleshy appendage to the SOFT PALATE, which hangs at the back of the mouth. See *Figure 1*, p. 11.

VANDAL: extinct language of the eastern branch of GERMANIC.

VELAR CONSONANT: one in which the PLACE OF ARTICULATION is the VELUM or soft palate, e.g. English *k, g*.

VELUM: the backward part of the roof of the mouth. Also called the *soft palate*. See p. 12 and *Figure 1*.

VERB: a word-class (*see* PARTS OF SPEECH). Examples of English verbs are italicized in the following sentences: (1) John *walked* down the road and *caught* the bus; (2) He *seems* very unhappy; (3) My hat *is* the black one; (4) His father *will come* to the party. Some grammarians would put the *is* of (3) in a separate category; and some would call *come* a verb in (4), classifying *will* separately as an auxiliary.

VERNER'S LAW: sound-change that took place in PROTO-GERMANIC round about the first century A.D. whereby the voiceless fricatives became voiced if they preceded the main stress of the word, but otherwise remained unchanged. See p. 116.

VOCAL CORDS: pair of muscular bands attached to the wall of the windpipe, which can be moved from wide open to fully closed. In one position they produce VOICE. See *Figure 1* and pp. 11–12.

VOCATIVE: one of the CASES of the noun in Indo-European, used for addressing somebody or something. There are no special vocative forms in English; but in Latin, if you call out to Titus, you say, not 'Titus!', but 'Tite!'

VOICE: musical tone produced by the air from the lungs passing through the vocal cords; see pp. 11–12.

VOICED SOUNDS: ones accompanied by VOICE (e.g. *v*, *z*).

VOICELESS SOUNDS: ones unaccompanied by VOICE (e.g. *f*, *s*).

VOWEL: a VOICED sound in which the mouth passage is unobstructed so that the air passes out freely. See pp. 12–15.

VOWEL DIAGRAM. See pp. 12–15 and *Figures 2* and *3*.

WEAK DECLENSION OF THE ADJECTIVE: in GERMANIC languages, a special set of INFLEXIONS for the adjective used in certain positions (e.g. after the DEFINITE ARTICLE). Contrasted with the *strong declension of the adjective*. See pp. 110–11.

WEAK VERBS: in the GERMANIC languages, verbs that form their past tense by adding an inflexion containing a *d*, *t*, or *th*, e.g. English *walk*, *walked*. Contrasted with STRONG VERBS. See pp. 112–13.

WELSH: a language of the Britannic branch of CELTIC. See p. 86.

WEST SAXON: a dialect of OLD ENGLISH. See pp. 126–8 and *Figure 11*.

WORD: there have been many definitions. For English, a useful working definition is 'a minimum free form', i.e. the smallest unit that is normally able to function as a sentence.

WORD CLASS: *see* PARTS OF SPEECH.

SUGGESTIONS FOR FURTHER READING

HERE are a few suggestions for further reading on the subject-matter of each chapter. They range from elementary works for beginners to text-books and advanced works suitable for students. Where several books are given on the same subject, they are roughly arranged in increasing order of difficulty. Foreign books I normally give only when they are available in English, but I have included a few books in French and German.

CHAPTER I: Language and Linguistics: E Sapir, *Language* (New York, 1921); Simeon Potter, *Modern Linguistics* (London, 1957); E. H. Sturtevant, *An Introduction to Linguistic Science* (New Haven, 1947); L. R. Palmer, *An Introduction to Modern Linguistics* (London, 1936); H. A. Gleason, *An Introduction to Descriptive Linguistics* (New York, 1955); C. F. Hockett, *A Course in Modern Linguistics* (New York, 1959); F. de Saussure, *Course in General Linguistics* (London, 1960); L. Bloomfield, *Language* (New York, 1933); A. A. Hill, *Introduction to Linguistic Structures* (New York, 1958). Speech Sounds: Ida Ward, *The Phonetics of English* (4th ed. Cambridge, 1945); Daniel Jones, *An Outline of English Phonetics* (9th ed. Cambridge, 1960); K. L. Pike, *Phonetics* (Ann Arbor, 1943). Animal Behaviour: N. Tinbergen, *Social Behaviour in Animals* (London, 1953); W. Köhler, *The Mentality of Apes* (2nd ed. London, 1948).

CHAPTER II: Origin of Language: O. Jespersen, *Language, its Nature, Development and Origin* (London, 1922); Sir Richard Paget, *Human Speech* (London, 1930); Leopold Stein, *The Infancy of Speech* (London, 1949); A. S. Diamond, *The History and Origin of Language* (London, 1959); A. Jóhannesson, *Origin of Language* (Reykjavik, 1949); G. Révész, *The Origins and Prehistory of Language* (London, 1956). The Alphabet:

I. J. Gelb, *A Study of Writing* (London, 1952); David Diringer, *The Alphabet* (2nd ed. London, 1949); G. R. Driver, *Semitic Writing* (Oxford, 1948).

CHAPTER III: P. E. Cleator, *Lost Languages* (London, 1959). Linguistic Change and its Causes: E. H. Sturtevant, *Linguistic Change* (New York, 1942); G. K. Zipf, *The Psycho-biology of Language* (London, 1936); André Martinet, *Economie des changements phonétiques* (Berne, 1955). History of English: L. P. Smith, *The English Language* (2nd ed. Oxford, 1952); G. H. Vallins, *The Pattern of English* (London, 1956); H. Bradley, *The Making of English* (London, 1904); O. Jespersen, *Growth and Structure of the English Language* (2nd ed. Leipzig, 1912); S. Potter, *Our Language* (London, 1950); A. C. Baugh, *History of the English Language* (2nd ed. London, 1959); H. C. Wyld, *A Short History of English* (3rd ed. London, 1927).

CHAPTERS IV and V: Mario Pei, *The World's Chief Languages* (3rd ed. London, 1954). H. H. Bender, *The Home of the Indo-Europeans* (Princeton, 1922); V. Gordon Childe, *The Aryans* (London, 1926); O. Schrader, *Prehistoric Antiquities of the Aryan Peoples* (London, 1890). A Meillet, *Introduction à l'étude comparative des langues indo-européennes* (Paris, 7th ed., 1934).

CHAPTER VI: H. M. Chadwick, *The Heroic Age* (Cambridge, 1912). E. Prokosch, *A Comparative Germanic Grammar* (Philadelphia, 1939); W. Streitberg, *Urgermanische Grammatik* (Heidelberg, 1943).

CHAPTER VII: P. H. Blair, *An Introduction to Anglo-Saxon England* (Cambridge, 1956); H. M. Chadwick, *The Origin of the English Nation* (Cambridge, 1907). J. W. Clark, *Early English* (London, 1957). P. H. Reaney, *The Origin of English Place-Names* (London, 1960). Grammars: G. L. Brook, *An Introduction to Old English* (Manchester, 1955); R. Quirk and C. L. Wrenn, *An Old English Grammar* (London, 1955); J. and E. M. Wright, *Old English Grammar* (3rd ed. Oxford,

1925); Karl Brunner, *Altenglische Grammatik* (rev. E. Sievers, Halle, 1942). Reader: H. Sweet, *An Anglo-Saxon Reader* (rev. C. T. Onions, Oxford, 1948).

CHAPTER VIII: A. Mawer, *The Vikings* (Cambridge, 1913); J. Brøndsted, *The Vikings* (London, 1960); T. D. Kendrick, *A History of the Vikings* (New York, 1930). E. Björkman, *Scandinavian Loan Words in Middle English* (Halle, 1900–2).

CHAPTERS IX and X: E. E. Wardale, *An Introduction to Middle English* (London, 1937). Grammars: J. and E. M. Wright, *An Elementary Middle English Grammar* (2nd ed. Oxford, 1928); R. Jordan, *Handbuch der mittelenglischen Grammatik* (Part 1 only, 2nd ed. Heidelberg, 1934). Readers: K. Sisam, *Fourteenth Century Verse and Prose* (Oxford, 1921); B. Dickins and R. M. Wilson, *Early Middle English Texts* (Cambridge, 1952).

CHAPTERS XI and XII: S. Robertson, *The Development of Modern English* (2nd ed. rev. F. G. Cassidy, New York, 1954). G. P. Krapp, *The Rise of English Literary Prose* (New York, 1915). T. H. Savory, *The Language of Science* (London, 1953); J. A. Sheard, *The Words We Use* (London, 1954); M. S., Serjeantson, *A History of Foreign Words in English* (London, 1935). E. J. Dobson, *English Pronunciation 1500–1700* (2 vols. Oxford, 1957). O. Jespersen, *A Modern English Grammar on Historical Principles* (7 vols. 1909–49). American English: E. H. Partridge and J. W. Clark, *British and American English since 1900* (London, 1951); T. Pyles, *Words and Ways of American English* (London, 1954); A. H. Marckwardt, *American English* (Oxford, 1958); G. P. Krapp, *The English Language in America* (2 vols. New York, 1925); H. L. Mencken, *The American Language* (2 vols. 4th ed. New York, 1936); W. Nelson Francis, *The Structure of American English* (New York, 1958). S. J. Baker, *The Australian Language* (London, 1945). English Dialects: W. W. Skeat, *English Dialects from the Eighth Century to the Present Day* (Cambridge, 1911); A. McIntosh, *An Introduction to a Survey of Scottish Dialects*

(Edinburgh, 1952); Harold Orton and Eugen Dieth, *Survey of English Dialects* (Vol. 1, Leeds, 1962).

CHAPTER XIII: J. Copley, *Shift of Meaning* (Oxford, 1961); S. Ullmann, *Words and their Use* (London, 1951); G. Stern, *Meaning and Change of Meaning* (Gothenburg, 1931); S. Ullmann, *The Principles of Semantics* (Glasgow, 1951).

CHAPTER XIV: Grammar of present-day English: C. C. Fries, *The Structure of English* (London, 1957); Barbara M. H. Strang, *Modern English Structure* (London, 1962); A. A. Hill, *Introduction to Linguistic Structures* (New York, 1958).

A fuller account of the changes going on in present-day English will be found in my own book *Linguistic Change in Present-day English*, to be published by Oliver & Boyd of Edinburgh during 1964.

These are PAN PIPER Books

Arthur Marwick
THE EXPLOSION OF BRITISH SOCIETY, 1914–1962

Pan Original. The fascinating story of fifty turbulent years and of the momentous changes that have revolutionised life in Britain. By a brilliant historian and University lecturer. (3/6)

Peter Fletcher
YOUR EMOTIONAL PROBLEMS

Specially written by PAN by an eminent Harley Street psycho-therapist, this book will help many sufferers from emotional tension, self-consciousness or over-anxiety towards a happier life. 'Stimulating, lucid, provocative' – Dr Eustace Chesser. (3/6)

Katherine Tottenham
THE PAN BOOK OF HOME PETS

Pan Original. How to choose, house, feed, handle, breed and keep healthy every kind of pet . . . cage birds, rabbits, hamsters, snakes, mongooses, ponies and scores more. *Illustrated*. (3/6)

Mary Ellison
THE DEPRIVED CHILD AND ADOPTION

A Pan Original. A vivid, outspoken introduction to one of to-day's major social problems, with full information for those considering adopting a child – including the latest legislation. Specially written for PAN by a leading London social worker and ex-Probation Officer. (3/6)

PICK OF THE PAPERBACKS

These are PAN PIPER Books

Sacheverell Sitwell

BRITISH ARCHITECTS AND CRAFTSMEN

For every lover of beauty and tradition. The best written and illustrated book on the subject – a classic. 'A "must" book' – *Sunday Graphic. Illustrated.* (5/–)

C. E. Lucas Phillips

THE SMALL GARDEN

A complete guide to the successful growing of flowers, fruit and vegetables. The book covers the whole range of normal small-garden activities from the initial stages of layout and design through planning and planting, propagation, greenhouse management, making paths, hedges, rock gardens and lawns. *Illustrated.* (5/–)

PICK OF THE PAPERBACKS